WALLACE NEFF

AND THE *Grand Houses* OF THE *Golden State*

WALLACE NEFF

AND THE *Grand Houses* OF THE *Golden State*

DIANE KANNER

THE MONACELLI PRESS

First published in the United States of America in 2005
by the Monacelli Press, Inc.
611 Broadway
New York, NY 10012

LIBRARY OF CONGRESS CATALOGING-IN-PUBLICATION DATA

Kanner, Diane.
Wallace Neff and the grand houses of the Golden State / Diane
Kanner.
        p. cm.
    Includes bibliographical references and index.
    ISBN 1-58093-163-4
    1. Neff, Wallace, 1895– 2. Architects—California—Biography.
3. Architecture, Domestic—California. 4. Eclecticism in architecture—
California. I. Neff, Wallace, 1895– II. Title.
    NA737.N37K36 2005
    720'.92—dc22   2005017670

Printed and bound in China

Designed by Sara E. Stemen

Frontispiece: *Sol and Marian Wurtzel House, Bel-Air, California*

CONTENTS

ACKNOWLEDGMENTS

A YEAR AFTER Wallace Neff's death in 1982, my study of his life and work began. I was a wife and full-time mother, with a background in journalism and a growing fascination with Los Angeles architecture. I found help at the University of Southern California, where the graduate program in writing introduced me to fine teachers. Instructor Robert Conot's maxim to his nonfiction writing students, "don't write in a vacuum," led me to study other architects and to explore California history. With the USC master's thesis project to recommend me, I visited a number of Neff's built works in Southern California.

Many of his clients from fifty years before were still living, and I was able to talk with remarkable people like Eleanor Boardman, Edith Mayer Goetz, Cary Grant, Sam Jaffe, Sol Wurtzel's daughter Lillian Semenov, and Claudette Colbert. Fortunately, there were also a number of his friends who were eager to share impressions—among them, John Elliott, George Brandow, Caspar Ehmcke, and Cliff May. They were open about his foibles as well as his strengths, adding a dimension to his personality that most clients would not have seen. The painter Harry Martin knew the profession from a different perspective than the architect Sam Lunden, but they had both worked in Southern California for over half a century and they were both kind enough to share their memories of Wallace Neff. The footnotes bear witness to dozens of personal interviews, for Neff's long life provided him with many associates, clients, and other contacts.

Within the Neff family, I interviewed Mary Nevins and Helen Belford, Neff's only niece, and his son Arthur and daughter-in-law Marvine. The latter opened the family papers to me and provided the names of Neff home owners. I owe Arthur, who passed away in 1994, and Marvine a huge debt of gratitude.

While my manuscript met the standards of the University of Southern California, and I was granted a master's degree, it was not up to the standards of several people whose opinions I value. Martin Ridge, a scholar of the American West, suggested that I deliver it to his wife's club. Was that the extent of my audience, I wondered? My friend Cheryl Johnson, with her experience writing on antitrust law and Los Angeles history, felt that more of Neff's personal history was needed. Dr. Robert Winter had other issues when he read it. With their help, and that of my husband, Ron Weinstein, an especially avid reader who analyzes documents in his legal work, a more animated Neff emerged.

Thanks also to my nephew, Jake Batsell, a journalist, and my mother, Nadine Bell, for reading the manuscript. Jean Ownbey offered her shoulder at countless lunch meetings. Dr. Wilbur Jacobs of the history faculty at the University of California at Santa Barbara admonished me to find a clear thesis. Occidental College's Dr. Andrew Rolle encouraged me to continue year after year. Penny Kirby introduced me to the phenomena of the Pasadena showcase house, with its glorification of period-revival architects, particularly Wallace Neff. And Dr. Doyce Nunis, the fine editor of the *Southern California Quarterly*, published an early draft of the first chapter.

When the 2003 BookExpo was held in Los Angeles, I attended and met the animated publisher Gianfranco Monacelli, who was immediately convinced that Wallace Neff's career was worthy of his press. Andrea Monfried took the matter from there and the deal was struck, thanks to the assistance of intellectual properties attorney Katherine McDaniel. What the reader finds in these pages is a collaboration between an exacting and patient editor, Noel Millea, an art editor who knows her fine arts, Elizabeth White, and a graphic designer with a discerning eye, Sara Stemen.

Above all, my ability to pull together Wallace Neff's life experiences and to review the record of his architectural output was made possible by research library professionals at several Southern California institutions. Thank you Lian Partlow, Kurt Helfrich, Carolyn Cole, Thomas Canterbury, Sarkis Badalyan, Romaine Ahlstrom, Diana Pam, Jill Cogen, Christopher Adde, Kathryn Henningsen, Leslie Anne Jobsky, Meredith Berbee, Mona Shulman, John Sullivan, Jean-Robert Durbin, Erin Chase, Jennifer Watts, Alan Jutzi, Robert C. Ritchie, Susi Krasno, Sarkis Badalyan, Dorothy Blakesley, and Mohammed Iqnabi. I am grateful to all of you.

Promotional brochure, written by Harry Brook and distributed at the World's Columbian Exposition in Chicago in 1893

CHAPTER ONE

COMING TO CALIFORNIA

There has been such a rosy glamour thrown over southern California by enthusiastic romancers
that many are disappointed when they fail to find an absolute Paradise.
—Kate Sanborn, *A Truthful Woman in Southern California*

𝓘N THE SPRING OF 1978, the leader of Pasadena's historic preservation community met eighty-three-year-old Wallace Neff at the distinctive igloo-shaped house he had designed and built in 1946 at the busy corner of Los Robles Avenue and Wallis Street. Claire Bogaard may have been widely feared by developers for her ability to rally public opinion against behemoth projects, but she was soft on the subject of Wallace Neff's work, and she was there to report on the tour of his houses that her group, Pasadena Heritage, had recently sponsored.

Dressed neatly in suit and tie, Neff was as handsome as ever, but his diminished physical and mental state made it difficult for him to converse at any length. Still, he was able to convey his gratitude for her group's attention to his work, and to suggest that the house in which they sat and conversed was the one he wanted to be remembered for. Confiding his fears that his work seemed to have been forgotten, he was close to tears. Should he have been more concerned with saving his records? he wondered aloud. Would his built work satisfy historians, without much in the way of letters or written output to supplement it?

Their conversation was notable, for Neff was an exceedingly private individual, and few of his admirers had been able to get much of a sense of the man behind the facade. His circumspection had served him well with celebrated clients who demanded that their privacy be protected, but by the end of his life his standard explanation of his success—"I just built California houses for California people"—left everyone who was interested in his work wanting more. While it was a credo that was easy to understand, it was just about the extent of what anyone knew about his motivation. But after a long life devoted to work above all else—almost to the exclusion of family and hobbies—he was gripped by a desire for praise, a longing for the acknowledgment that his accomplishments had affected, if not transfigured, California's built environment. He hoped, he told Bogaard, that the igloo-shaped house, which was known as the Bubble House, would someday become a museum devoted to promoting the principles of affordable housing. That such a museum would also help publicize his own work couldn't have been far from his mind.

A REVIVALIST AMONG MODERNISTS

Critics had written off Neff as an architect of palatial houses with little social relevance. They carped that the Spanish colonial aesthetic he worked in had no real basis in the history of Southern California. How could Los Angeles take itself seriously, the criticism went, if its most popular style was so uninspired? Neff had

Entry vestibule of the Carroll L. and Fannie Post House, San Marino, California

been hearing this lament since he began his career during the building boom of the 1920s. Los Angeles houses like the ones he designed were, of course, widely derided by modernist architects such as Richard Neutra, who described them as "Georgian mansions on 50 by 120 foot lots adjoining Mexican ranchos."[1] They were also parodied by writers like S. N. Behrman, who included a thinly veiled portrait of Neff's 1931 Wurtzel House in his novel *The Burning Glass*, calling it "a perfect little Renaissance castle, the kind of house which a grand duke might build for his mistress."[2] Nathanael West, a leading author of Hollywood fiction, lambasted the city Neff's work had been so influential in creating, complaining that it had "monstrous" tastes and that "not even the soft wash of dust could help the houses. Only dynamite would be of any use against the Mexican ranch houses, Samoan huts, Mediterranean villas, Egyptian and Japanese temples, Swiss chalets, Tudor cottages, and every possible combination of these styles that lined the slopes of the canyon."[3] He may not have mentioned Neff by name, but the implication was clear.

Neff had spent a lifetime fending off a widely held bias against California architecture, but even in Southern California his work was suspect. California architectural historian Esther McCoy overlooked Neff while promoting the work of Greene & Greene, Rudolph Schindler, the modernists, and the Case Study House architects.[4] Another preeminent architectural historian, David Gebhard, sought Neff's opinion several times during the 1960s and 1970s when he was preparing a monograph on the one Southern California architect Neff considered his peer, George Washington Smith. Gebhard and his coauthor, Robert Winter, declared Smith to be "the acknowledged master" of the Spanish colonial and Mediterranean style in *Architecture in Los Angeles: A Compleat Guide.*[5] Neff had hoped to be singled out in the book and was disappointed to

discover that he had been lumped in with all the other Southern California revivalists.

Instead of being credited for the best of the Spanish colonial revival in Southern California, Neff found himself being blamed for the overembellishment that encouraged modern architecture to flourish in reaction, long before the rest of the country had embraced its revolutionary principles. In fact, Neff abhorred overembellishment. The house he built for his family in 1928 was almost devoid of applied ornament. Neff houses were usually dramatic in scale and proportion, however, which may be why the house he designed for the director King Vidor and the actress Eleanor Boardman struck F. Scott Fitzgerald as the perfect setting for a Hollywood story. "There was an air of listening as if the far silences of its vistas hid an audience," the writer rhapsodized. "Under the high ceilings, the situation seemed more dignified and tragic."[6]

When asked, Neff would cite as his most famous work Pickfair, a residence that had not pleased him during the 1920s when the actress Mary Pickford and the doyenne of the world's interior decorators, Elsie de Wolfe, had insisted he transform it to reflect the style of the imperial French regency. Pretensions notwithstanding, Pickfair was, in fact, the best-known house in Neff's portfolio, and Pickford had done a great deal to further his reputation, financing the development of a modular house called the Honeymoon Cottage during the Depression.

Neff took solace in the credit he received as a pioneer in pneumatic housing, not only for Pickford's Honeymoon Cottage but also for its successor, the Bubble House. Officially known as the Airform, it had a social vision as compelling as that of any mid-century public housing scheme, and it meant more to him than any building he created for clients of means because he felt it proved that he was a significant twentieth-century architect. "No one knows more than I about gunite," he would say of the material the Airform was constructed of, and with good reason: he had studied the properties of the concrete derivative for almost half a century.

Neff worked for fifty-five years, until 1975, when he was no longer able to keep a grip on the thick, colored pencils he used to draw terra-cotta tiles and "Neff blue" shutters. During that time he published one book, distilling his love of the Southern California landscape into seven optimistic paragraphs and filling the volume with photographs. "Nowhere else is found such freedom in planning, gaiety in color and beauty in conception," he wrote of the region where he spent nearly all his life. "It is as if all the restrictions and shackles of the past had been lifted to let a new style emerge."[7]

In his own life, though, Neff was never truly able to escape the shackles of the past. By the time he was seventy-five, he had taken to signing correspondence "Wallace McNally Neff," in the belief that the association with his maternal grandfather, Andrew McNally, who had founded the famed Chicago map company over a quarter of a century before Neff was born, conveyed more cachet than simply "Wallace Neff." He had also tacked Rand McNally & Company maps to the walls of his Hollywood office to reinforce the connection and had begun handing visitors autographed atlases.[8] It was, of course, Andrew McNally's empire that had provided the family with its financial security, for Neff, like many architects who devote themselves to residential design, had prospered in fame rather than fortune. By 1978, the day was fast approaching when the proceeds from Andrew McNally's trust would be shared among his heirs, and Neff's sons were so at odds with each other over their stakes that they had taken their grievances to the downtown superior court. Neff had been subpoenaed more often than his nerves could bear.

The real story of Wallace Neff's influence in South-

ern California would seem to begin there, with the family fortune, but in fact it can be traced back even further, before Andrew McNally settled in Los Angeles in 1888. Neff's story actually begins with William Rand, his grandfather's business partner, who started his journey west much earlier.

THE GOLD RUSH

On April 5, 1849, young William Rand left Boston Harbor aboard a wooden sailing ship called the *Areatus*, and battened down for the half-year-long sojourn to far-off California.[9] Months after the ship rounded Cape Horn, Rand found himself in San Francisco, the most thriving city in the soon-to-be American state.[10] He soon set off for the gold diggings at Sonora, where he earned fifteen hundred dollars a month when his luck was good. After the strikes played out, Rand returned to his original trade, setting type and writing, for the *Alta California*, while he considered whether to remain in the West.

Los Angeles's first paper, the bilingual *Star*, or *La Estrella*, had been on the streets for two months when Rand got word that the editors were desperate for a typesetter who could work their ancient Washington Hoe press. The paper covered the local scene, as well as the state capital and the gold country. The editor was a relative of Rand's by marriage, and his partner had bunked with Rand when he worked for the *Alta*. Like Rand, they were newsmen and printers who had come west for gold and stayed on as journalists. Rand jumped a steamer and headed for the pueblo.

The Los Angeles that twenty-three-year-old William Rand discovered on July 20, 1851, was "a regular old Spanish-Mexican town," one visitor wrote. "The houses are but one story, mostly built of adobe or sunburnt brick, with very thick walls and flat roofs."[11] Because the streets were neither paved nor graded,

*William Rand, cofounder of
Rand McNally & Company*

dense clouds of yellow dust formed when caballeros engaged in the most popular local diversion, horse racing. Wild mustard and willow trees needed little irrigation, and the water that could be saved from mountain runoff and winter rains was hauled from open canals and used for drinking. The population of 1,610 used the remainder for bathing.[12] The economy thrived as feudal ranchero barons spent lavishly.

Rand's quarters at the Bella Union Hotel, one of the few two-story buildings in town and a *Star* advertiser, were deluxe. Floors were wood, not dirt, and the beds were set on frames. The paper was printed in a wood house on Los Angeles Street, where *imprenta* (press) was inscribed on an unbleached cloth nailed above the door.[13]

Every week, the *Star* broadened its scope. Among the new features was a Spanish section edited by a Spanish-speaking attorney. California's statehood had been approved by Congress in September 1850, and the paper had been charged with printing the state's laws in English and Spanish for the enlightenment of residents south of the Tehachapis, the mountains separating Northern and Southern California. The paper did its best to bridge the interests of the pueblo's diverse communities.[14] Rand went to work printing the laws of the city common council and the

proclamations of the mayor, Benjamin D. Wilson, who owned a share of the paper and was throwing government contracts its way. News from the north could take three weeks to arrive by mail, so the editors focused on local happenings—rites like fandangos that were as foreign to Rand as the finer points of American law were to rancheros named Sepulveda, Abila, Lugo, and Yorba. As a stakeholder in the paper, Rand appears to have written unsigned editorials that often rang with the disenchantment with frontier life a Yankee would have felt. "With all our natural beauties and advantages, there is no country where human life is of so little account," one editorial read. "Men hack one another with pistols and other cutlery as if God's image were of no more worth than the life of one of the two or three thousand ownerless dogs that prowl about our streets and make night hideous."[15]

On a good day, Los Angeles was murder-free, but attorneys often battled one another in court, where it was not unusual to encounter flying bottles of ink, while outside vigilantes hanged inebriated Gabrielino native Californians. Drinking, gambling, prostitution, and lynching were as commonplace as death by shooting or knifing. The city's reputation for lawlessness was on a par with that of Tombstone or Deadwood.

Rand found himself elected to public office after he made a name as a self-styled lawman.[16] Figures like Don Abel Stearns, a New Englander who prospered after Mexico defeated Spain to win possession of Alta California in 1821, and Hugo Reid, the chronicler of the native Gabrielenos who supported his family growing grapes for wine at the San Gabriel Mission, became Rand's allies.[17] When the clerk of the common council proposed building a water system, and the *Star* reported that the pueblo could not afford the terms, Rand probably wrote the editorial.

Rand's powerful position meant little to him, however, without the spiritual and emotional life he had left behind in Massachusetts. A strict Protestant, he found no place of worship in Los Angeles, for every preacher who came to town left in disgust. Romance was also out of the question, since Rand remained true to his fiancée back east. And the tensions between Californios and Americans that made for good copy would have created great discomfort for a Yankee on the largely Hispanic city council.

Rand's reprieve came when he learned that one of his brothers in Massachusetts had contracted to print a promising new book by a woman making a name for herself as a newspaper columnist, Harriet Beecher Stowe. Rand, who opposed slavery but was outnumbered by its advocates in Los Angeles, gave up his city council seat and his interest in the newspaper and left to help produce *Uncle Tom's Cabin*.[18] After he married his longtime love, Harriett Robinson, in 1856, they moved as far west as Chicago, and he invested his earnings in a print shop. Meanwhile, in Southern California, the great rancho lands fell victim to drought, and falling prices ruined the sheep and cattle industries. The Hispanic residents, besieged by challenges to their titles, watched as their influence on culture, society, politics, and religion began to diminish.

THE BIRTH OF RAND MCNALLY

Andrew McNally happened upon Rand's little shop in 1858 and was reportedly hired on the spot. Eight years Rand's junior, he was nearly broke after a transatlantic trip from Northern Ireland to New York, followed by a brief stint as a compositor in Manhattan and a run-in with anti-abolitionists who bombed the Memphis print shop where he was working after the newspaper printed there adopted a strong editorial stance against secession.[19]

McNally was born on March 4, 1836, near Belfast, to a dirt-poor Protestant Scotch-Irish farmer and his

Andrew McNally

Dutch wife, the eighth of thirteen children. By the time he was sixteen, he had witnessed the massive Irish exodus precipitated by the potato famine, and he realized he would need to learn a trade if he were to advance in life.[20] For seven years, he apprenticed to an Armagh, Ireland, printer, learning all aspects of publishing. With his freedom and forty pounds in his pocket, he then made the pilgrimage to America.

About the time Rand hired McNally, an event took place that, unbeknownst to them, would have great significance to their future: the first reliable, comprehensive map of the American West was published as part of the *Pacific Railroad Reports*, a thirteen-volume set that amassed all the information discovered during the previous fifteen years of western exploration.[21] Soon after, in 1859, Rand gave up his little shop to manage the job-printing department at the *Chicago Tribune*. With McNally as the shop foreman, they prepared maps, tickets, and annual reports for railroads headquartered in Chicago, the hub of America's transportation system.

Two years before the May 10, 1869, ceremony at Promontory Point, Utah, when the Golden Spike was pounded into the tracks of the Central Pacific and Union Pacific railways, creating a transcontinental

James W. Steele's Sketches and Stories of Frontier Life in the Old Times, *one of the original works published by Rand McNally & Company for consumption by westward travelers*

route, Rand and McNally bought out their *Tribune* partners in the job-printing department and created Rand McNally & Company. "The *Tribune* gave father a gold watch," McNally's daughter Nannie wrote of the day her father left the paper and its publisher, his friend Joseph Medill, to establish his own business. "They gave him a scroll telling him how much they thought of him."[22]

Their timing was serendipitous. The West had long been considered a place for the young and adventuresome, but after the Golden Spike, anyone who could afford a train ticket could visit the frontier. "Intrepid men had pushed the railroad through the forbidding barrier of the Sierras," the writer Sarah Bixby Smith noted in her classic 1931 chronicle of early Southern California, *Adobe Days*, "giving for the first time easy access to California, and thus making inevitable a changed manner of life and conditions."[23]

By the time the two men observed the first anniversary of their partnership, thirty-one thousand miles of track had been laid by 350 railroad companies at a cost of $1 billion.[24] Much of the land was donated by the federal government in exchange for the construction of a national rail system. As the various railroads opened up new territory, they published guide-

books and travel literature that depicted only their own lines, with no sign of the competition. Rand and McNally's earliest attempt to market to the rail industry involved advertising "consecutively numbered railroad coupons and local tickets, an entirely new feature in the West."[25] Their first actual commission was the annual report for the Chicago, Rock Island and Pacific Railroad Company.

Three years into their partnership, disaster, in the form of the great Chicago Fire, brought out their tenacity. "By Monday morning, October 9, at 2 a.m.," according to Andrew McNally III, "it was licking at the floors of 51 Clark Street, where Rand McNally had their business. By that time, Rand had moved two ticket printing machines from the firm's location to McNally's stables three miles from the heart of the fire. My great grandfather carted them to the shores of Lake Michigan and dumped them on the sand. The entire plant was gutted and destroyed, but three days later they were back in business."[26] Rand's house remained intact, but McNally's was destroyed.

The price of their financial survival was Rand's health. While he sought a cure for exhaustion in Switzerland's spas, McNally took the helm. After printing a railroad map on the back page of the December 1872 *Railway Guide*, a periodical that listed timetables for railway and steamboat lines throughout the west,[27] the company found its niche, and pocket maps became its stock-in-trade. It also began producing guidebooks for America's emerging cities. Mother Goose verse sold briskly as well, as did tall tales of the west, which were devoured by passengers traveling by train, along with original fiction commissioned by the railroads from authors of the stature of Bret Harte, who were paid huge fees. The company also printed practical booklets for farmers, such as *The Locust Plague in the United States*, and brochures like *Cheap Farms and Free Homes in Northern Nebraska*, which—along with the ubiquitous tickets, handbills, maps, and flyers—lured buyers to remote parcels far beyond established settlements, hastening the demise of the frontier. And to insure that the Rand McNally name found its way onto the pages of newspapers, the company mailed complimentary maps to editors. (In July of 1877, the *Los Angeles Evening Express* reported receiving the "most complete map of the Russo-Turkish war that has been published.")[28]

McNally's first visit to California, in 1880, coincided with the establishment of a state commission to regulate the rates and business dealings of the freewheeling rail barons, who had been called "the curse of California" because of their economic stranglehold on the region.[29] (The word "tourism" would soon be coined to describe the new industry spawned by railroad-owned resort hotels.)[30] Andrew, his wife, Adelia, and one of their four children, seventeen-year-old Nancy (also known as "Nannie"), traveled across the country, from Chicago to San Francisco, in Pullman cars outfitted with amenities comparable to those of the best hotels and restaurants. As it happened, they were two days behind Mrs. George Mortimer Pullman herself, an acquaintance whose husband had patented the deluxe rail car, who was traveling with an entourage of children and servants, en route to a rail-industry gathering at San Francisco's Palace Hotel. On March 22, the McNallys disembarked in the grandest metropolis in the west, a city with a quarter of a million inhabitants. "To us, the Palace Hotel and San Francisco seemed like heaven," their daughter recalled years later.[31]

After four days at the hotel,[32] the McNallys boarded a steamship for Santa Barbara, continuing south to Los Angeles after winds prevented a landing.[33] From a mudflat called San Pedro, where shacks circled a bay, a tug took them north to an unimposing town called Wilmington. There they secured a horse and buggy and headed to the home of friends, the Congers, who lived at the intersection of Orange Grove and Colorado boulevards in a community founded seven years earlier by teetotaling Midwesterners—Pasadena. For the first time, McNally experienced the heralded colony system.[34]

One of the first citrus trade fairs was about to convene in Pasadena, and on his second trip west, in late 1880, McNally attended to learn more about citrus farming. His impressions of the fair went unrecorded, but he did describe the weather and the built environment. "I shall always remember New Year's Day of 1881," he later wrote. "I lived at the Sierra Madre Villa, on the foothills of the Sierra Madre mountains. The day was bright, warm and genial; a cloudless sky of the deepest blue. Flowers, wild and cultivated, everywhere, which, with the bloom of the orange and lemon trees, were as grateful to the sense of smell as the unrivaled scenic effects were to the eye."[35]

Los Angeles's unpaved streets and its "dirty and untidy ranches" made a less favorable impression. There was insufficient water to sustain a larger population, the harbor facilities were meager, and industry was almost nonexistent. Still, McNally was "determined to own some of it" because, he said, "it seemed to me a mid-winter paradise." The Southern Pacific Railroad had arrived in 1876, and with it like-minded settlers who shared his dream that Southern California could live up to the potential advertised in the popular guidebooks.

The McNallys returned the next winter, and the next. They experienced the episodic flashes of rain so typical of Southern California in January and February—when dry riverbeds become flood basins overnight—as well as the sublime sunny weather that is the region's greatest asset. Two years after the family's first visit, Rand McNally & Company published *From River to Sea: A Tourists' and Miners' Guide from the Missouri River to the Pacific Ocean*, the first of many Rand

Los Angeles's Chinatown in 1890, photographed by one of Nannie McNally's friends

Nannie McNally and several friends on a train caboose, during a rail excursion through Southern California in 1890

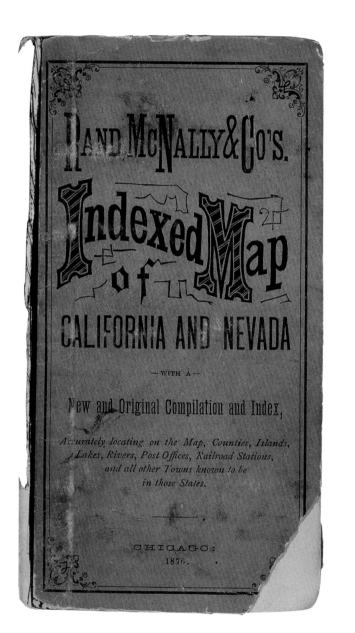

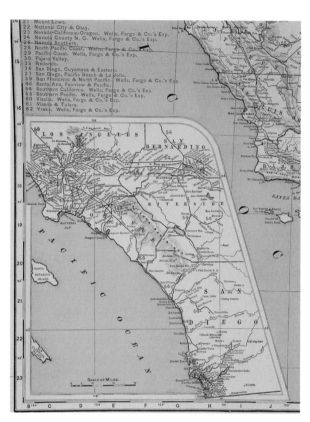

McNally travel guides to describe Utah, Colorado, and other states along the rail routes.[36]

But California was the ultimate destination. Railroad depots throughout the country were plastered with posters beseeching the curious to "Come to Southern California." To direct the flow toward their own hotels, railroads like the Southern Pacific published travel magazines with names like *Sunset.* The extension of the Southern Pacific Railroad line from Northern California stimulated talk about the region's charms, and by 1886, when the Atchison, Topeka & Santa Fe arrived to give the Southern Pacific a run for its money, a land boom was already under way.

Rand and McNally had reached a new pinnacle of financial success the year before, when they became the first mapmakers to adopt the revolutionary Linotype wax-engraving process of copper lithography, which cut the cost of creating maps from five dollars apiece to pennies, because compositors could set them so much faster. Railroad executives, seeing a more accurate, less expensive product, commissioned millions.

By now, Los Angeles had become more Anglo than Hispanic, and newcomers were importing customs, architectural styles, and religious institutions. Land prices soared as the railroads lowered ticket prices, and a thousand passengers arrived each month. After Chicagoans were besieged by blizzards during the winter of 1887–88, McNally prevailed upon friends and business associates to join him in investing in Southern California land.[37] Some of his investments never amounted to anything, but one settlement in particular held his interest: Altadena. He purchased fifteen acres surrounding the dusty intersection of Mariposa and Santa Rosa avenues and engaged the architect Frederick L. Roehrig to design first a garage and then a house. (The garage served as a makeshift living quarters for the family while the three-story, Queen Anne confection was completed and reservoirs were created to irrigate the new rose gardens and orange groves.)[38]

Joseph Medill, McNally's long-ago employer at the *Chicago Tribune,* came west to take the waters and invested in land directly north of the McNallys.[39] G. G. Green, whose almanac was printed by the McNally presses, invested as well. Alfred Armstrong, of the Atchison, Topeka & Santa Fe, who also did business with Rand McNally, purchased five acres. McNally tried to persuade Rand to join the enclave, but Rand had given up his California dreams; the colony of Chicagoans on the West Coast represented an "expensive folly" in his mind, and he never ventured west again.[40] While McNally trekked across California's Sierra Madre, Rand climbed Switzerland's Matterhorn to clear his soot-filled lungs, and in 1899 he resigned from the company he had cofounded.

Rand's suspicion that land investment in Southern California was risky proved accurate. The population more than quadrupled in 1887, and inevitably the fervor died down. The rail lines became so hungry for passengers that they practically gave seats away. For a few days, one could travel from Saint Louis to Los Angeles for a dollar.[41] "For Sale" signs dotted the countryside around Los Angeles, and half-finished hotels were the only buildings on stretches of land that the railroads hoped to sell.

For Rand McNally, however, 1888 was a boom year. After taking in more than a million dollars, the company signed a ninety-nine-year lease with Marshall Field for four lots on Adams Street in Chicago and commissioned Burnham & Root to design a ten-story building. It was to be the world's first tall building supported by an all-steel frame, and the first covered entirely in terra-cotta burnished with color.[42] With a near-skyscraper in downtown Chicago, an upstanding reputation, and strong civic connections, McNally was able to claim a place in the hierarchy of men responsible for organizing the World's Columbian Exposition

TOP LEFT AND RIGHT: *The ten-story Rand McNally & Company Building in downtown Chicago under construction, 1889–90*
BOTTOM LEFT: *The vestibule, which featured an Islamic motif popular in the late nineteenth century*
BOTTOM RIGHT: *Northeast entrance arch, 1891*

Randy McNally & Company's office in Chicago, 1891

CALIFORNIA BUILDING, AT THE WORLD'S FAIR, CHICAGO, 1893.

The California State Building at the World's Columbian Exposition

in Chicago, the fair honoring the four-hundredth anniversary of Columbus's discovery of America. He hosted planning sessions in the Rand McNally Building, positioning himself on the boards of directors, ways and means, and press, printing, and manufacturers. By raising money to stage the fair, he assured that his company would be commissioned to print the guides visitors needed to find their way around the huge event.[43] Twenty-eight million came from all over the world, including California.

"The rush of Californians to the World's Fair is steadily increasing," the *Los Angeles Express* reported breathlessly on May 3, 1893, "and every eastbound train out of Los Angeles is now run in sections and every berth occupied." Occasionally an impartial voice issued from the Southern California press. The fair's California State Building, an *Express* reporter wrote

on May 22, was in "a chaotic state. Worse, still, those in charge seem to be entirely unmindful of affairs or unwilling to remedy them. The building is not finished and the interior resembles a huge junk shop. Exhibits are scattered everywhere or piled up in heaps, fruit is rotting unopened, while wine from broken bottles is soaking the floors."

By June, though, the conditions had improved so much that the California State Building was nearly as crowded as the bawdy Midway Plaisance, where earthy pastimes prevailed.[44] Visitors jammed the aisles of the building for glimpses of Golden State products. Parapets and trefoil windows and tile roofs, cupolas and towers and domes: the structure had all the vocabulary of a California mission. Its plaster was applied to resemble weathered adobe.

The gloom cast by the Southern California reces-

One of the hundreds of thousands of maps and guidebooks Rand McNally & Company printed for visitors to the World's Fair

sion diminished in McNally's imagination as the glow of the fair's revenues erased doubts about the wisdom of investing in the region. In the California State Building's amazing popularity, he saw opportunity.

On October 25, the *Evening Express* reported that McNally had purchased 1831.54 acres south of Los Angeles from the Stearns Rancho Company for $54,926.20. The utopia-like colony system that provided pre-drawn parcels for investors intent on growing citrus was booming in Pasadena, Anaheim, Riverside, and Long Beach. Taking to heart the literature his company printed, which claimed that "more money can be made on a small farm in Southern California than on a majority of eastern farms of ten times its area,"[45] McNally set out to create a place where dozens of midsize farms might coexist within his personal enclave of olive and lemon groves.

He told the *Evening Express* that he would spend a hundred thousand dollars on his house.[46] "His costly residence," another paper noted, "will be built of red brick and granite and covered with tile. The plans were taken from one of the World's Fair Buildings."[47] A few miles south of the crumbling adobe built by California's last Mexican governor, Pio Pico, McNally had embarked upon a gamble that had the potential to make him one of the most influential men in the region.

Citrus label from Andrew McNally's La Mirada venture

CHAPTER TWO

LEMON GROVE GAMBLE, LA MIRADA DREAMS

Mr. McNally's men were sinking a well on his fruit ranch at La Mirada when, about 600 feet below the surface,
they struck a spring of whisky; not a very high quality, but good enough for cooking purposes or external application.
You can find almost anything in California, but the most gratifying discoveries have been accidental.
—*The Chicago Record* (May 16, 1899)

Mcnally and his chicago company ultimately invested at least a hundred thousand dollars, buying twenty-four hundred acres to create a citrus and olive colony.[1] The Santa Fe's Southern California Railway spur had been routed through the parcel,[2] an advantage McNally would have cited to his Chicago board as reason enough to invest. A wealth of agricultural ventures—dairy farms to the west in Norwalk, a German colony of vineyards to the south in Anaheim, vegetables planted by Chinese in the same community, the entrepreneur Gaylord Wilshire's almond-and-walnut farm in Fullerton, and a Quaker settlement to the north in Whittier—had made it worth the railroad's time to lay the line. And the new Fulton Wells spa near Norwalk, with its springs of sulphur water and its grand hotel, had begun attracting patrons looking for rest and recuperation.

The area was part of the onetime Rancho Los Coyotes, named after the animals that once loped across fields of mustard on the trail of grazing sheep. Pio Pico's brother, General Andres Pico, had purchased a half interest in 1850, the same year California became an American state, putting title to the land, and all the ranchos, in limbo. Pico's claim was validated, but the lengthy litigation was so expensive that he lost the property to foreclosure, and Don Abel Stearns assumed title. Years later, William Rand dismissed Stearns as a mere "cattleman with a Mexican wife,"[3] but Stearns, in fact, had a hand in nearly every significant mid-nineteenth-century real estate venture in the area. In the early 1860s, he had foreclosed on a fifteen-thousand-dollar tract of land that belonged to Pio Pico, adjacent to Pico's rancho. But after the famine of 1865, Stearns was forced to sell 177,000 acres to a syndicate of five businessmen: Alfred Robinson, Edward F. Northam, Samuel Branon, Charles Polhemus, and Edward Martin. Their 1869 scheme to carve out a town called Savanna went nowhere. One potential investor came and left after writing about "a solitary coyote on a round-top knoll gazing despondently down the street upon the debris of a deserted sheep camp. The other inhabitants of the city of Savanna had not arrived, nor have they to this day put in an appearance."[4]

It took a man of McNally's moxie to finally make something out of the mostly treeless land. Prospecting for artesian water, he found it in abundance, hundreds of feet below the spearheads left by migrating pre-Columbian Native Americans in his topsoil.[5] There was enough to nurture six wells and a lake he named Windermere, after the largest body of water in England. Wise to what would appeal to the press, McNally reported this claim as a "whiskey spring" to the press.[6]

He called his settlement La Mirada, after standing in the Coyote Hills to the east and delighting in the

FROM ROSES TO SNOW.

These two Photographs were taken on March 1, 1894, within two hours. The lower picture at Altadena, Andrew McNally's residence ; the upper in the Sierra Madre Mountains, reached by the Lowe Electric Railroad.

The Country Gentleman in California, *a fifty-page brochure for prospective buyers, produced by Rand McNally, showed the McNally house in Altadena* view of his new acquisition.[7] To make it more attractive, he imported flowering plants and trees. His Chicago writers composed a prospectus titled *The Country Gentleman in California*, directed at Southern California's financial community: "These lands will be sold in tracts of not less than twenty acres on the following terms: 25 per cent cash, balance in three annual payments, with interest at 6 per cent per annum. The price includes the cost of trees and planting of same, care of the trees for four years, and shares of stock in the water company."[8]

On Monday mornings, McNally usually made the trip from Altadena to La Mirada to check on progress at the ranch. After boarding his personal Pullman on a spur of the Altadena Railway that ran through his property, he would hook up with the Santa Fe and head south, perusing copies of the *Norwalk Call* and the *Rural California* while en route, to see what his competition was up to.[9] (The local papers were filled with advertisements that posed questions like "Do you want a home in Ontario in 5, 10, 20 or 40-acre tracts?") Once his new depot—jointly financed with the railroad, after he decided the original one was unremarkable—came into sight, he would prepare to disembark, anxious to survey the improvements to the roads surrounding the colony and to meet with county officials to discuss sharing the expense.

To be sure, McNally was not shouldering the responsibility alone. His second of three daughters, Nannie, intended to marry, and it appeared that her new husband, who had worked as a stockbroker at the Chicago board of trade, was willing take charge of sales in La Mirada. Nannie had met the thirty-one-year-old Edwin Dorland Neff at an athletic match at the Chicago YMCA in 1891, when his calisthenic prowess caught her eye. Edwin Neff, who was born in Cincinnati and had lived in New York and Boston, may have turned to exercise to preserve his health. How sick he was—and with what exactly—remains unknown, since mention

Neff family coats of arms depicting the Swiss anti-Catholic warrior Adam Naef

of the most likely possibility, tuberculosis, was usually avoided because of the fear it generated. TB had brought so many to Southern California that the president of Stanford University lamented that its victims must have been "banished from the East by physicians who did not know what else to do with their incurable patients."[10]

Courtship commenced despite the chasm caused by a difference in religious faiths. Edwin's beliefs, while not as strongly held as Nannie's, were deeply grounded in a family history that embraced some of the first Protestants: Adam Naef had retrieved the banner of Ulrich Zwingli when the Reformation leader was martyred in Zurich, Switzerland, in 1531, in a battle between two thousand anti-Catholics and eight thousand Catholics. (Naef received an imposing Tudor-style chalet for his efforts, and his armor and sword are still kept under glass at the Swiss National Museum.) Ed's mother's Dorland ancestors were among New Amsterdam's early Protestant settlers, and he proudly displayed the family crest on his stationery.

The devoutly Roman Catholic Miss McNally, on the other hand, had rejected her Protestant roots. Raised in Chicago's St. Peter's Episcopal Church by an Irish mother and Scotch-Irish father, she may have awakened to Catholicism during the forays she made among the languishing remnants of Latin traditions in California. Was it the state's twenty Franciscan missions ("the noblest ruins in the United States," as Charles Lummis of the *Los Angeles Times* later called them, in the *Landmarks Club Cookbook*)[11] that opened her mind to a new faith? Or was it the authentic adobe houses? Nannie's fascination with the pastoral Hispanic California of old came at a time when the novel *Ramona*, by Helen Hunt Jackson, was feeding a similar interest in millions of readers. The book was as significant to 1880s culture as *Uncle Tom's Cabin* had been to the Civil War era.

Nannie's decision to relinquish one Christian faith in order to take up another, however, was as characteristic of her as marrying at the ripe age of twenty-nine. Although she was bound by the conventions of her class, she remained true to her convictions, despite the reaction from her family, who received her decision to convert with the skepticism mainstream faiths reserve for obscure religious sects. "No one could figure where it came from," a bemused niece recalled a century later.[12]

In Chicago, Nannie regaled her beau with tales of citrus groves in Pasadena and gold in the streams of the Sierra Madre. The gold was no more than a fingerful, but to a young man with limited means, the idea that you could find gold in the mountains behind your house seemed like a dream. Marrying Nannie promised the dual benefits of a Southern California recuperation and a financially rewarding future.

The impending union was announced in the *Pasadena Daily Evening Star* on January 7, 1893. The groom, the story noted, was delayed in Flagstaff,

Arizona, while his train was undergoing repairs. (Neither his mother, Lavinia Dorland Neff, nor his sister, Carrie, could make the trip, since his father, Edwin Wallace Neff, had died just a few weeks earlier.) Joseph Medill's *Chicago Tribune* covered the McNally-Neff nuptials in the January 12, 1893, edition, describing the "beautiful winter home" of the McNallys where the event took place and the private midday ceremony presided over by a priest. It was reported that an orchestra played on the veranda while guests, including Mrs. T. S. C. Lowe, a noted collector of Southwestern artifacts and the wife of the inventor and entrepreneur Dr. Thaddeus Lowe, sipped coffee and nibbled chocolates. Eight hundred invitations had been sent out for the afternoon reception.[13]

A congratulatory telegram from Medill in Chicago became a family keepsake. So did a letter from Nannie's new sister-in-law, Mrs. Fred McNally, in Chicago. "The streets are one sheet of ice," she wrote. "Do you wonder that we all long for California?"[14] Unable to make the trip, she missed seeing Nannie in white silk brocade, her luxuriously thick brown hair pulled back in a fashionable psyche knot and trimmed with orange blossoms.

The newlyweds took the Surf Line south to the Hotel del Coronado near San Diego, a destination created by the railroads. Ed hunted and fished, while Nannie developed film in a darkroom provided for box-camera amateurs. Later they journeyed cross-country by Pullman to the World's Columbian Exposition in Chicago. Returning west, they settled temporarily in Altadena, where they rode in the Arroyo Seco, a deep riverbed that attracted hunters with its quail, rabbits, coyotes, and wildcats. Ed Neff's participation in the fledgling Progressives Club was cut short, perhaps after admonitions from the McNally family to remain politically neutral. Their stake in the railroad was, of course, at odds with the rising public pressure

ABOVE: *Nannie McNally's wedding portrait*

RIGHT: *Correspondence from Nannie's sister-in-law, who was not able to leave Chicago to attend the wedding*

P.S. Mamma & I were very sweet, your sister entertained us, and while not the same as we here — no finer than. We missed you all.

Nannie. Please ask your Hubby where any box of candy.

VMC
140 Astor Street.

Chez Moi.
Monday.
February 27-1893.

My dearest Nannie:

We enjoyed your welcome letter, and interesting description of your wedding, immensely.

It was indeed sweet and kind in you to write me about it.

I think a wedding at Pasadena. and especially within the beautiful grounds of Fairyland itself. or La Mirada. must indeed. have been an

Seated to the right, a pensive Nannie Neff appeared in a Greek-inspired dance at Pasadena's Grand Opera House on April 7, 1893

to free the land, the economy, and the government
from the control of the mighty rails. Ed's new member-
ships in the California Club, the Valley Hunt Club, the
Los Angeles Chamber of Commerce, and La Fiesta de
Los Angeles, which staged fairs, parades, and balls,
suited his boosterish father-in-law far better.

Fifteen hundred spectators watched Nannie and a
dozen other ladies perform in a new civic celebration
called the Pageant of Roses on April 7, 1893, at the
Pasadena Grand Opera House.[15] Nannie wore a loose,
gauzy gown, embellished with a Grecian key motif to
accommodate her increasing girth, for a child was on
the way. Andrew McNally Neff, named for his maternal
grandfather, was born on November 9 at the Altadena
house. With a number of maiden McNally aunts living
there, caring for the infant was a shared responsibility.
Visitors arrived constantly, among them a writer from
the *Chicago Herald* doing a story about progress at the
La Mirada settlement. "Now the labor is begun," he
reported, "of setting out thousands of orange and
lemon and walnut and almond trees, in long rows as
straight as a surveyor can make them. Mr. McNally will
be assisted in it by his son-in-law, E. D. Neff, who is
about to build himself a substantial and elegant
dwelling on the place."[16]

The norm in architectural styles in La Mirada was
the jigsaw-decorated, wood-sided house constructed
from plans ordered out of a pattern book. What was
being built for the Neffs, however, was a custom-
designed, two-story, wood-frame house covered by
creamy portland cement applied to emulate mud-
based adobe. They had hired Frederick Roehrig, the
same architect who had designed the McNallys' house
in Altadena.[17] Ed, Nannie, and young Andrew were in
residence, and ready, by the time Nannie bore her second son, on January 28, 1895.

TOP: *Depicted in* The Country Gentleman of California, *the
Roehrig-designed Neff house was constructed in 1894*
BOTTOM: *Roehrig also designed the Southern California Railway's
La Mirada depot*

The first four of Nannie and Ed Neff's six children: from left, Wallace, Della, Marie, and Andrew

WEANED ON THE NEW "OLD MISSION"
STYLE OF ARCHITECTURE

A teletyped message announcing the birth of the healthy, eight-pound, blue-eyed Edwin Wallace (named after his paternal grandfather) was immediately sent over the depot wire.[18] The weather that morning was a booster's nightmare. Twenty-eight-degree temperatures greeted Ed as he ran down to the depot to send the telegram. There was no sign of the balmy Mediterranean climes depicted in the La Mirada literature, and snow blanketed the Sierra Madre Mountains in the distance. Controlled fires had blazed in the groves throughout the night to keep the lemon trees from freezing.

Nannie rested in the birthing room, where she was to endure two more deliveries. On April 14, she bundled the infant into a carriage and rode with Ed to Saint Mary Catholic Church in Whittier, where the baby was baptized while grandmother McNally and two great aunts looked on. The infant's second venture outside the family home occurred when the Neffs rode the dusty bridle paths to Altadena for Easter Sunday luncheon on April 20. The meal was interrupted when someone smelled smoke. The Raymond Hotel, which they could see from the veranda, was in flames on a South Pasadena hilltop a half-dozen miles south. By three o'clock it was a shell.

The specter of the inferno remained in Nannie's mind for the next sixty-four years.

Time passed, and the baby's given name, Edwin, was forsaken for his middle name, Wallace. His circle grew larger with the birth of Delia in 1896, named for her maternal grandmother, and Marie, in 1898. Marie was a blue baby, in the parlance of a time when rest was all that could be offered to infants with congenital heart disease. Sometime after her birth, Wallace's brown curls were snipped off, so he wouldn't be mistaken for a girl. The result pleased his mother so much that she sent his portrait to Chicago, where his grandfather included it in a Rand McNally McGuffey-type reader. As he matured, Wallace grew to resemble his mother, with her broad Irish jaw and prominent nose.

Wallace's growth was casually documented in the kind of book mothers rely upon to record first steps and words. Photos show his brother, Andrew, at his side, sharing toy trains, dolls, dogs, and even a baby lamb. The two pitched a tent in the orchard on January 28, 1899—Wallace's fourth birthday—and shared cake inside with friends. As a brilliant orange sun set, Wallace asked his brother, "Was that heaven?" According to Wallace's baby book, Andrew replied, "It was hell," referring to the heat.[19]

A CORNER IN LEMON ORCHARD, WINDERMERE RANCH, LA MIRADA.

TOP: *Panoramic view of McNally's olive and lemon trees with the Neff house and barns on the left*

BOTTOM LEFT: *The first label used on crates of lemons grown at La Mirada*

BOTTOM RIGHT: *Lake Windermere, described in* The Country Gentleman of California *as "a beautiful lake, surrounded by a park planted with rare tress and shrubs"*

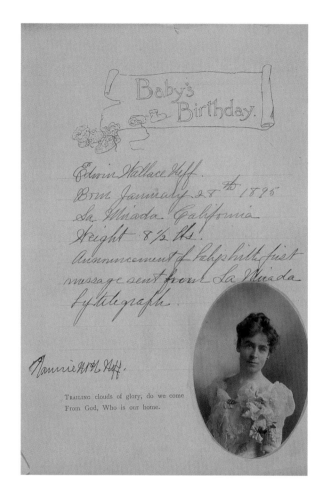

Wallace Neff's baby book

TOP: *Andrew, left, and Wallace in a La Mirada cornfield*
BOTTOM: *From left, Wallace, Della, and Andrew in the yard of the Neffs' La Mirada house*

Together they made the rounds of the ranch with their father, observing cows giving milk and boisterous hogs being fed. Ed watered his exotic palms by hand, carrying a .22-caliber rifle to fend off linnets that pecked at the fruit in the orchard. At the blacksmith's bench at the stables, the boys watched the smithy shoe mules and mend harnesses. When the corn was high, the cook prepared corn omelettes and waffles according to Nannie's recipes. (Nannie contributed some of these recipes to a cookbook assembled to raise money and awareness for the mission restoration cause.)[20]

In the groves, Andrew and Wallace watched Japanese day laborers spread canvas under the trees before shaking the olives from the branches. Inside the mill, they saw juicy green olives being pulverized by five-foot-round steel wheels. The mill was far and away Roehrig's most distinctive accomplishment at La Mirada. With its quatrefoil window, compound round arched portal entry, and scalloped gable overhead, it was eye-catching enough for an exposition. While the boys had no conception of architectural quality, they knew air quality, and the rancid mill could make them gag. Wooden vats held the smelly but prized olive oil until it was divvied up into quart bottles that sold for $1.50 apiece to the Owl Drug Company and Jonathan and Occidental clubs. The Hotel Green and Raymond Hotel were also customers, and sixty carloads of olives and lemons were sent east annually.[21]

Extending overhead from the mill to the citrus packing plant was an arch with a sign that proclaimed "McNally's Olive Oil." It looked like one of the gateways city fathers were building over the main streets of various new California towns. Passengers could catch a glimpse of it as they disembarked at the depot on the other side of the tracks. Inside the packing plant, Ed Neff maintained a laboratory where he experimented with a new citrus product called the pomelo, dabbling with a salve made from the rind to

TOP: *The mill designed by Frederick Roehrig*
BOTTOM: *The packing plant, dominated by an arch that advertised McNally's Olive Oil*

TOP: *Packing plants at La Mirada were typical of those in Southern California's citrus colonies*
BOTTOM: *Japanese grove workers at La Mirada resided in quarters that had a kitchen, reading room, and sleeping porch, with a bathhouse at the rear; the courtyard above features a Japanese garden*

ease the pain of skin lesions.

A pair of sphinxes flanked the entrance to the driveway leading to the Neff house. They were unlike anything in Southern California—except the sphinxes at the entrance to the McNally house in Altadena. Sphinxes and mission-like buildings were among the devices used to draw attention to the settlement in remote, dry, flat southeast Los Angeles County.

During the scorching days of summer, the children found shade on the wide veranda of the house, where they were shielded from the heat by potted plants. Ten times a day, a Southern California Railway whistle would announce the arrival of northbound and southbound trains. During the winter months, the children could be found in the foyer, by the fireplace, which had a broad, arched opening that resembled that of the World's Fair's striking Transportation Building.

In the hot summer months, the family traveled to the shore at the Del Coronado or Long Beach. One summer when Wallace was four, his family set off on the Santa Fe to visit the McNallys in Chicago's posh Lincoln Park and Lake Forest neighborhoods. In the winter months, the Neffs journeyed north by carriage to the Altadena house, where they could find three generations of wintering McNallys. Along the route, young Wallace saw Pio Pico's adobe on the banks of the Los Angeles River. Little more than an empty, crumbling building with peeling plaster, it had been stripped of its furnishings by vandals.[22] Above Alhambra, where they hitched the horses to a tree and had a picnic lunch, the Neffs passed another famed local adobe, El Molino Viejo, which had served as the flour mill for the Mission San Gabriel.

In Altadena, Wallace and his cousins would be underfoot as McNally and his cronies relaxed on the veranda. Colonel G. G. Green of Woodbury, New Jersey, was among the most colorful of them. He was so taken

ABOVE: *The sphinx gates at the McNallys' ranch were reproduced on
many of the La Mirada citrus labels*
RIGHT: *The sphinxes faced Stage Road, an old stagecoach route*

The abandoned adobe of Pio Pico, who had once served as governor of California

three-story McNally house, a pleasing meld of early Queen Anne and late shingle style, was the size of a small hotel, yet the family called it "the cottage." McNally saw that its clapboard siding was regularly repainted and photographed, and sent images off to magazine editors and postcard printers.[25] But McNally's real avocation was horticulture, and since almost anything would grow in Southern California if watered, the transformation did not take long after he piped in a supply from the Sierra Madre. By 1898, his grounds were so enveloped in roses and orange trees, a Chicago reporter noted, "There is not a bare spot as large as a saucer."[26] Deodar cedars planted along Santa Rosa Avenue by the founders of the community were cared for by McNally's Chinese gardener.[27] No one dared eat the mysterious green fruit on the trees McNally brought from Mexico, so the avocados dropped to the bottom of the reservoirs and rotted.

Looking at images of the McNally compound in magazines and newspapers, those unfamiliar with Southern California must have reacted with disbelief. How could a house have roses growing in the garden if there were snow-covered mountains in the immediate background? Photo captions such as "Inhaling the rich fragrance of ten thousand times ten thousand sweet scented flowers" made the scene even more unbelievable. McNally did his best to persuade prospective travelers that the aridity of Southern California did not inhibit horticulture. If they came, they could expect to find the vegetation of home.

So many visitors streamed in and out of the McNally house—grandchildren, reporters, and guests—that the furnishings had to hold up like a hotel's. Carpeting laid in 1888 was dense enough to last into the Eisenhower years. Windows were draped with lace curtains to frame views of the San Gabriel Valley. Oak and redwood mantelpieces, wainscoting, and floors held up to the wear. Sheltered from the sun by

with Altadena that he named both his daughter and his Pullman car Altadena. Green dabbled in patent medicine concoctions like Green's August Flower and Boschee's German Syrup. Hotels were another of his investment outlets. Picking up E. C. Webster's failed establishment in a foreclosure sale, Green added his name to the confection of turrets, terra-cotta, and Moorish-Turkish embellishments designed by the increasingly ubiquitous Frederick Roehrig, and created a Pasadena institution, the Hotel Green. Green's house west of the McNally property was notable for the massive rocks of its perimeter walls.[23]

The industrialists did their best to remake life in Southern California according to an East Coast model. They began by changing Spanish street names to English, and then organized electric railroads, starting with the Los Angeles, Pasadena and Altadena Railway Company.[24] Altadena's Millionaire's Row featured an explosion of architectural styles that would have been at home in shingled Newport, Rhode Island. The

The smoking room, added to the McNallys' house in the mid-1890s

green-striped canvas awnings, the McNallys played bridge on the veranda. "I never understood it," their granddaughter Helen Belford remarked about their general obliviousness to authentic local pastimes. "They might as well have been in Chicago."

Such creatures of habit from Chicago as Charles Wacker, Jacob Rehm, R. T. Crane, Edward P. Ripley, and R. R. Donnelley congregated in the octagonal Turkish-style smoking room on the east side of the house.[28] The exotic site of Easter egg hunts, it featured gold-leaf Arabic inscriptions on the cornice, piles of Oriental rugs, brass urns, tasseled cushions, and a phonograph that screeched Gilbert and Sullivan

operettas. Rumors that McNally had taken the room from the Ottoman Empire's Kidiva on the Midway Plaisance at the Chicago World's Fair have never been confirmed.[29] Perhaps Roehrig created it using the room from the fair as inspiration.[30] While the mystery of its origins remains, it continues to provide a rare vision of late-nineteenth-century West Coast life. The mania for Moorish style among the wealthy had spread across the continent, and the smoking room was one of Wallace Neff's earliest experiences with the fascination for things that were Hispanic or from the Iberian Peninsula.

*Sketch drawn by five-year-old
Wallace Neff*

*Three-year-old Wallace Neff on
his first trip outside California,
at his grandparents' home in
Chicago surrounded by siblings
and cousins*

SUNDAY RITUAL

The McNally women were responsible for overseeing the children's activities. Religious studies were essential, although which religion was never agreed upon to anyone's satisfaction, since each of the women—Mrs. McNally, her husband's two maiden sisters, Nannie, and her two sisters—went her own way to worship. The Sunday luncheon at the McNally dining table became a family tradition unhampered by questions of faith. Week in and week out, grandmother Adelia served chicken fricassee. Following dessert, the children ran through the orange groves, sailed miniature boats in the reservoirs, caught trout stocked in the ponds, and explored the aviary with its goldfinches, songbirds, and pheasants.

The attractions of Altadena began to outnumber those of La Mirada. Several factors determined the Neff family's decision to move north. The foothill air was considered therapeutic for fragile, young Marie, who continued to suffer from a heart defect. And beyond that, the two-room schoolhouse in La Mirada, which served all ages and economic levels, was not providing the academic rigor Nannie wanted for her children. But the main reason was economic: Ed had not been able to find a market for the Country Gentlemen Estates. The boom of the 1880s, when people bought land sight unseen and then lost their savings, had left Southern California with a sullied reputation for land ventures.

After the Neffs relocated to Altadena, the Robert McGill family moved into the vacated Neff house, and for the next forty years, McGill managed the ranch. He watched citrus and olives thrive one year and then struggle the next. To pay La Mirada's bills, the undeveloped parcels were leased to tenant farmers. La Mirada joined the cooperative California Domestic Water Company to supplement the water supply, but in the process gave up eighty-four acres for its shares. There were still the lemon and olive groves to care for, and

Students from first through eighth grades posing in front of the La Mirada schoolhouse

the headaches that often afflict growers—insects, scale and mold, rot, viruses, frost, and the wait for an orchard to mature—were as prevalent and tiresome as the responsibilities of irrigation, spraying, and cultivation.[31] Roads that McNally had named La Habra, Araucaria, Acacia, Cypress, Windermere, Rubra, and Goldmella were seldom traveled. Rand McNally & Company nevertheless continued printing maps that showed La Mirada on a par with the growing neighboring towns of Norwalk, Downey, and Anaheim. Its 1903 *Guide to California* praised La Mirada for its "attractive homes surrounded by beautiful grounds" and "miles of shade trees from twenty to thirty feet high."[32]

Bosqui Eng. Co. S.F.

Illustration from a pamphlet printed by the Pasadena Improvement Company, luring prospective investors to Altadena

CHAPTER THREE

PASADENA RITES

Pasadena was the universally understood symbol for the gilt-edged well-to-do.
—Morrow Mayo

ANDREW MCNALLY NEVER MISSED an opportunity to announce to those within earshot that Southern California living could cure what ailed you. With reporters at his tail and a service in Chicago clipping stories on his whereabouts, he and his wife, Adelia, boarded the Santa Fe for Chicago every year just before Easter, proclaiming that Southern California's winter had added years to their lives.[1] In truth, like William Rand, Joseph Medill, and many of his friends from Chicago, McNally was battling heart disease aggravated by the pressures of boardroom decision making. After the Chicago papers accused him of giving thousands of dollars to a mayoral candidate to make sure that Rand McNally textbooks found their way into public school classrooms, his sojourns in the West became protracted.[2]

McNally's heart troubles and Marie's shortness of breath were worries the Neffs faced each day, but there were also pleasures like visits to Los Angeles to have the children photographed professionally and attending the annual fiesta. As the years passed, life in Los Angeles and Pasadena was becoming less arduous and more enjoyable: streets that had been illuminated by electric lights for twenty years were now being paved to accommodate the noisy horseless carriages. Men and women commuted to work on Huntington's trolley cars. The few remaining adobes around Los Angeles's central plaza were either crumbling from moisture

damage or being torn down in the name of slum clearance. (Adobe brick was not a material that the dozens of architectural firms on Main, Broadway, and Spring streets would consider using. Fired brick and mortar better served contemporary needs, as did rusticated stone like that found on the County Courthouse and City Hall.) At the Chamber of Commerce Building on the southeast corner of Fourth and Broadway, the Neff family marveled at an elephant made of walnuts that had originally been shown at the World's Columbian Exposition. Each month, some ten thousand visitors gawked at the curiosity before the novelty wore thin.

Pasadena was young compared to Los Angeles: middle-class Midwestern Prohibitionists had incorporated the city in 1886 to fight a proposed saloon, whereas the history of Los Angeles went back to 1781, when poor farmers of mixed blood came from the Mexican provinces of Sinaloa and Sonora to establish the pueblo. But by the early twentieth century, the civic agendas of Pasadena and Los Angeles were in sync: sell land, build industry, promote commerce. Ed Neff served on the board of one of the institutions promoting those values, La Fiesta de Los Angeles, which sponsored concerts and parades.

The Tournament of Roses, another well-known civic institution in which the Neffs and McNallys participated, helped the region shed its provincialism

Echo Mountain and the Mount Lowe Railway appeared in countless publications promoting exciting destinations in Southern California

when it became a national event. The celebration began when the Valley Hunt Club sponsored a parade on January 1, 1890, and three thousand curious spectators showed up to join the fun. Children scattered homegrown rose petals along Orange Grove Boulevard before a caravan of flower-decked carriages. That afternoon, on a lot east of Los Robles between Colorado and Santa Fe, mounted horsemen carrying twelve-foot lances set out to replicate a Spanish contest, competing to spear three rings hung thirty feet apart. Picnicking under giant oaks, guests were given oranges to take home.

By the following year, the club had dubbed the event "Dead of Winter." The next year, after frost ruined the rose season, the name was changed to the Orange Tournament. By the time Nannie Neff took the stage of the Grand Opera House with the Women's Guild in 1893, the celebration had become more than the Valley Hunt Club could handle. With visions of generating revenue for its hotels and restaurants, the Pasadena Board of Trade took over the Tournament of Roses in 1896.[3]

Another Pasadena mainstay in which the Neffs and McNallys invested time and funds was the Mount Lowe Railway. The brainchild of their brilliant, eccentric friend, Thaddeus Lowe (a professor who pioneered the use of balloons in warfare), it involved two counterbalanced cars on parallel tracks, which took passengers up thirty-two hundred feet to the top of Echo Mountain, where an electric car running over thirty-seven bridges continued the excursion six miles into the mountains. A searchlight at the 4,715-foot-elevation Inspiration Point was said to project a beam so powerful that a newspaper held in its path thirty-five miles away could be read at night.

Enticed by plenty of hype, much of it printed by Rand McNally & Company, thrill seekers made Mount Lowe a major tourist destination, although the hazards created by the harsh terrain were apparent.[4] The Neff children, blithely unaware of any risks the funicular represented, financial or otherwise, eagerly accompanied their grandfather on the cable car. The trip up the steep hillside was as thrilling as any twenty-first-century roller-coaster ride. At the top of the mountain, they dined at the Mount Lowe Alpine Tavern before retiring for the night at Echo Mountain House. The effusive editor of the railroad's newspaper regularly reported on their visits.[5] On the way back, McNally would blast a stag's horn through the canyons to let his wife know they were coming. Hiking was in vogue, and the tenacious McNally, even with a heart condition, often led a pack of men down the mountain, their wives on horseback, while the children took the rails.

For young Wallace Neff, Grandfather McNally appeared a supreme patriarch. He provided houses, vacations, servants, groceries, and clothing, as well as philosophies for living. The tenets of social Darwinism, which asserted the inevitability of the survival of the fittest, were preached at the dinner table. Wallace learned from his grandfather that

A bearded Andrew McNally, with companions including Marshall Field, returning from Mount Lowe to Altadena

reward came with effort and that the rich were rich because they had proved themselves superior.

Los Angeles was known for its antiunion leanings, and McNally talked about moving his business out of Chicago after negotiations with the typesetters' union grew testy, but he ran out of time. On May 5, 1904, while lunching at the California Club, he developed chills. He returned home to Altadena, abandoning plans to visit La Mirada later that day. He was diagnosed with pneumonia and died two days later, at the age of sixty-eight, worlds from the economic uncertainty of his Northern Ireland homeland.

A Santa Fe Pullman took the body to Chicago, where McNally was interred in the burial ground of the mighty, Graceland Cemetery. Marshall Field, C. H. McCormick, and others paid respects at the McNally home,[6] and some two hundred American newspapers printed his obituary. "If ever there was a noble man on this earth," McNally's fellow Los Angeles and Pasadena Electric Railway bondholder Moses H. Sherman wrote to Fred McNally, "it was your dear father. The tears are in my eyes as I mention his name."[7] A resolution from the Rand McNally & Company board called him the "real founder of the house, the one who in the truest sense has been responsible for its prosperity and enlargement."[8] William Rand, who was to live eleven years longer,[9] wrote to McNally's widow that her husband had possessed "a good heart, remarkable business ability and a strength of character."[10]

McNally's brother James sent Nannie copies of the Chicago newspapers that had published her father's obituary. "In years to come," he wrote, "all these marks of esteem for your father may be an incentive for your children to follow in the footsteps of their grandfather, than whom a kinder one never lived. His whole life had been devoted to the best interests of his children and grandchildren."[11]

McNally never achieved the prominence in Southern California that he had had in Chicago. His real influence came from his publishing house: Rand McNally & Company's travel literature was instrumental in shaping public perceptions of Southern California. Maps, handbills, and books extolling the region's virtues at the expense of its shortcomings contributed first to tourism and then to an expanding population. When McNally distributed photos of his turreted Altadena house to magazine after magazine and the published pictures showed a garden of roses and well-dressed people, they conveyed an image of a genteel, carefree destination.

The World's Columbian Exposition on which he labored set tastes well into the twentieth century and propelled trainloads of visitors to California, for the fair's California State Building was as good a vehicle for travel promotion as a Rand McNally map. Finally, for those who made the trip, McNally provided architectural and horticultural attractions. They became the standards by which young Wallace judged the natural and built environment.

McNally's seven hundred thousand dollars' worth of assets, recorded in Cook County Probate Court, were nowhere near the financial stratospheres of the railroad barons. His share of La Mirada was valued at $315,000. Nannie Neff received half the net proceeds of the rents, interest, and dividends from McNally's Chicago properties, and a percentage of the trust, which held shares in the map company. McNally's grandchildren would be provided for ten years after the last of his children died.[12] McNally's one male heir, Frederick George, took the helm of the map company, which had just begun producing the industry's first folded highway map.

GROWING UP IN ALTADENA

By the time the Neffs settled in Altadena in 1904, Los Angeles's population was reported to have quadrupled from its 1890 level to two hundred thousand. The growth would not have been possible without Henry Huntington's octopus-like system of electric streetcars (the Pacific Electric) and rail lines (the Southern Pacific). McNally and his partners in the Los Angeles and Pasadena Electric Railway sold out to Huntington, I. W. Hellman, and Huntington's uncle Collis on December 30, 1898, for one million dollars.[13] The Neffs and the McNallys had prospered largely because of their investment in such railroads, but the growing resentment of the rail trusts, which concentrated wealth with the few, may have accounted for their eagerness to sell. Of course, this was of little concern to eight-year-old Wallace, who was more focused on how his life had changed with his family's move. After the freedom he had enjoyed in rural La Mirada, life in Altadena seemed much more regimented.

It was an existence that resembled small-town life in any other part of America, for those who had means. The Neff house was called White Friars, for its painted white shingles.[14] From the veranda on Santa Clara Avenue, Wallace could watch Mount Lowe's rail cars moving across the Sierra Madre. He could gaze east upon hillsides brilliant with orange poppies and populated with picnickers who arrived on Sundays in their new horseless carriages. The dry, clear foothill air was especially appealing to asthmatics, who came in great numbers to live in tents rented for two dollars a month or in one of the area's many sanatoriums. It may have been during this impressionable period of his life that he noticed how the intense Southern California sunlight cast deep shadows in the afternoon. The contrast between the brightness of a white wall, like those of the Neff house, and the deep shadows created by overhangs brought recreational painters by the dozens into the

Andrew McNally's house and garage before the addition of the smoking room

foothills to capture the effects of the light.

The Neff house, complete with telephones, plumbing, and electricity, was a smaller version of the McNally house. Since electricity was unreliable, dual lighting fixtures were installed so that gas could take over when the electrical power failed. The parlor, filled with such Rand McNally titles as *The Little Lady of Lagunitas, Cloisters of California, Early California Hospitality,* and *Californian Trails,* was used to receive guests, who called on Wednesdays. The fragrance of roses was omnipresent when Nannie arranged vases in anticipation of an afternoon hand of euchre. To escape the female onslaught, Ed would leave to supervise the efforts of the Rubio Canyon Water Company. For his unpaid efforts, he was made a "director."

Horses and fraternal clubs were also significant to Ed, much as child rearing and religious faith were to Nannie. A high point for him was the year he served as president of the Tournament of Roses. Movie cameramen fought for space on the side of the road that January 1, 1906, as he led the floats past Orange Grove

ABOVE: *McNally at left, in his gardens, with his grandson Alexander Belford and his daughter Helen McNally Belford, at right*

OPPOSITE, TOP: *McNally's house, 1888, with the Sierra Madre Mountains looming a mile to the north*

OPPOSITE, BOTTOM: *The house in spring, circa 1895, with Christmas Tree Lane on the left*

Flowers at Altadena and Snow at Mt. Lowe,
Southern California.

Flower Beds and Snowbanks,
Beautiful Winter Scene in California.

Ed Neff as president of the Tournament of Roses, January 1, 1906

Boulevard's mansions, through the city's commercial center on Colorado Boulevard, to the parade's conclusion at Tournament Park. May Sutton, a tennis star, was the queen that year. A young architect named Myron Hunt, who served as one of the judges, awarded Altadena High School the trophy for best float. Wallace and his siblings brought up the rear on bicycles they had covered with flowers.

After the parade, Ed served as a judge of a race between chariots—a tournament first. A rider named Ed Off, who was slated to be president the following year, rode on one of two four-horse rigs. Unfortunately, when Off got to the finish line, his horses wouldn't stop. In the second race, the competitors and their steeds landed in a pile of mud. It was the beginning and the end of chariot racing in Pasadena.

Wallace and Andrew, who were growing up quickly, delighted in typical adolescent pranks like soaping railroad tracks, despite numerous warnings that their grandfather had once ridden on an electric car that had screeched to a halt because of just such an infraction.[15] They also attended cotillions, including one held in the third-floor ballroom of the Up de Graff house on Columbia Street. In 1904 and 1906, Nannie bore two more sons, William and John, and how she was able to control her brood on Sunday mornings at St. Andrew Catholic Church without the help of her husband, who did not attend, is uncertain.

In 1907, Nannie's brother, Fred, died suddenly, and her brother-in-law, Harry Clow, assumed the presidency of Rand McNally. Mapmaking was so much a part of the family's lives that Fred's son Andrew spent his honeymoon mapping the route between Chicago and Milwaukee. The bride idled in the horseless carriage while he photographed white arrows painted on trees and buildings. The film was sent to Rand McNally to be reproduced in the company's auto guides, an early version of the road map.

The Neffs, meanwhile, debated what to do about Marie, whose heart remained underdeveloped. At the time, the German medical establishment was considered the world's best. Germany had a vast network of scientists and research facilities that attracted American doctors, and its mountain spas were famous for their restorative mineral water. Having settled in California for Ed's health, they decided to leave for Marie's. The rest of the children would have the opportunity of a lifetime to broaden their education.

Their departure in 1909 coincided with a number of momentous changes in the United States. The first motion picture made in Los Angeles, *In the Sultan's Power*, had been filmed two years earlier in a rented mansion at Eighth and Olive streets. Moviegoing was becoming a national pastime, and studios like the Selig Polyscope Company and the Bison Company had set up for business on the Pacific Coast. The mighty Southern Pacific Railroad, whose political influence had once extended from local sheriffs to the United States Senate, was among the casualties during the years immediately after the Neffs left town, as Hiram Johnson, who won the governorship of California in 1910 on the Progressive ticket, proceeded to remove railroad supporters from state offices. During these years, class conflict was evident in battles between labor and management throughout the United States, but by October 1, 1910, when the Los Angeles Times Building was dynamited, the Neffs were tackling the Swiss Alps in their Franklin automobile. And they were still in Europe in 1912, when frost wiped out the entire citrus crop at La Mirada.

Marie, Della, Nannie, John, Bill, Ed, and Andrew Neff at the beginning of their trip through Europe

‹ CHAPTER FOUR ›

THE GRAND TOUR AND BACK

*Any notion that these early Pasadenans were merely vulgar and tasteless
social pretenders fades when you stop in front of a Greene & Greene house.*
—Jack Smith, *Los Angeles Times* (October 10, 1983)

*I*N 1909, THE SIX YOUNG NEFFS and their parents
set sail for Europe from the port of New York. A new
air-cooled Franklin automobile, which they had
arranged to have shipped from a factory in Syracuse,
New York, awaited them in Munich. Ed preferred the
Franklin because it didn't require manual cranking,
but it was still a horseless carriage and it made for
rough riding over the treacherous Alpine roads.[1]
Whenever the car gave out (as it frequently did, to judge
from photographs in the Neffs' family albums), oxen
had to be found to pull it to the nearest garage.

After enrolling Wallace and Andrew in an American school in Munich, the family drove to a Bad
Nauheim spa where congenital respiratory and heart
ailments were treated and where the aged and ailing
came to restore their youth and health. Jack and Bill
pedaled a miniature-airplane-like toy up and down a
hillside while their parents consulted with physicians
on Marie's behalf. A governess and a therapy program
were arranged. The family returned for regular visits,
and at one point, Nannie arranged for an extended stay
with her ailing daughter.

Still, the Neffs managed to enjoy their travels in
Europe. At Oberammergau in Bavaria, they watched
the Passion play with the Crane-Gartzs of Altadena,
before taking in the Salzburg music festival. Later, they
all crowded into the cockpit of a zeppelin and flew off
over the countryside. They also motored to the Eiger

Glacier and posed at the entrance to its cave.

In Zurich, they visited the timbered chalet of
Swiss hero Adam Naef, where the banner he had carried into battle four hundred years earlier was displayed, and jigsawed balustrades wrapped around
myriad porches. In Ireland, the vicar of Sawrey,
Reverend F. G. McNally, and his maiden sisters,
Matilda, Annie, Elizabeth, and Frances, welcomed their
niece and her family. The Neffs also visited St. Patrick's
Cathedral in Armagh, which had hymnbooks printed
by R. P. McWaters (with whom Andrew McNally had
apprenticed) in the pews. In Holland, they saw the
windmills. In Paris, Nannie captured the 984-foot-high
Eiffel Tower with her Brownie.

Andrew and Wallace joined the tour during school
vacations, visiting Rome for Easter break of 1910, where
they got to see the pope and the grandeur of Saint
Peter's. Their suits and ties and celluloid collars were
covered with soot after a day in the Franklin, yet Wallace, photographed by his mother, remained bandbox
handsome. She saw to it that the youngest Neff boys
were well groomed and dressed identically in lederho-
sen. Della wore nautical blouses, with huge bows in her
Gibson girl-style hair. Nannie wore an enormous black
auto veil over a large hat, secured with a long pin.

In March of 1911, Wallace left Munich to enroll at
the Institut Sillig in Vevey, Switzerland. The reason for
the move is unclear, but it may have occurred because

53

Swiss hero Adam Naef's Zurich chalet

friends from Pasadena, brother and sister Thaddeus and Louise Up de Graff, were enrolled at Sillig while their father, a doctor, studied medicine in Switzerland. The two families visited Oberammergau together, and it was there, according to family lore, that the sixteen-year-old Wallace and the attractive eighteen-year-old Louise began a romance.

Back in Vevey, Wallace's family set up housekeeping in a chateau known as the Villa Valerie, on the northeast shore of Lake Geneva. The children were given tutors, and Bill and Jack learned German and French well enough to converse with the locals. Della studied the harp. All became accomplished skiers. And hurtling down the mountainsides, Wallace and the Sillig bobsled team won competitions at Saint Moritz and Les Arant.

Marie's health continued to worsen despite the care she was receiving. No amount of healing water could create what was never there—a healthy body. Marie and her mother made a pilgrimage to Lourdes, but late in 1912, after three years in Bad Nauheim, Marie died. Her burial brought the immediate family together, and Nannie and Ed determined that they should remain together. Wallace left the school at Sillig and the family moved to Munich, where Andrew was excelling in chemistry at the German-American Romers Institute.

Wallace roamed the city, which some were calling the new Athens, with sketch pad in hand. Munich had none of the attributes of an industrial city—no evident poverty and scarcely a single factory. Instead, it had a university and, according to the novelist and California émigré Gertrude Atherton, "an atmosphere of independence and beauty, beauty everywhere."[2] Europe's landed aristocracy still ruled the city's cultural life.

"In Germany," Neff later recalled, "architects go out in the country in the summertime and study drawing

and painting. I went, expecting to spend a couple of
months with these famous professors. One of them,
Peter Paul Muller, was probably one of the best painters
in Germany. He showed me all kinds of little tricks.
'Don't paint your trees too tight,' he told me. 'Get some
life in them.'"[3] The professor's cryptic advice to the
young Neff to loosen his hand, scribbled in rune-like
German on one of his drawings, was, Neff said, "the best
lesson I ever had."

Another mentor, Fritz Noekaner, an architect for
whom he clerked, encouraged his aptitude for invention, and on February 19, 1913, the eighteen-year-old
submitted an application to patent a device that measured an automobile's angle of incline on a slope with a
tube filled with fluid and inscribed with a cross line.
Neff received his patent from the U.S. Patent Office the
following year.[4]

He devised a self-sharpening pencil and sought a
patent for that as well. Drawing was his passion. A new
kind of architecture—modernism—was being discussed in German architecture classrooms, but it did
not seem to catch his interest, if, in fact, he was even
aware of it. He gravitated to villages like Naumburg,
Ritzbuhel, Gruyeres, Thun, Frabertsham, Grand Villars,
and Steffisburg—far from where the new architecture
was emerging—to sketch on weekends. Sometimes he
took a 2:00 a.m. train from Munich to the Alps, ten
hours away, to ski, subsisting on rolls and sausages,
and returned the following day.[5]

When the family toured France and Italy in their
faithful Franklin, he observed the region's vernacular
forms: steeply pitched roofs in the mountains, flat
roofs on seaside villas, wood houses in the Alps, stucco
ones in the Mediterranean, straw roofs on the farmhouses of the Dolomites in northeast Italy, and tile
roofs in the Po Valley, Italy's only sizable flat land. In
southeast Italy, he saw beehive-shaped *trulli*, thatched
like English Cotswold cottages.

Early sketch by Wallace Neff

TOP: *Young Neff in Europe*
BOTTOM: *Wallace Neff, at right, in the cabin of a dirigible*

It was in Italy, the traditional final stop on the grand tour, that Neff committed himself to the study of architecture. In Venice first and later in Florence, immersed in drawing ocher-colored villas, burnt-sienna-shaded cathedrals, and taupe-pigmented garden walls, he was captivated. The settings, which recalled the hillsides of Los Angeles and La Mirada's olive trees, were not unfamiliar.

Pompeii's ruins also brought out his sketch pad, as did Roman Catholic shrines and Andrea Palladio's villas in the northern countryside. Nearly all Italy's offerings inspired him, as they had the architecture critic John Ruskin, who associated learning with things that had been seen rather than read or heard, with places rather than men or institutions.[6] Neff learned with a pencil in hand, not a book; he never had much patience for reading. A scribble of a thought suited him. A message on the back of a postcard was his idea of a letter.

He sent his father one from the Alz River with a note about the good weather, fishing, and swimming, noting that he would be home soon. By "home" he meant Munich, for California was long removed from his experience.

Then, in the summer of 1914, Germany was gripped by fear. Archduke Francis Ferdinand of Austria-Hungary was assassinated in Sarajevo in June, and war broke out in August. Ambitious Germany dominated the alliance of the Central powers that included Austria-Hungary and Turkey. The Western powers, France and England, their ally Russia, and soon Italy formed the opposition.

The Neffs left the German side of Lake Constance for the Swiss side so quickly they had to abandon five years' worth of acquisitions, their clothing, and all of Neff's drawings. In Switzerland, Neff sketched furiously, filling tablet after tablet. He never saw combat as a soldier, but as a civilian, in the company of his father and Andrew, he visited a French battlefield where he came face to face with the wounded.[7] Like the Neffs, a hundred and fifty thousand other Americans also found themselves stranded, without funds, and an institution was born: Herbert Hoover oversaw the American Citizens Committee in London, which attempted to aid such refugees by issuing cards—possibly the first credit cards—that identified them as U.S. citizens without funds.[8] Six weeks later, ships packed with Americans sailed for home on the strength of $1.5 million in credit.

Five years in Europe had provided Neff with a perspective on culture, humanity, and geography that he would have missed sitting in a Pasadena classroom. He had learned a smattering of Italian and French and a great deal of German. He had seen England and most of the continent.[9] The suffering of his sister Marie, the family's flight from Germany, and his own interaction with the wounded added to his resolve to make something of his life.

The Neffs returned to Pasadena before Christmas in 1914 and took up residence at the Maryland Hotel. "The war did not drive Mr. and Mrs. Edwin Dorland Neff and their delightful family of young people back to America," the hotel newsletter reported. "It only delayed their coming by four long months, and even at that, their most precious possessions are left behind in their trunks in Munich. Think of gathering gifts for five long years, picking up this treasure and that in out of the way places, selecting with care and discrimination gifts for a Christmas reunion in the home land, and then to be obliged to leave your Christmas presents behind you. Hard luck, but anyone who has had even a glimpse of the cruel war on the other side, as Mr. Neff and his sons had in visiting the wounded on the French frontier, will not complain of losing Christmas gifts."[10]

The bobsled team at the Institut Sillig, winter 1912, with Wallace Neff at the helm

CHANGES AT HOME

When Wallace Neff had left for Europe at the age of fourteen, railroads and horses were the prevailing modes of transportation, but by the time he returned at the age of nineteen, the automobile was in ascendance. The years between 1900 and the outbreak of World War I had seen a growing discontent among the less privileged in America, who were frustrated by the wealth and power of capitalists like the McNallys and their heirs. Politicians wrote laws restricting business practices considered monopolistic, stripping industrialists of their economic control. In 1912, the Progressive Party had tried to send Theodore Roosevelt back to the White House, but a more low-key candidate, Woodrow Wilson, had won the election instead. And in 1913, the Internal Revenue Service was created to collect taxes on personal income.

Southern Californians had been largely unperturbed by Archduke Francis Ferdinand's assassination. Wasn't he from somewhere in Central Europe? Public interest in national and world affairs was still minimal

Ed Neff's expertise with a shotgun was news in the Los Angeles sports pages

E. D. Neff, All-around Sportsman,
is to shoot on the Southern California Rifles team against Company I of the National Guard, today, at Devil's Gate, Arroyo Seco.

on the West Coast in early 1914, and Governor Hiram Johnson's Progressive Party was too busy fighting to stay in power to pay much attention to the tensions in Europe. Then, in late July, locals awoke from the days of summer somnolence and ice-cream socials. World War I had begun.

Anticipating the entry of the U.S. into the war, Californians like Ed Neff began preparing. He had been a crack shot since his days at La Mirada, and at the age of fifty-five, he organized Company 40 of the California Military Reserve, becoming captain of the unit. None of this sharpshooting held the allure for Andrew or Wallace that it did for their brothers Bill and Jack, who won awards under the guidance of their father.[11] Father and sons practiced shooting in the deep gorge of the Arroyo Seco, the geographic boundary between Pasadena and Los Angeles.[12]

The arroyo's pristine natural beauty had begun to erode after the Valley Hunt Club gave up riding there in the 1890s and moved to Orange Grove Boulevard, focusing on social activities instead of sport. With no one giving thought to its welfare, the winding valley began deteriorating. Although the City of Pasadena had

set aside 620 acres as a natural reserve in 1910, it made no effort to protect them. Vandals looking for firewood stripped the valley of its giant sycamores and native live oaks. Rubbish, garbage, and dead horses were dumped unceremoniously in the fields of wildflowers. In fact, Pasadenans had not looked out for the arroyo since 1903, when Teddy Roosevelt had come to town and suggested that it be turned into a park. In 1913, the Colorado Street Bridge had opened 150 feet above the gorge, and the streambed had continued to dry up as water was impounded for the reservoirs of the Los Angeles Water Company to supply the area's growing population.

While the Neffs were overseas, the rest of the local landscape had continued to evolve as well, as city fathers annexed region after region. Los Angeles, which soon had a population of 320,000, became the first U.S. city to regulate industry and residences with a zoning ordinance.[13] After years of dispute over where to locate the Port of Los Angeles, it had finally been dredged in San Pedro in 1912 and had opened Los Angeles to international trade. The city had tapped the lakes and rivers of a High Sierra valley called Owens, bringing water through a conveyance system 250 miles long. Where the previous water supply provided enough for no more than 250,000 people, now millions could be accommodated.

Following the introduction of the Model T in 1909, California voters had approved an $18 million bond issue to create a system of paved highways. Climate and scenery combined with low gasoline prices and good roads made the state a drivers' paradise, and oil companies began encouraging driving by commissioning mapmakers like Rand McNally & Company to print highway maps.

REDISCOVERING SOUTHERN CALIFORNIA

In the summer of 1915, driving a fresh new Franklin, Ed Neff took the family north on the new Ridge Route to see the Panama-Pacific International Exposition in San Francisco celebrating the completion of the Panama Canal. The road was dangerous but Ed, who was used to the byways of the Alps, was in his element. Afterward, they left twenty-one-year-old Andrew at the University of California across the bay in Berkeley, where he was continuing his studies in chemical engineering.

In the wake of the earthquake that had ravaged the city on the morning of April 18, 1906, spawning fires that destroyed twenty-eight thousand buildings, San Francisco was experiencing an economic revival. The centerpiece of this new growth was the fair, which featured gardens, sculpture, fountains, and a dozen brand-new neoclassical palaces along a two-mile stretch of waterfront. The electrically illuminated, domed, and arched Palace of Fine Arts was the public's favorite. According to California historian Kevin Starr, the exposition evoked a new California and bade farewell to the frontier.[14] Roaming the fair, twenty-year-old Wallace Neff might have safely concluded that Renaissance and classical European architecture served America's cultural needs. Visitors had been falling in love with San Francisco since the gold rush, and Neff was determined to discover its virtues for himself, sketching and walking its forty-two hillsides.

He chose to return to Pasadena, however, along with the rest of the family, to plan his future. Driving along the Camino Real, they all stopped and waited while he sketched the Mission Santa Barbara and, later, the mission in San Fernando, trying to master a sense of depth in his romantic renderings of the eroded mud-and-saw *padrillo* bricks damaged by time and vandals.

Back in Southern California, he discovered the work of Charles and Henry Greene. Street after street was dominated by their grand bungalows, lavish versions of humbler houses that had sprung up in the area while the Neffs were overseas. (One of these wood-shingle edifices had been commissioned by Dr. and Mrs. Arthur A. Libby Jr., the aunt and uncle of Neff's friend Louise Up de Graff.)[15] Their intricate craftsmanship was prohibitively expensive for all but the wealthy. Rich woods, without a hint of a nail, enfolded interiors and exteriors. Tons of rock scavenged from local riverbeds were set into concrete to decorate retaining walls. Many of the Greenes' designs sat on the community's flattest and most visible lots, where they were as horizontal in profile as Frank Lloyd Wright's Prairie houses were in Chicago.

Some considered the Greenes' woodwork as fine as that of Japanese cabinetry, while others complained they could not see the woodwork for the dark interiors created by low-hanging eaves that kept out the year-round sun. "They stand as a strange paradox," one critic wrote. "The newcomers who came westward for the sun built homes in which they get practically none."[16] One natural phenomenon of the bungalows that impressed Neff was the shadows created by beams projecting from gables.

The Neff family settled in the same Altadena house where they lived before their sojourn overseas, for the renters who had occupied it in the interim had returned to their native Scotland after war broke out. The two youngest Neff boys went off to Pasadena's Throop Elementary, which had been reorganized as the Throop Polytechnic Institute. Eighteen-year-old Della remained at home, where she was sheltered by her mother, Nannie, for as long as Nannie lived. She was the one living daughter, and as attractive as she was, she never seemed to be interested in finding a man or a vocation. In one of her rare public acts, she donned a plumed and ribboned hat and rode in the 1915 Tournament of Roses in the Maryland Hotel's horse-drawn carriage.

Wallace Neff at the wheel of the Franklin automobile the family used in Europe, circa 1911

A "SPECIAL STUDENT" AT MIT

Pasadena had a number of architects who would take on young men who wanted to learn the profession, but Neff was not interested in apprenticing with a master builder. He intended to pursue "the study of the art and science of buildings," as the curriculum was described at the Throop College of Technology, a twenty-two-acre campus kitty-corner from the school his younger brothers attended. The letter *T* on the south ridge of Mount Wilson announced Throop's presence below.

Throop applicants needed a high school diploma, however, a document Neff could not produce, despite his extensive studies in Europe, so he applied to Polytechnic High School as well. At the same time, he sent his portfolio to the exalted Massachusetts Institute of Technology. He "wanted to learn mathematics," he told a reporter years later. "They gave me a test, designing a library. Fortunately I had been studying with architects in Florence who had given me a similar problem. When the professor saw it he said, 'All right, bring him in.'"[17]

He was accepted to MIT as a "special student" in the class of 1918. He could attend, but without a high

school degree he could not graduate. Still, he had not only had gained admission to the first school in America to teach architecture, established in 1868—the alma mater of such architects as Louis Sullivan and Myron Hunt—he had passed muster with steely Ralph Adams Cram, its dean. Cram viewed the admissions process as his opportunity to keep prospective architects *out of* MIT, for he had seen too many genteel young men like Wallace Neff chose architecture over medicine or law because it required fewer years of study. Fashionable and gentlemanly, architecture school was certain to bring employment from fellow members of the leisure class. "If I found that if a candidate seemed inclined towards architecture because of any of these," Cram warned, "I tried to dissuade him from the course."[18]

Cram had turned to teaching after designing college campuses and a remarkable seventy cathedrals and churches with his partners, Bertram Goodhue and Frank Ferguson. He held such strong opinions that teaching was a natural outlet for him. Or it would have been if he wasn't so outspokenly opposed to the architectural philosophy espoused by most of his fellow academics. At MIT, the faculty members were primarily influenced by the École de Beaux-Arts in Paris, where the apprenticeship-atelier system was predicated on the study of the architecture of ancient Greece and Rome. The curriculum stressed simplicity of form and plan: spaces and voids were considered as important as solid matter, and balance prevailed. The Beaux-Arts ideal was one of tautly symmetrical, rectilinear buildings, with central entrances and fenestration subordinated to the mass. Where glass was employed, the openings were so deeply recessed—often up to a foot—that what appeared to the eye was a voided space, dark and mysterious against the solid mass of the strong building. New York City's Grand Central Station, the Library of Congress in Washington, D.C., and the Chicago World's Columbian Exposition buildings epitomized the Beaux-Arts standard of well-defined axes, large open spaces, and simplicity, providing a view of all elements in a single glance.

Like Frank Lloyd Wright and Louis Sullivan, Cram despised the Beaux-Arts, which he called the "French School." This aversion was not because he was championing a new style of his own. Cram actually believed that all the architectural styles that could be devised already had been. He was enamored with an era that came centuries after ancient Greece and Rome—the Middle Ages. For Cram, the Gothic style's time-honored forms (particularly those found in Gothic churches in England, France, and Germany) not only conveyed quality and authenticity, they also communicated a sense of spirituality, which was their greatest draw.

Cram believed that too much time was spent on academic renderings of romantic columns and classical orders, and not enough on practical tasks like designing apartment houses and banks, which were more likely to be requested by the average client. And instead of rendering someone else's work in the studio, as Beaux-Arts instruction advocated, Cram expected his students to go into the field and draw from life.

He assailed America's only architect president, Thomas Jefferson, for attaching Ionic-columned porticoes to clapboard at Monticello, without a transition of form or material. "Like all amateurs," Cram complained, "he severed design and style from construction and function."[19] Among the few American architects whose work Cram admired were 1891 MIT graduates Charles and Henry Greene.[20]

Cram peppered his lectures with news of the Great War, and after the Reims Cathedral was almost totally destroyed, he feared that neither side would be willing to spare the historic churches between northern France and western Germany. Raging against America's failure to become involved, Cram considered leaving

the country. It was idealistic students like Neff who kept him in Boston.

Neff thrived in the pressured atmosphere of MIT. He wrote to his parents that Cram was pushing his students to compete with Harvard to design a chapel and a monastery. A church Cram executed in the Boston area, St. Elizabeth at Whitehall, left an impression that influenced his work years later. Ornately Spanish, it was noticeably out of place in Puritan New England.

As German and Swiss buildings had been Neff's weekend destinations when he was an adolescent, now Boston's structures served the same purpose. He absorbed the ideas of Francis Bond, an academic who wrote, "Good architecture is the art of building beautifully and expressively and bad architecture is the reverse."[21] Neff saw more seventeenth-century buildings in Boston than he could have found anywhere else in the country, as well as the work of masters like H. H. Richardson and McKim, Mead & White.

When MIT expanded its campus from Copley Square to Cambridge, he set out with pencil and pad to document the expansion, beginning at Boston Commons, where he drew the Old North Church. His sketches of the old and new campuses were good enough to be used as illustrations in the 1917 yearbook.[22] The scale and perspective of the drawings, which demonstrated an understanding of Beaux-Arts-prescribed symmetry, were worlds away from his admissions presentation two years earlier.

With MIT on both sides of the Charles River, and the Department of Architecture still in Boston in the Rogers Building, he covered the chilly territory in layer upon layer of heavy sweaters. The course load was demanding, as Cram was capable of assigning four or five of his own books at a time. Second- and third-year students took nine courses each term, including life drawing. Fourth-year students took eight and were

STUDY OF THE IONIC ORDER: ENTRANCE TO A GALLERY OF SCULPTURE.
E. W. NEFF

Wallace Neff student project, included in the 1917 MIT yearbook

expected to spend between 75 and 310 hours on their senior theses. Under Cram, Neff was able to study the Spanish tradition, discounted by many in the architectural mainstream because it was so overtly influenced by Roman Catholicism. Cram did not share the belief that its aesthetics represented the excesses of the Catholic Church.

Neff never had the chance to write a senior thesis, for after the United States entered the war in the spring of 1917, he left school and returned to his parents' home in Altadena. Cram's lectures about the noble cause of freedom and democracy had not persuaded him to enlist. Instead, he signed on as a loft molder at the port of Wilmington, California, as part of a team that designed and built the ferro-cement ships that carried munitions to France.

"Ships are very difficult to design," he told interviewers at the Pasadena Oral History Project years later. "You make one little mistake on one of those frames, you have to do the whole thing over again." The experience was so challenging that he enrolled in a night course in shipbuilding at the University of Southern California. "There was a shortage of...designers so they were pushing to get me to work all day. I had an Indian motorcycle I went back and forth on."[23]

Then, a year and a half later, the war ended abruptly. Spirits soared along Pasadena's Colorado Boulevard when the armistice was declared on November 11, 1918. Oversized American flags suspended from buildings conveyed momentary optimism, while Model A's paraded side by side with Pacific and Electric red cars. Members of organizations like the Friday Morning Club (which Mrs. Andrew McNally belonged to) prepared themselves for the shock of welcoming home maimed loved ones. "The Problem of Returning Disabled Soldiers" was the sobering topic of the club's December 1918 program.[24] More politically incendiary organizations, such as the Communist

Labor Party, recruited members in the postwar atmosphere of disenchantment that followed the armistice. The Neffs weren't political zealots, but others, like Nannie's friend Kate Crane-Gartz—"Aunt Kate," as the Neff children called her—became embroiled in revolutionary politics.

Andrew Neff, who was widely considered both handsome and brilliant, appeared to have the most promising future of any of the Neff offspring. With a bachelor's degree from the University of California in hand, and war service in the U.S. Army Chemical Corps at New Jersey's Edgewood Arsenal Laboratory, he pursued his studies in chemistry at the Ph.D. level at the University of Chicago. He would serve his country as a chemist in the Second World War, and would later help to establish Pasadena's first symphony and a multitude of its arts organizations.

Wallace, on the other hand, had no degree and no desire to receive one. "I wasn't much of a student," he insisted so often it seemed to have become a badge of

honor.[25] In any case, by 1920 he was twenty-five years old—perhaps too old, in his mind, to return to college. (Later he must have rued his failure to match his brother's scholastic achievements, because he insisted that MIT had, in fact, given him a degree. MIT's files are confidential, and no diploma of any kind exists among Neff's papers, so the claim can't be verified. It seems unlikely, however, that he would have been granted a college degree without first earning a high school diploma.)[26]

Although he was advised by many to pursue studies in engineering, he jumped at the chance when his mother offered him an opportunity to put his design skills to work building a house in Santa Barbara. He later told the curious that she had virtually forced him to take up the profession of architecture, but that was simply his way of downplaying his gift.[27] Fortuitously, he began his career in architecture just as Southern California was entering the biggest population boom of the twentieth century.

The young Wallace Neff, probably as a student at MIT

CHAPTER FIVE

SANTA BARBARA INTERLUDE

California architecture is not, as legend so often has it, an organic representation of such regional conditions as the land, the climate, or native building materials. Rather it is a visual projection of the continuing world-wide immigration that today, as always, is the central fact of California culture.
—Harold Kirker, *California Historical Society Quarterly*

W HILE OPPORTUNITIES FOR TRAVEL and education were provided liberally to the young Neff, he had no reason to believe he could go through life on the Rand McNally dole. The bounty of the McNally trust had limits, as the heirs were marrying and multiplying. Since the terms of the trust called for its dissolution twenty years after the demise of the last Andrew McNally child, it could be expected to run out in Neff's lifetime if he survived his mother and her sisters. Like the Chicago cousins who worked their way up the Rand McNally company ladder, he was expected to earn a living. In his early to mid-adult years, he never received more than a few hundred dollars at a time from his mother's share of the company dividends.

To be sure, his entry into the workforce was orchestrated by his mother, who commissioned him to design a cottage in Santa Barbara, eighty miles north-west of Los Angeles on the coast. As it is today, Santa Barbara was a haven for the leisure class, and its majestic eighteenth-century mission drew crowds of school-children and tourists. Its Montecito enclave, where grand Mediterranean villas began proliferating in 1903, still draws film industry types and social-climbing Angelenos, and Santa Barbarans continue to consciously reject the runaway growth and industrial energy that define Los Angeles, in favor of something smaller and more refined.

When Neff arrived in late 1919, a half dozen licensed architects could be found on the city's main thoroughfare, State Street. Neff, who did not have an architectural license, arranged to collaborate with one of them, William A. Edwards, six years his senior, who did. Today the shake-roofed, half-timbered cottage they designed for Nannie and Edwin Neff looks incongruous among the sea of tile-roofed houses, but at the time the Mediterranean style of the villas in the hills had yet to infiltrate the rest of the town.

Where did Neff get his ideas for his first house? "I was looking through some books," he said later, "and I always came back to one picture of a fireplace, a big fireplace the full width of the room, a real English fireplace. I built the house around it."[1]

Remarkably, this unknown duo soon found their humble little design featured in three magazines. Its publication in *Country Life*, which focused primarily on grand East Coast estates—"substantial buildings," as one advertisement noted—contributed to the assumption that Neff had paid to get his name out.[2] The credit, which read "E. W. Neff," with no mention of Edwards, reinforced the suspicion.

"Sincerity in architecture is nowhere expressed more strongly than in the frank exposing of its supporting framework, and it is because of this sincerity that the timbered room always appeals," the article

TOP: *Architect George Washington Smith*
BOTTOM: *Smith's Otto E. Osthoff House in San Marino*

read. "These two views of a Santa Barbara living room show it to be an unusually good example of the charm inherent in such work." Neff's design philosophy, which was reported in *California Southland* as well, was a dogma he followed, sometimes successfully and sometimes not, for the rest of his architectural career. "Throughout, an endeavor was made to reduce the architecture to its simplest form; moldings, cornices and all forms of ornamentation were omitted, leaving merely an organic structure in which each member has a definite purpose."[3]

These were the ideals of modernism as well, but without its steel, glass, reinforced concrete, and angu-

lar planes. Like an architect of any era, Neff responded to the social and economic forces of his day, and his mother was the most immediate economic force on the horizon. As one might expect of a woman of her social position, Nannie Neff wanted something familiar, and northern Europe's architecture was part of her experience. She did not want a mission revival–style house like the one in La Mirada, for that style's popularity had faded with the onset of World War I. She wanted a view of the Pacific, which was available from the broad, brick terrace, and a house that appeared to be centuries old. Never again did Neff design a house with such pronounced arts and crafts qualities, for that vogue, too, was vanishing.

Neff threw historians a curve in his old age when he credited George Washington Smith, not William Edwards, as being the first architect with whom he collaborated. Smith, he claimed, had taken him into his Santa Barbara design studio and acted as his mentor for some eight months.[4] Whether or not this was true, Neff may well have found Smith's personality irresistible. Smith cultivated attention by dressing in white three-piece suits and driving an open convertible with a fluffy dog at his side and a scarf blowing around his neck.

The most sought-after residential architect in Santa Barbara at the time, he was also a habitué of its fanciest clubs. The style of his houses, in contrast, was gravely austere. He nearly eliminated windows from the facades, providing only the smallest of circular openings to let in light. The bumpy, white portland-cement exterior of Smith's two-story residences contrasted sharply with their black, wrought-iron balconies above the darkly stained front doors. Smith was inspired by the primitive farmhouses of Andalusia in southern Spain, where lengths of whitewashed walls connected building after building. His ascetic style and courtyard entries, so unlike the overembellished mansions in swank Montecito, impressed young Neff.

Smith was drawn into local politics after advocating a uniform Hispanic-style design code for all of Santa Barbara. The trend toward building in the Spanish colonial aesthetic had begun in San Diego only a few years before, when Bertram Goodhue, one of Ralph Adams Cram's East Coast associates, designed the Panama-California Exposition buildings in an ornately romantic version of mission architecture's churrigueresque style. It was the first time a major assemblage of buildings in that style had been erected in California, and the popularity of such Mediterranean design was about to explode.

Smith's proposal to preserve Santa Barbara's nineteenth-century adobes and replace the rest of its buildings with new structures designed in the Spanish idiom resulted in the formation of a planning commission to look into establishing a new building code.[5] Such personal conviction meant almost nothing to Neff. Building permits, not legislation, were his focus when he visited a city hall. That indifference toward politics—even at the lowest level—remained constant throughout his career.

Neff lived in the house he built for his parents while he befriended locals like John K. "Jack" Northrop, a young aeronautical draftsman who had designed a twin-engine seaplane for the Lougheads, two brothers trying to get experimental airplanes financed. Most aspiring architects and designers, however, found Santa Barbara's tourist economy too slow to foster their careers. The Lougheads eventually moved their company to Burbank, and Neff soon returned to Pasadena.

Five years later, after hundreds of buildings were destroyed by the Santa Barbara earthquake of June 29, 1925, he returned to inspect his parents' cottage. "A great deal of damage was done to the masonry facades of the commercial buildings," he noted, "caused by the roof swinging at a different speed and batting the facade out. Means should be taken to tie gables and roofs together so that they will swing as a unit and not break apart."[6] Structures with steel reinforcement fared better, he reported, although his parents' house, which had been constructed with a conventional wood frame, was unscathed.[7]

Following the earthquake, Santa Barbara was rebuilt according to the Mediterranean ideals of George Washington Smith. Critics have since questioned whether the neo-Spanish style was appropriate to Southern California. The historian Carey McWilliams has scoffed at its "epidemic" vogue.[8] It was not the "real architecture" of the region, he said, and he awaited "real homes."[9] The outspoken Frank Lloyd Wright considered it a "cheap opulent taste,"[10] but in fact, Smith's restrained and unpretentious compositions contrasted starkly with the ornate residential designs that had become the norm in the mid-1920s. In the end it was the consumers, not the historians or the architects, who decided what was popular, and during that era more than a dozen California towns were built or rebuilt according to the Spanish period style that Santa Barbara had chosen.[11]

Because his sensibilities had been fed by a lifetime of practicing Roman Catholicism, Neff was not prejudiced against profuse aesthetic display. Although he did not visit Spain until well into middle age (while attending the World's Fair in Brussels in 1958), that did not hamper his imagination. Unlike the hordes of migrating architects who descended upon Southern California just as he opened his practice, Neff had spent his formative years in the presence of authentic Hispanic architecture. The old mission or mission revival style—the Anglo version of the indigenous Spanish—had been advanced through the efforts of Neff's own family with their La Mirada rail and agricultural investments. Neff was now anxious to see whether he had the talent to make a difference in this or any architectural idiom. His stylistic preferences were wide open—effect was what he hoped to achieve.

Entry hall, Keith and Eudora Spalding House, Pasadena

CHAPTER SIX

BUILDING ON BALLYHOO

In 1922 and 1923, white-collar clerks in southern California everywhere deserted good office jobs to become real estate salesmen.
Rows of tiny flags waving before every piece of acreage gave southern California a red, yellow and gala appearance.
—W. W. Robinson

THE BULGING *LOS ANGELES TIMES* rotogravure sections on New Year's Day, 1920, provided evidence that Wallace Neff and everyone else in Los Angeles had an opportunity to prosper in the decade ahead. The construction industry news supplement was now as thick as the motion picture industry news section. Tract map preparers at City Hall were hard-pressed to keep up with the mass of applications from land speculators, and "old-time, high-pressure, lunch-and-lecture salesmanship" reigned, according to one developer. "The land boom was on."[1]

The *Times* counted on advertisers like the real estate developer Frank Meline, whose ads bombarded the high-end buyer with hyperbole. For Pasadena's Oak Knoll district, he advertised on November 28, 1920: "Select a location and build your residence in this paradise for homes protected by proper surroundings, exclusive and permanent residence restrictions." For Beverly Hills, he advertised on July 9, 1922: "If all the people of Los Angeles really knew how reasonably they could purchase a delightful home site, my organization would be overworked to meet the demand." And in *California Life*, the ad he ran on February 3, 1923, boasted, "We can build anything from a bungalow to a hotel."

Between 1919 and 1930, Meline sold houses promoted by the Rodeo Land and Water Company, while he developed expensive property in Bel-Air and Castel-

lammare for a savvy developer named Alphonzo Bell.[2] Lot after lot in Meline's Beverly Hills tracts held substantial fifteen- to twenty-five-thousand-dollar Italian- and Spanish Renaissance–style houses.[3] "He was selling property, and he tried to sell architecture too," architect Clifford Hoskins said.[4] "If you buy," ads advised, Meline had nine offices covering the Southland to meet your needs. "If you build," the ads went on, "our architects have been trained in the best American and Continental schools."[5]

Meline had worked his way into real estate after dressing the windows of Hamburger's Department Store. With a little of his own money, and much more from the cornucopia of Los Angeles's banks, which were eager to cash in on the building boom, he bought land, subdivided it, moved the earth with dynamite and mule power, dug gullies for utilities, graded streets, designed and built houses, and then marketed, sold, mortgaged, and insured them. He used his own designers and construction crews, cementing his political clout when he won a seat on the new Los Angeles Harbor Commission.[6]

Early in 1921, Wallace Neff, who was just back from Santa Barbara, signed on as a draftsman at Meline's office on Hollywood Boulevard.[7] He worked side by side with the other draftsmen, designing projects from the ground up, doing everything from site and plot

Wallace Neff's rendering of a First National Bank design, preserved by Nannie Neff in his baby book

plans to elevations and working drawings. Riding to work on a motorcycle, Neff passed the Garden Court Apartments and the Fifth Church of Christ, Scientist, on Hollywood Boulevard, Meline creations that had helped transform Hollywood from an outpost of orange groves and farms into a city of banks, film studios, and residential developments, although the hillside roads were still as narrow and unfriendly to pedestrians as those on the hillsides along the Mediterranean.

Meline's award from the Southern California Chapter of the American Institute of Architects for the design of a First National Bank should have been accepted by his young draftsman Wallace Neff, its designer.[8] But Meline took credit for his staff's work. Within months, Neff concluded that Meline needed him more than he needed Meline. He could take the principles of proportion he had learned at MIT, along with his instincts about how to shape space and handle the disposition of voids and solids, and employ them for his own profit. After designing dozens of buildings anonymously, he left Meline's office in early 1922.

Studying for California's architectural licensing exam by night, he set up an office in Pasadena by day. On March 28, 1922, he took the test, and by April 14 he had been awarded license number B-1119. At the time there was only one proficiency examination, not the nine that architects endure today.[9] Neff was one of some 250 registered architects in early 1920s Los Angeles, who were responsible for housing a population that grew from just over half a million in 1920 to 1.2 million in a single decade.[10] Jockeying for commissions brought out their best, and these architects created such landmarks as the Hollywood Bowl, the Rose Bowl, the Samson Tire and Rubber Company Building, Bullocks Wilshire, the Los Angeles Central Library, Grauman's Chinese Theatre, and the Renaissance revival buildings at UCLA and USC.

Many worked on downtown's Hill and Spring

Streets. Some, like George Wyman, who designed the breathtakingly original Bradbury Building, had been around since the previous century. Others, like twenty-nine-year-old Paul Williams, were as unheralded as Neff.[11] In addition to the registered architects, there were numerous "architectural designers," draftsmen who moved from office to office as commissions came and went.

Never again in the twentieth century was designing residential architecture in Los Angeles so lucrative. In 1919, building permits showed the total volume of construction to be near $28 million. By 1920, permits reflected an increase to $60 million. In 1922, the number was $121 million. By 1923, Neff's second year of solo practice, the value of construction in Los Angeles had reached $200 million, exceeded only by that of New York and Chicago.[12] The harbor was receiving so many shipments of lumber, a commodity lacking in semiarid Southern California, that ships often had to wait days to unload it. The new port in San Pedro had become an essential part of the building boom.

In 1925, successful realtor-developer Harry Culver (soon to be a Neff client) took a roomful of realtors to task for taking their windfall for granted. "The trouble with a California realtor is that he is calloused with opportunity. He needs a year in the East where the property owner says, 'Get rid of it, even at a loss, I am going to California.' Back there it takes real, honest-to-goodness salesmanship to put the name on the dotted line."[13]

One architect claimed that "almost anything with four walls and a roof and an adequate number of rooms could be sold,"[14] as the city's forty-three thousand real estate agents benefited from the unprecedented surge in population. Along for the ride were building contractors like Karl Moller, Frederick H. Ruppel, William Warmington, and Frank Hogan, men whose pride of workmanship produced lasting monu-

ments to the decade of spectacular growth. They vied for the commissions to build the Pasadena City Hall, the Pasadena Playhouse, Pasadena Junior College, the Pasadena Civic Auditorium, the Pasadena Library, and the Rose Bowl.

Neff, who was a member of Pasadena's chamber of commerce and the Annandale Golf Club, built his practice on referrals from realtors,[15] although his own office, in the Slavin Building on North Fair Oaks Avenue, was in a part of town the chamber and many realtors would have been loath to acknowledge. Gilmor Brown's nearby Community Playhouse had been evicted from the Savoy on North Fair Oaks after the onetime burlesque house was declared a fire hazard. And one block east on Raymond Avenue, the last of Pasadena's grand old architects were holed up: Frederick Roehrig, who had designed the house in which Neff was born, G. Lawrence Stimson, who was known for his boxy neoclassical villas, and Henry Greene, of Greene & Greene, all continued practicing in the Central Building. In 1926, Neff joined the old masters, moving into a space on the second floor. Like his first office, it had its drawbacks, for the Santa Fe ran through the alley behind the building and he could set his watch by the rattling of the window-shade weights against the glass.[16]

"Though he opened an office for himself only last January," the *Pasadena Star-News* had reported on April 15, 1922, "E. Wallace Neff has already six houses in the course of design and construction." Just a year later, on April 21, 1923, the *Star-News* had reported that Neff was working on "Homes Totaling Quarter Million," with an average price of thirty thousand dollars. By January 5, 1924, Neff noted that he had already designed thirty houses—nearly one a month. Around the same time, an article in the *Pasadena Star-News* on the construction of a new Neff house in the posh Flintridge district had run side by side with another piece documenting

*The Spalding House yard and reflecting pool, adjacent to the
Pasadena City Hall and the Maryland Hotel*

the remarkable influx of residents that had made such productivity possible: "During the past year more than 132,000 people have come to Los Angeles, bag and baggage, with the intention of making this their permanent home."[17]

FAMILY TIES AND SOCIAL CONNECTIONS
Referrals by realtors notwithstanding, it was established Pasadenans like the Linnards, the Macombers, the Torrences, the Scovilles, the Newcombs, the Burdettes, the Stowells, the Blankenhorns, and the Up de Graffs who were the backbone of Neff's initial clientele. Pasadena's mayor, A. R. Benedict, resided in a half-timbered Neff cottage near Caltech, with a steeply pitched roof that would become a Neff trademark. Former mayor Horace M. Dobbins considered implementing a Neff plan to replicate a Mediterranean hill town on Pasadena's Jumbo Hill. Keith Spalding of the sporting goods Spaldings, and his wife, Eudora Hull, commissioned Neff to build a Mediterranean house that was so grand that five other houses had to be removed from the site to make room for it.[18] Developer David Blankenhorn ordered three speculative American colonial revival houses in the Oak Knoll district, named for the ancient oak in its midst and its view of growing San Marino below.

Neff acquired clients from the Midwest through referrals from this network of friends and contacts. Carroll L. Post, of the Michigan cereal family, for instance, was investing in local property when he heard about Neff from Stephen Vavra, who lived in a new Neff house on Bel Air Road. Midwesterners like Post, who eventually commissioned Neff to design a stately colonial in Oak Knoll, considered his close connection to Rand McNally & Company an asset. They also valued his knowledge of Pasadena and his bias against high Victorian taste, which matched their own.

Working his way up the ladder from office boy to chief draftsman in Neff's office, Clifford Hoskins often heard his employer disparage the American colonial revival style that had evolved from Queen Anne Victorian. "You could see [that style] in any book you picked up," Neff would complain. Its form was more or less that of a stiff, rectilinear box incapable of melding itself to a hillside lot or any site that was not square and flat. Even the roofs were nearly flat—or at the very least had a minimal pitch—because architects didn't have to contend with melting snow in Southern California.

Neff could master generic historic styles, but adhering to any one of them in a doctrinaire way frustrated his artistic side. Given the opportunity to put his stamp on the blossoming Spanish-Mediterranean style, however, he showed a gift for inventiveness. His talent was in taking common, vernacular forms, such as farm buildings, and adding his own vocabulary. The portland cement used in Mediterranean styles allowed architects more flexibility than they had with wood. Early in the decade, many of the new tract developments in Los Angeles County—some fourteen hundred—restricted home owners from building in any style except the Spanish revival.[19] Magazines like *Sunset*, attempting to lure buyers from other parts of the country, published renderings of typical California Spanish architecture meant to convey the widespread availability of the style.

One early Neff Spanish effort fell flat stylistically, although the client who commissioned it was herself an innovator in thought and action. Kate Crane-Gartz appeared to be a conventional dowager, and in some ways she was; she frequented the Valley Hunt Club, where she played bridge with Neff's aunt Helen. Yet she devoted most of her time to political causes, agitating for the release of Sacco and Vanzetti from prison and for governmental assistance (a hundred dollars a month was the figured she proposed) for the financially strapped. Married at the McNallys' house around the time Nannie wed Ed, she had lost two of her children in the 1903 Iroquois Theater fire in Chicago, which seems to have inspired her to speak out against injustice and poverty. She opposed war and supported Communist principles, and the Sunday afternoon salon she held at her house, across from the McNallys', attracted guests like the Richard Neutras, who came to hear what Upton Sinclair had to say about the California economy.[20] Like Sinclair, she became a pamphleteer, denouncing Caltech scientists as warmongers and castigating the Los Angeles police department. Editors who dared to ignore her printed manifestos incurred her wrath.

Gartz, whose share of the Crane Plumbing Company was rumored to be $30 million,[21] would eventually commission Neff to design a villa overlooking the Pacific in Palos Verdes, but first she asked him to develop her idea for producing housing that was within the means of the working class. In most of the courtyard housing that appeared in Los Angeles early in the twentieth century, identical bungalows were arranged in a U shape around a strip of open space that served as a common garden. After these courtyard apartments became nearly ubiquitous, developers and progressives turned to architects like Neff to improve the image of the bungalow court. The complex Neff designed for Aunt Kate's out-of-town guests, a short distance from her own house, however, showed only a fraction of the originality he was capable of displaying.

More interesting to him was the opportunity to transform a whistle-stop of an outback town into a resort. By April of 1923, Pasadena newspapers were reporting that Edward Drummond Libbey had commissioned Neff to design a luxury retreat. Libbey had convinced residents of Nordhoff, sixty miles northwest of Los Angeles, that they should rename their little town Ojai (pronounced "oh hi"). With Libbey's stockpile of shares in Libbey Owens Glass, it was a mere petty cash item to grade Bristol Road, which wound through meadows thick with live oaks, to connect the Ojai Valley to the state's main road, El Camino Real.

Libbey had already begun remaking the community in the image of a Spanish town, and he asked Neff to design a golf-course clubhouse on a hill overlooking the verdant valley. While the club was embellished with wrought iron and furnished with deluxe amenities, it had the simple form of the adobe haciendas Neff had seen as a child. The shallow, almost flat pitch of the roof and the dearth of windows created a severe form, but Neff provided visual contrast with a curving exterior staircase.

A stable he designed for Libbey served as a jumping-off point for the French Norman aesthetic he employed so regularly during the 1930s. When he created the illusion of exposed adobe brick on the exterior walls of the stable, some believed he had sold his soul: such studied irregularities were untrue to the materials. Although it may have resulted in a tour de force, the instant aging was widely considered to be disingenuous and Neff did not resort to it again.

BUILDING A PRACTICE

The Southern California Chapter of the American Institute of Architects awarded Neff certificates of honor for both Libbey structures, and for the H. L. Walker House in Pasadena.[22] The twenty-nine-year-old architect's work was published in six magazines, and his reputation was established. Business was so good, he began to turn away commissions for buildings with budgets of less than twenty-five thousand dollars.[23]

Preparations for all Neff's buildings began on site, where he sketched ideas for plans while an associate surveyed. Most important was determining where the entrance court should be sited. If there is a hallmark of Wallace Neff's work, it is this approach: his houses were generally oriented around a circular court that set the mood when visitors arrived.[24] The auto court was to the Neff house what the interior courtyard was to George Washington Smith houses. Like Smith, Neff wanted a studied relationship between the building and its landscape. Entries flush with the ground or with a minimum of steps were his preference. How the building addressed the site meant more to him than any spectacular views from within.

Armed with the knowledge of where the site could best accommodate a flat courtyard, Neff would turn his attention to the orientation of the house. A series of quick, rough pencil sketches of a tentative plan would materialize on a four-by-six-and-a-half-inch page of his ever-present, all-purpose, black leather vest-pocket book. Among the geographic conditions that would be noted were air currents that might affect the direction kitchen appliances would vent.[25] (Before the kitchen became a gathering place, hostesses wanted to make sure that cooking smells drifted away from, not toward, the guests in the dining room.)

Presentation drawings could win or lose a commission, so Neff did them himself when he could find the time. Sometimes that meant retreating to the office in the middle of the night to draw without distraction. Quickly and without artistic anguish, Neff used soft leaded pencils to define light and shadow, with no hint of a pencil stroke. He used orange pencils to depict terra-cotta roof tile, and deployed a certain hue of blue pencil to depict trim so often it became known among the staff as "Neff blue." To animate a tableau, he sketched birds overhead or in the entry courtyard. Without fail, he exaggerated the height of the chimneys for effect.

During the day, secretaries in white smocks churned out purple-inked specs from duplicating machines. In a practice that derived from the Beaux-

Arts tradition, the draftsmen hunched over their drawing boards wore green smocks. When a dozen buildings were in the works and the load had become overwhelming, Neff contacted the Los Angeles Architectural Club for prospective draftsmen. They had to be male, under the age of thirty-five, and able to design well, develop freehand sketches into finished drawings, and work effectively without supervision. Applicants might as well have been in practice for themselves, the requirements were so stringent.

Chief draftsman Joseph Kucera supervised a crew that counted among its numbers Arthur Fisk, Orin Stone, Edwin Westberg, Mark Ellsworth, Marion Dale Hughes, Harry Balthesar, George Young Cannon,[26] Douglas Honnold,[27] and Alexander Gollitzen.[28] Cannon doubled as construction supervisor. Two of the finest, Robert Ainsworth and Everett Phipps Babcock, left after several years to practice architecture on their own. There were no engineers on staff, but Neff's draftsmen were expected to be grounded in the basic principles of engineering technology.

When they drafted one-eighth-inch-scale working drawings, they were expected to make sure that major elements, particularly chimneys and exterior staircases, remained exactly where Neff had sketched them on the presentation drawings. Neff would stand over a draftsman's shoulder for hours until the results satisfied him. "Keep it simple," he advised.

"By the time we got through with the challenge," Clifford Hoskins recalled, "the plan worked. It was kind of stretching it sometimes, fitting in all the rooms with his elevation, but we got the chimney where he wanted it."[29] The long hours ate into profits, and Neff, who was known to pay well, personally absorbed the costs.

For a building contractor, there were no plans easier to work with than the precise drawings created by the Neff office, with their hierarchy of notes and numbers that defined the degree of importance of each element in the construction process. "The actual craft of producing such sheets of drawings is lost today," the architect Stefanos Polyzoides lamented in a monograph of Neff's work. "In a world beset by the practice of working drawings as legal documents, the drawings of Neff's draughtsmen are works of art."[30]

Neff personally envisioned the articulation on his buildings; it was he, not his draftsmen, who selected the exact details. Wrought iron was of paramount importance, and he insisted that full-scale patterns be drawn in charcoal and taped to the walls of the office. "Once I drew a proposal for a wrought iron stair railing that turned out to be as elegant as a railroad tie," Hoskins recalled. "Neff suggested that I keep a piece of wrought iron at my drafting board to consider its qualities."

"Only my eyes can tell me if it is right," Neff explained. In at least one case, however, his idea of what was appropriate did not suit one of the draftsmen, who complained that "someone" had drawn a weather vane "too crudely."[31] Neff overheard him and took responsibility, without displaying any irritation.

Contractors often phoned Neff before 8:00 A.M., because once he had left the office to visit construction sites, he lost track of time.[32] His fastidious clerk of the works, William S. Byers, who oversaw the fieldwork, wore a three-piece suit, no matter how dusty the site, to show that he meant business. Neff trusted his younger brothers, Bill and Jack, to serve as office managers.

At day's end, the staff adjourned to the back room of the office for a hand of bridge and no doubt a drink. "They all liked the boss, especially the women," Hoskins remarked. Everyone got a bonus at Christmas, although one year "one fellow didn't get his raise because Wallace wasn't happy with his work, so he quit."[33] Not one to confront those who displeased him, Neff used such tactics to weed out his least desirable

employees, especially during the 1920s, when he knew other jobs were readily available.

Two days after Thanksgiving in 1925, a full-page advertisement appeared in the *Pasadena Star-News* proclaiming in the largest typeface available that sixteen nine-thousand-dollar Wallace Neff houses were on the market. Neff's brothers Bill and Andrew each bought one of the lovely, modest houses on Berkeley Street in Pasadena, financed by the Lincoln Mortgage Company. Neff's office had used mirror images of each plan to produce two plans from one idea, a time-saving ploy commonly used by developers.

The idea of commissioning a well-known architect to design relatively inexpensive houses originated with Lincoln Mortgage Company's vice president, Harry H. Culver, the most resourceful developer Neff had ever encountered. Culver had brought a mere three thousand dollars of his own money to the table when the town that bore his name, Culver City, was created in 1913.[34] Supposedly he conceived the idea of developing a town devoted to filmmaking after noticing the director Thomas Ince shooting a film on a barley field near the area's Ballona Creek. Ince bought into Culver's plan, building a studio. He was followed by D. W. Griffith, Mack Sennett, Louis B. Mayer, Marcus Loew, Samuel Goldwyn, and David O. Selznick. As a result, "Culver City achieved," historian Kevin Starr concluded, "the most compelling identity of all, an actual connection with the dream-producing film industry that was motivating the movement of so many migrants into Southern California in the first place."[35]

Skeptical observers, however, believed that Tract 2444—the legal designation of Culver City—was overrated. Gloria Swanson dismissed it because it was miles from Hollywood.[36] Anita Loos, seeing it from the perspective of a Metro-Goldwyn-Mayer scenarist, called it "a shabby suburb built on a salt marsh leading down to the Pacific."[37]

Culver City was subdivided to accommodate bungalows, not mansions, although Culver had earned enough to build the latter for himself. He trucked a bungalow to a lot that overlooked Culver City, in an area christened Cheviot Hills, and awaited the completion of the Culver family dream house, described in detail in the *Southwest Builder and Contractor*:

"Two-story, 30-room, brick residence at 3216 Club Drive, for Harry Culver, owner, Culver City. Wallace Neff, architect, Pasadena (Terrace 0174) 180x180 ft., tile and composition roof, art stone, staff, ornamental iron, plate glass, wood shutters, marble, tile, hardwood and pine floors, hardwood and Oregon pine trim, 8 tile baths, tile showers, lavatories, mantels, drain boards, kitchen and pantry wainscot, electrically controlled unit gas furnace heating, 16 furnaces, gas radiators, 250 gallon Rudd automatic water heater, water softener, pipe organ, solarium, gymnasium, laundry, garage (Wayne air compressor and fuel pumps, cement floor), stables, swimming pool, dressing rooms, landscaping; $125,000."[38]

It was the most costly residence Neff designed during the 1920s. Culver had in mind a grand, American colonial–style house with federal details, but Neff convinced him that a villa or a castle would better convey his real-estate aspirations. The architectural elements ran the gamut from an intricately detailed, gold-leaf coffered ceiling in the dining room to grand entries on both Club and Shelby drives.

John C. Brasfield, a promoter as brash as Culver, featured the house in his new magazine, *Architectural Digest*, where architects like Neff were given editorial space in exchange for drumming up advertising among contractors and subcontractors.[39] Because Neff could be counted on to have cultivated the painters, plumbers, and craftsmen who worked on his houses, he could easily oblige.[40] The large-format,

To attract buyers, Wallace Neff's Berkeley Street development was advertised in Pasadena and Los Angeles newspapers

J. K. Baillie House, built by the president of the Lincoln Mortgage Company

Three of the sixteen houses in the Berkeley Street development, still extant in Pasadena

black-and-white magazine was a far cry from today's thick, glossy, color version. Instead of articles that described property owners' lifestyles and interior decorating choices, readers found headlines, lists of construction team members, and austere photographs of buildings, with no inhabitants in sight. The idea of publicizing lifestyles and the architects who designed the mansions was years from reality. Neff handled his own publicity.

Culver, however, paid publicists to issue press releases and plant stories. (One Sunday morning, when Neff opened the *Los Angeles Times,* he was surprised and pleased to find an image of the Culver House, with himself credited as the architect.)[41] But Culver's business did not survive the Depression, and he lost the grand house. With the Santa Monica Freeway at the door in the post–World War II era, and Spanish-style mansions out of favor, Neff's grandest creation was torn down and the grounds were subdivided. It was becoming a Southern California tradition.

California Security Loan Corporation Building

CHAPTER SEVEN

PUBLIC NOTICE

California is now engaged in one vast and spectacular experiment in domestic architecture.
—Frank A. Waugh, *Garden and Home Builder* (December 1924)

He paints from a bold palette. Delicate detail would be entirely out of keeping with the virile atmosphere which is characteristic of all Mr. Neff's work. Broad rough surfaces of white-washed walls are pierced with deep embrasures, edged with the crisp, irregular shadows of heavy roof tiles. He uses vigorous arches of varying shapes, curving ramps, solid beams of timber, thick wooden shutters, projecting balconies, wrought iron in forms that are strong and simple.
—Harris Allen, *Pacific Coast Architect* (August 1924)

REVIEWS OF NEFF'S WORK began appearing after he sent photographs to Southern California publications, where the critics put away their swords in favor of florid rhetoric. It was tempting to wax poetic when writing about the Spanish colonial—castle-like houses perched on hillsides overlooking landscapes unspoiled by major roadways or tall buildings. The critics were living in a Southern California that was still wide-open country, at least compared to America's other major metropolises.

Neff's projects shared space on the printed page with those of his peers Roland E. Coate and Gordon B. Kaufmann, who designed grand projects Neff did not covet because of the proposal writing and panel review they entailed. Coate designed David Blankenhorn's houses in Pasadena and Santa Barbara, commissions for the children of Edward Doheny, the Frederick H. Ruppel residence, houses for the O'Melvenys of the law firm, Myron Selznick's mountain residence at Running Springs, and Jack Warner's and William Wellman's houses. Kaufmann tended toward more architectural formality, capturing grand-scale commissions like Edward Doheny Jr.'s sandstone estate in Beverly Hills and hilltop reveries for Jewish families who prospered in banking and film.[1]

Neff's work was first featured on a magazine cover in August 1924, when *Pacific Coast Architect* published images of Libbey's stables and a half dozen photos of the Ojai Valley Country Club to illustrate a story titled "An Artist in Adobe." (In fact, Neff had not yet used adobe in his work, but the alliteration must have been too tempting for the editor to resist.) The following December, *California Southland*'s cover reproduced a color rendering of Saint Elizabeth Church, built on a sloping stretch of Lake Avenue dominated by plant nurseries. The September 1927 issue, which pondered the best method of building a monument to Charles Lindbergh, had Neff's Petifils House on the cover, looking down from the Los Feliz hills. Photos showed three views each of Neff's California Security Loan Corporation Building and his Saint Elizabeth Church, ten images of the Mr. and Mrs. Fred Thomson House, two of Mr. and Mrs. Norman Chandler's house, four of the Petifils Residence, six of the J. C. Anderson House, one of the living room of the Stephen Vavra House, and two of the villa of Mrs. Charlotte Pickford. The magazines surveyed architecture, not ideas. Neff was never questioned, and he preferred it that way.

The magazines did, however, criticize other builders and designers for copying Neff. "Countless humble home builders have hung little brown balconies on their houses and have dared to leave undecorated a large expanse of plastered wall," *California Southland* complained in September 1926. Neff's fellow Pasadena architect, H. Roy Kelley, who was also a well-

Ojai Valley Country Club

respected critic, decried the unfortunate "deformed egg-shaped landscape windows, parasite second-story chimneys, bunion buttresses, skyhook balconies."[2] As Kelley wrote in the *Los Angeles Times*, "The vast majority of people have an astounding lack of good taste and knowledge of style in decorating their homes."[3]

The magazines themselves were not entirely without culpability. Like *Architectural Digest, Pacific Coast Architect* and others signed up contractors and iron foundries as advertisers after featuring houses they had built. And it followed that those who advertised were more likely to receive editorial coverage. One of the most heavily featured was the pricey Cheesewright Studios of Pasadena—the manufacturer of the elaborate period furniture found in many Neff houses. Edward Cheesewright, the company's owner, advertised frequently. He was also something of a dealmaker and was personally responsible for bringing Neff a rare commercial project—a savings and loan.

The California Security Loan Corporation Building on Colorado Boulevard in Pasadena was commissioned by a banker named Byrne, after Cheesewright provided an introduction and admonished Neff to "do a good job for them."[4] Neff more than complied: the gem-like proportions of the finished project made the neoclassically columned bank next door look like a hulking elephant. The abundant cast stone that adorned the roofline of Neff's building was like that of a baroque church and made the modest structure appear monumental. The bank was nothing less than a "basilica," *California Southland* editors concluded, "an example of the height of the period."[5]

In his invitation to four thousand depositors to come and take a look, the bank president declared, "Our aim has been to make this one of the finest buildings of its kind in California."[6] It is impossible now to judge Neff's bank building in three dimensions, for management ordered it demolished in 1961 and

Interior, Saint Elizabeth Church

Saint Elizabeth Church, Altadena

replaced it with a brutish nine-story structure that would have been considered modern at the time.

Another Neff building from the same period—and one that is still vibrant with activity—is Saint Elizabeth Catholic Church on Lake Avenue in Altadena. (Its location, considered the gateway to the city, was equidistant from the old McNally house and a new house Neff was designing for his own use on Mendocino Street.) Selected by the WPA as a destination in its Depression-era guide series, the church shows Neff at his baroque best. Its low-pitched, one-story roof, topped by a hundred-foot tower, repeats a profile he used in dozens of structures, where steep chimneys or towers created contrasting drama: high and low, light and dark, strong horizontal, strong vertical. The light-dark contrast materialized at Saint Elizabeth in the recessed arched entry, which looked black against the white structure. The arch form reappeared in the bell tower. Next to the dour, poured-concrete Gothic Westminster Presbyterian Church on the opposite corner, Saint Elizabeth appeared as friendly as a stuffed piñata.

The Marion-Thomson House, possibly the first film-industry estate designed by an architect

< CHAPTER EIGHT >

THE SEARCH FOR THE STYLE OF WEALTH

While Neutra was fashioning eyries out of a minimum of inexpensive materials, the Spanish Colonial Revival style continued to be admired;
it was reassuringly heavy and yet romantic—a past that Americans had never known helped them to shoulder the burden of the present.
—Brendan Gill, *The Dream Come True*

The development of a private estate requires the most thorough study of the many conditions involved. Be sure you secure competent service.
—Clarence P. Day, *California Southland* advertisement (April 1923)

$\mathcal{M}$UCH WAS ONCE MADE of the dichotomy between the Pasadena social set on the east side of Los Angeles and the film industry on the west. Anita Loos, who wrote the comedies that propelled Douglas Fairbanks to stardom, saw in Pasadena "a winter resort for snobbish families whose lineage had been established by brand names such as Heinz's Pickles, Smith Brothers' Cough Drops, and Chalmers' Underwear."[1] But for slings and arrows, there is no Los Angeles authority like Carey McWilliams, whose *Southern California: An Island on the Land* remains the textbook on the history of the region. Movie people did not "live" in Los Angeles in the early years of the industry, he wrote. "They merely camped in the community, prepared, like Arabs, to fold their tents and steal away in the night."[2]

Film pioneers began to overcome their reputation as itinerants once that great equalizer, money, put them in the same rooms with the upper crust. Gloria Swanson's torrid romance with plumbing-fixture heir Craney Gartz, for instance, began at a nightclub near the beach, and as it progressed he began escorting the actress to the Pasadena Country Club.[3] Film industry people were initially able to enter such institutions only on sufferance, while shooting movies. As the cameras rolled, they ran roughshod over Oriental rugs in grand estates rented for the day. The Marx Brothers and Harold Lloyd defied the country's upper-class

social conventions when they crashed balls staged in Orange Grove Boulevard mansions. Pasadena took the money, and the filmmakers were saved the trouble of building sets.[4]

But old money and new were now united in the quest to live well, and the amount of architectural talent available to build dream houses was overwhelming. The avant-garde who had descended upon the city during the decade of its most creative architectural boom, the 1920s, included Frank Lloyd Wright, Richard Neutra, and Rudolph Schindler, and they all dreamed of attracting a clientele unbound by preconceived notions of how to live. Architects of Neff's ilk whose practices thrived included Reginald Johnson, Gordon B. Kaufmann, and H. Roy Kelley, as well as Carleton Winslow, Arthur Kelly, Stiles Clements, Roland Coate, John C. Austin, Myron Hunt, Paul R. Williams, Sylvanus Marston, Elmer Grey, and Garrett Van Pelt. Dozens of lesser-known men—Clarence P. Day, A. F. Leicht, Marshall Wilkinson, and William J. Dodd, among them—covered entire hillsides with their period-revival output.

Wallace Neff had too much faith in his own abilities to view these architects as competitors. He did not seem to want to emulate any of them. "When 'Modernism' was virtually unheard of," he later recalled, "I applied the lessons I learned in five years' study of the traditional architecture of Europe."[5] Architects who had long served the Pasadena establishment found themselves losing out to the younger, less rigid Neff.

Confident that he could design in the traditional styles, he kept himself interested by tweaking the expected. At the root of his success was his experience growing up in Los Angeles. Neff was familiar with the spartan adobes built by *pobladors* of mestizo, African, mulatto, and Native American blood. He knew an authentic hacienda had a floor of packed adobe. He had witnessed the Landmarks Club's efforts to protect the missions from earthquakes with a crude seismic-retrofit method employing wooden pillars and metal rods. He knew that the prevailing view of an eighteenth-century California where pure-blooded Spaniards oversaw opulent haciendas was naive. And he had no illusion that his was a new way of building: his Mediterranean or Spanish colonial style was a revival.

Conjecture among today's social scientists that clients like Neff's were appeasing their consciences by identifying with those they had displaced would have left Neff chuckling.[6] Most of his clients wanted nothing more than pure fantasy—the ideal dream house. Early in his career, two couples, both newly married, came to him for just that, encouraging him to reach for the heights of Hispanic fantasy. The first couple valued leisure, while the second worked diligently. Both endeavors were shadowed by tragedy.

AN EARLY PLAYBOY MANSION
Arthur "A. K." Bourne of Connecticut was heir to a stake in the Singer Sewing Machine Company fortune.[7] He and his wife, Emily, came west for the climate, which allowed him to play golf nearly year-round. A. K. chose the venerable Annandale Golf Club of Pasadena as his headquarters. The only amateur in the PGA until Bing

Crosby achieved the honor in the late 1930s, Bourne lavished his generosity upon the club.[8] His golf cronies traveled by chartered bus to see him play at the Los Angeles and Midwick country club tournaments.

Bourne's vision of a grand estate in San Marino was a brash one, for the new community was already known for its conservatism. When a magazine writer described the furnishings of a San Marino house Neff had designed as being "harmonious" and "quiet," she was articulating the standard for San Marino art, architecture, and social interaction. The exemplar of San Marino style was the individual who had invested more capital in Los Angeles than any other—fabulously rich, politically conservative Henry Huntington, heir to the Southern Pacific Railroad fortune.

THE ORIGINS OF SAN MARINO
The same year residents of Beverly Hills voted to incorporate on the west side of Los Angeles, people on the east side, in the San Gabriel Valley, went to the ballot box for the identical reason. Prospective San Marino residents sprung to action in 1913, when Alhambra's citizens began planning a "Greater Alhambra" that would have swallowed up their property. Six of them huddled to plan their municipality, including Huntington, who proceeded to move dozens of families onto his grounds as his employees in order to achieve the population required by Los Angeles County to qualify for incorporation. The proposal to incorporate carried 126 to 5.[9] Because Huntington paid 75 percent of the property taxes, the community took the name of his estate, San Marino. Manufacturing was forbidden, and retail was confined to a few streets. Bars, gambling, and apartment buildings were prohibited.

Huntington now began planning other communities on a grander scale, announcing that he was determined to "join this whole region in one big family."

RIGHT: *Bourne House plan, as published in* Architectural Digest
BOTTOM: *Bourne House entry courtyard*

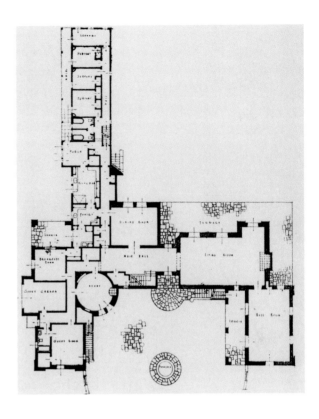

With investors who included his friend and neighbor George Patton, he bought enough land to become the largest landowner in the state. His consolidated trolley line, the Pacific Electric Railway Company, provided more frequent service and greater short-haul efficiency than steam lines. Trolleys traveling forty and fifty miles an hour whizzed by his stately grounds—southwest to Los Angeles and northwest to Glendora—making the office, theater, beach, mountains, suburbs, and downtown readily accessible to the Southern California commuter.

THE BOURNES ARRIVE

Disembarking from a train at Pasadena's depot, Emily and Arthur Bourne were greeted by African American porters ready to haul their trunks.[10] The Bournes sought out the Huntington Hotel, owned by the transportation mogul and arts patron. In the lobby, Mrs. Bourne was approached by a real estate broker, a practice, she noticed, that was commonplace. "As soon as anyone [new] appeared at the hotel," she said, "William Wilson Realtors sent someone over to sell them a house. We were no exception. We found one on Hill Street near Caltech, where our neighbors became our closest friends. We decided the style of their home was what we wanted."[11]

While the Bournes' house had been designed by well-regarded local architects,[12] it paled in comparison to the house Wallace Neff had designed for their neighbors within months of opening his practice. The Neff design, with its courtyard and rustic surfaces, mimicked century-old adobes. Lintels over the window frames and *rejas*, or wrought-iron grilles, were among the house's early Spanish elements. Redwood *vigas*, or beams, radiated from the peak of the entry arch. An adze hammer used on the wood beams after they were hewn created the appearance of hand-sawn timber.

TOP: *Bourne House, Lombardy Road facade*
BOTTOM: *Exterior stairs and gated archways in the courtyard*

Tiles of brilliant blue and orange wrapped around the baseboard in the circular entry hall, where the staircase drew the eye up to the wide-beamed ceiling. A breakfast room surrounded by windows overlooked an expansive rear yard, and a sixteen-foot-high stucco mantel was the focus of the living room. Expansive surfaces of unadorned stucco were used to evoke adobe, cast broadly at the base to support the weight of the upper levels. Deep-set windows reinforced the image of an adobe building, although the structure was, in fact, wood frame covered with stucco. This appearance of impenetrability appealed to the Bournes, and they commissioned Neff to design a house.

AN ICON OF NEFF STYLE

A few doors south of the original Bourne residence, Lombardy Road begins a picturesque ramble from Pasadena to San Gabriel, passing San Marino along the way. (The ebullient architectural historian Robert Winter has observed that the street sets an example of "the way all people should live, even if they do not wish to.")[13] Bourne liked Lombardy's flat grade, imagining that it might be appropriate not only for a house, but for the pitch-and-putt eight-hole course he longed to build.

The Bournes purchased four and a half acres of Ardengrove tract 7988, extending from California Street to Lombardy Road, for seven thousand dollars. Notice of a permit to build was published in the October 31, 1924, edition of the *Southwest Builder and Contractor*. By Thanksgiving, a scale model of the project was on display in the window of a real estate office at Colorado Boulevard and Marengo Street.[14]

Amenities comparable to those of a civic center were incorporated into the house. Architecturally, it united the most diverse of vernacular forms, from sta-bles to castles. The penned enclosures of a Spanish farm met the thick walls of a Mexican fortress. Molding portland cement stucco over the wood frame, and rounding as many corners as he squared, Neff simulated whitewash over adobe. Not one, but two exterior stairways added another level of mystery to a facade that seemed to go on forever, with one-story arms extending from either side of the two-story central volume.

It was the depth of the arched entry vestibule that particularly appealed to Neff's devoted following. From its Gothic arch to its olive-green walls, its built-in benches, and its rustic, paneled front door, it seemed to evoke the Kasbah. The fewer the windows, Neff knew, the more dramatic the effect. It was also more practical, since less sun could penetrate the building if only a couple of windows punctuated the facade. The plain, white walls that contrasted with the deep entry, along with Neff's masterful manipulation of light and shadow, made for architectural greatness. And the shadows cast by the projecting roof tiles were reminiscent of those produced by the beams projecting from the gables of Greene & Greene's houses.

Neff chose a landscape designer named Katherine Bashford, who he believed was capable of translating his architectural vision into horticulture. Bashford scattered potted plants around the fountain in the circular courtyard and used the minimum of shrubs and trees so that the structure, not the vegetation, would be the focus.

Nearby, rail baron Henry Huntington's house was covered by a tile roof as shallowly pitched as the Bournes', but there the similarity ended. The Huntington and Bourne houses demonstrated how drastically tastes had changed in twenty years. The first achieved Beaux-Arts propriety with columns and keystones and the massive proportions of a robber baron's estate. The second confounded symmetry, exuberantly mixing forms of every shape in the Hispanic idiom. The editor of the *Western Architect,* Rexford Newcomb, rhapsodized that the Bourne House "transports us to a land of oriental delights, for a certain quality almost of the desert, pervades its forms. Its almost barbaric trimness recalls in spirit, if not in form, unforgotten scenes in sun-bathed Algiers or Tripoli."[15]

"Here," the architect Charles Moore later wrote, "is one of the most satisfying examples of the Spanish Colonial ever built."[16] With one house, Neff had produced the standard by which all his work would be measured. Soon other meandering Spanish-style houses with low walls went up in the immediate neighborhood, and then they began appearing in Pasadena, Los Angeles, and Beverly Hills as well.

The Bournes celebrated the completion of the construction by throwing a party in a wine cellar hidden behind false walls and reached through trapdoors and myriad passageways to evade liquor prohibitions. Lath-and-plaster journeymen mingled with tile setters and golfers and socialites. The Aeolian pipe organ that dominated the living room—a fixture of early-twentieth-century life among the wealthy in America—played into the night, in honor of Bourne's father's love of music.[17] (The senior Bourne, a parishioner at New York's Trinity Church, had sung in the choir as a young man.)

Amelita Galli-Curci, the opera star, came to see the new house during the run of a production in downtown Los Angeles in which she was performing. Mary Pickford also came to size it up, as she and her family were considering building a number of residential projects.

Unfortunately, the Bournes encountered more disappointment than happiness in their houses. When one of their three children fell from a horse and broke his arm, he did not receive immediate treatment because of Emily's mistrust of physicians. A nurse engaged to care for the child eventually became romantically involved with A. K. In spite of their unsettled marriage, the couple expanded the house with a bar, a recreation room, and a lap pool, creating a total of twelve thousand square feet of living space. Instead of hiring Neff, they selected Evert Phipps Babcock, a former Neff employee, for the Depression had begun and they believed Babcock needed the work more than Neff did. A. K.'s growing collection of Duesenbergs and Rolls-Royces was sheltered in a phalanx of new garages. Guard towers were erected over the servants' quarters after the kidnapping of Charles Lindbergh's son on March 1, 1932, made the Bournes increasingly security conscious. Where the cost of the original, Neff-designed Bourne compound had been estimated at $38,250, the additions cost $30,000. Ten years after commissioning Neff to design the Lombardy Road house, the Bournes ended their marriage. Emily's second marriage, to a man who was rumored to have been her chauffeur, was a success, and the two remained in the house until 1944, when her son went off to fight in World War II.

Bourne and his second wife, Alberta McCune, retreated to a Glendora citrus ranch he purchased, which Neff expanded from its modest proportions to ninety-eight hundred square feet of American federal grandeur. With the security of his children still on his mind, Bourne ordered that an underground tunnel be built to link the caretaker's quarters to the house. Neff designed a third residence for Bourne, Ranchora, in the shadow of the San Jacinto Mountains, adjacent to one of the first golf courses in Palm Springs. The U-shaped plan centered on a pool, so that the courtyard acted as a living room. The desert design was also notable for its use of the soon-to-be mass-produced sliding-glass Arcadia doors that integrated indoor and outdoor spaces. Neff would never have admitted it, but he was borrowing a trick Richard Neutra had hit upon in 1935 when he used sliding glass the size of airplane hangar doors in his Corona Avenue School in southeast Los Angeles.

BREAKING INTO SHOW BUSINESS

The Bournes led quiet lives compared to Frances Marion and Fred Thomson, members of the film industry. Like many who had left New York to come to Los Angeles, they lived a transient life, moving from hotel room to rented bungalow, because they had always felt that it was not the kind of city where they could settle down. (Marion's biographer, Cari Beauchamp, described the Los Angeles of the day as "a boomtown where large houses and clusters of businesses were indiscriminately interspersed with lean-to refineries and thousands of oil wells, and the occasional barn or deserted building on vacant land taken over by a roving band of moviemakers.")[18] Actors, producers, and directors finally began buying property after it became clear that film was a bona fide industry that could pay very, very well. "Having risen from stoop, porch, piazza, and veranda," Marion wrote in her autobiography, "[they] now rode in cars of foreign make, staffed their homes with liveried butlers, French chefs, and maids in trim uniforms, and built pools with water heated to a temperature that permitted swimming even on cold winter days."[19]

Marion and Thomson's marriage seemed to have the makings of film fantasy. She was a film writer who had appeared before the camera in 1915 in *A Girl of Yesterday* with Mary Pickford, at the same time she was writing *Daddy-Long-Legs* and *Stella Maris* for the actress.[20] "It isn't the slightest exaggeration," fellow screenwriter Adela Rogers St. Johns observed, "to say that without Frances Marion, there would have been no Mary Pickford."[21] William Randolph Hearst had so much faith in her ability, he paid her two thousand

dollars a week to write screenplays for Marion Davies.[22] Frances Marion's Oscars for *The Big House* and *The Champ* proved that her talent extended beyond melodramatic two-reelers. "No one was more in demand or more prolific from 1915 through the late 1930s," her biographer wrote. "For over two decades she was the world's highest paid screenwriter—male or female—writing 200 produced films."[23]

Thomson, an Occidental College athlete, had served as a World War I chaplain with the field artillery. After Pickford cast him opposite herself in *The Love Light*, which she directed, he gave up the cloth for acting and turned his talents to western serials. ("There was never a confirmed preacher who wasn't a confirmed actor," his wife noted.)[24] "Boys across the country identified with him as a great western rider," the historian Andrew Rolle wrote of Thomson, whose horse, Silver King, was equally famous. "He enriched himself by making more than 65 films under a label controlled by an Irish financier from Boston, Joseph P. Kennedy."[25]

After they were married in 1919, the couple began looking for land where they could live and board as many as a dozen horses. Thomson approached Alphonzo Bell, a friend from Occidental College days, whose hilly Bel-Air enclave allowed horses. "Hilltop property had become the rage," Marion wrote in her memoirs. "Wherever you went, you met groups from the picture colony trudging up the steep wooded hills in full mountain-climbing regalia."

It was also common, however, to find deed restrictions prohibiting sales to actors in 1920s Los Angeles, just as it was to find prohibitions against selling to racial and religious minorities. Bell reportedly told Thomson, "I'm terribly sorry you became an actor, but I've made it a law. Not one acre of my land is to be sold to actors or Jews."[26] Bell's intolerance was founded, historian John Pohlmann believed, on a "sincere, if mis-

Frances Marion and Fred Thomson's Enchanted Hill estate included two guest houses, tennis courts, a large swimming pool, stables, and a riding paddock

taken, feeling of responsibility for the morality of the public as a whole."[27] (Presbyterians like Bell used their economic power to fight the film industry after the murder of the director William Desmond Taylor and the trial of the comedic actor Fatty Arbuckle. The faithful boycotted all but the tamest of films.) Thomson found a developer who had no preconceived ideas about actors, but not before letting Bell know what he thought of his laws.

Around 1921, the couple bought four acres in the Beverly Terrace tract above Benedict Canyon for four hundred dollars an acre. Later they bought twenty more, after the price had escalated to forty-five hundred dollars an acre. "Within a month," Marion wrote, "bulldozers chugged up the hill . . . Forty laborers cleared the underbrush and uprooted native trees, gnarled and scaly with age. When the twenty-four acres looked like a large nude head rising above its fellow hills, we could study the topography and find the best location to house Fred's horses."[28]

The architect they had selected to design a riding ring, stable, and house had gone to Mexico on an extended trip, recommending Neff to design the gatehouse entry and the guests' and servants' quarters. The plan Neff devised suited the couple so well that they scrapped the original architect's plans and hired Neff to design the house.

Nicknamed the Enchanted Hill, it was the first substantial house owned by anyone in the film industry to be designed by a licensed architect. "I must confess, with embarrassment," Marion wrote in her memoir, "that Fred Thomson and I built the largest house on the highest hill in Beverly Hills." Neff's design was wild with architectural ornament, minarets rising from the roof wherever a right angle appeared. Coats of arms decorated with a horse's head, a movie reel, and a horseshoe were cast in stone and placed over the entry vestibule. "In a short while our hill

resembled a gigantic wedding cake," Marion wrote.

The estate was remote and difficult to reach, and Neff oriented the facade around a courtyard where automobiles arrived after passing through an arched opening in the front of the house. It was the same ogive-parabolic-elliptical (some would say Gothic) arch used in the Bourne entry, an arch that was becoming a Neff trademark. Walls were punctuated with balconies and windows of varying shapes. Wrought iron blossomed into flowerlike forms. Inside the voissoired portal entry and vestibule, a two-story hall marked by arches on all four sides was enveloped in patterns of tiled Moorish stars that recalled those of the exotic buildings of the Alhambra. There was a ballroom, a screening room in the basement, an office where Marion could write screenplays, and a workroom for Thomson. Thomson's bathroom shower, which had a dozen spigots on the wall and an overhead tap ten feet high, was considered a marvel, the kind of thing friends like boxing champion Gene Tunney wanted to see when they came to visit.

All this excess meant that a number of building-material suppliers wanted to be associated with the project. Tile manufacturer Gladding, McBean & Co. took out a page in *Architectural Digest* to advertise its work on the house. So did the manufacturer of the refrigerator, Servel. Venerably stuffy *Architectural Record* devoted page after page to the house in its November 1927 issue. It also appeared in a book called *The Spanish House for America*, which depicted residences in locations as far-flung as Pennsylvania.[29]

None of Marion's contemporaries at MGM, including Louis B. Mayer and the producer Irving Thalberg, had built such grand houses, and when Thalberg heard she was organizing the Screenwriters Guild, he was livid. "Those writers are living like kings," he exclaimed. "Why would they want to join a union, like coal miners or plumbers?"[30] Marion was

The Marion-Thomson House, as published in Architectural Digest

supposedly the industry's best-paid screenwriter until Ben Hecht received $260,000 from Samuel Goldwyn to rework *The Front Page* as *My Gal Friday* in 1938, but grand living ultimately made her uncomfortable. Although at the time she sought her English butler's advice—waiting in the drawing room, where she had been coached to say, "Charmed you could come this evening, cherie," after he had greeted Rudolph Valentino or Greta Garbo at the door—she eventually renounced this lavish lifestyle, calling her mansion "the house that bunk built." The pretensions were bad enough, but what really irked her, she later wrote, were friends like Pickford and her husband Douglas Fairbanks, who had become so accustomed to being the center of attention that they failed to take note of others' accomplishments.

It all came to an abrupt end when Thomson became ill. Despondent over his inability to obtain a new contract, he awoke with pain and a 104-degree temperature one night. After surgery for kidney stones at the Queen of Angels Hospital, he prepared a will. On Christmas Day of 1928, after the symptoms of tetanus were finally diagnosed, he died.

Frances Marion sold the estate before Black Thursday and the stock market crash for a reported $540,000.[31] Texas oil driller William "Lejene" Barnes, who bought it, lost his fortune and walked away from the property.[32] While the house was uninhabited, the eight-bedroom quarters for equestrian hands burned to the ground.[33] After World War II, another buyer appeared: Paul Kollsman, the inventor of the airplane barometric altimeter, saw an ad for the property in a New York newspaper. He flew to Los Angeles and, when he was unable to reach the broker who had placed the ad, drove straight to the estate. Climbing over the wall, he peered into the vacant mansion and walked the grounds under a full moon. The following morning, he bought the property. As time passed, Kollsman bought

View from the entry portal to the auto court, where guests disembarked

a hundred undeveloped acres around the estate. After his death in 1982, his widow chose to live in New York, and the house was once again vacant.

After years of speculation about who could afford a site that big, Microsoft Corporation cofounder Paul Allen purchased it for $20 million in 1997.[34] Placing a call to Frances Marion's biographer, he requested pho-

tos of Neff's structures. It came as a shock to her when she opened the *Los Angeles Times* on January 23, 2000, and discovered that Allen had demolished the house.[35] He had decided to build another one, fifty thousand square feet in size.

ABOVE: *Entrance of the Marion-Thomson House, as seen from below the auto court*

LEFT: *The living room, decorated by the Cheesewright Studios of Pasadena*

Manufacturers such as Gladding, McBean & Co. and Servel advertised in the issue of Architectural Digest *that featured the Marion-Thomson House*

Entry hall of the Neffs' house on Orange Grove Boulevard

CHAPTER NINE

TUSCAN PASADENA

There is but one standard of criticism, the standard of beauty of line, proportion, texture and color.
—Reginald D. Johnson, *California Southland* (February 1926)

ℛEALTORS MIGHT DESCRIBE Neff creations as Spanish or Italian design, but Neff came to prefer "Californian" as a word to describe his output. "The architecture of Southern California is characterized by long, sweeping, seemingly unbound lines flowing to conform to the surrounding terrain," he wrote poetically of what he was trying to accomplish.[1] His Southern California did not lend itself to pediments, columns, and classical orders. But some of his clients did not want houses that flowed to conform to hillsides, no matter what he thought. Rectangular villas to rival the opulent, Venetian-style palazzos Addison Mizner was designing in Florida—like those Andrea Palladio had designed in the Veneto countryside centuries before—were their idea of what Southern California needed.

The stately Italian villa had, in fact, become Wallace Neff's stock-in-trade, despite his aversion to its pretenses and his indifference to re-creating such precise axial geometric styles.[2] Neff designed several dozen villas for his clients, who included a doctor, a car dealer, a land speculator, a film star, a director, and captains of industry like Dr. Milbank Johnson, the first president of the Automobile Club of Southern California, who retired to his villa in the sylvan San Rafael district of Pasadena with his wife, Isabel, in 1924. Neff satisfied his own need to be creative by selecting identifiable elements of Italian villas—a grand stone pedi-

ment entry, for instance—and exaggerating their proportions. Compared with their model, Neff's pedimented entries would be overblown, but they would have gained importance in the viewer's eye.

Neff may have disagreed, but developers had been claiming that the Italian villa was a natural in Southern California since the 1880s. The tracts of land they plotted were called "villa lots" to capitalize on the Mediterranean analogy that was the refrain of travel boosterism. When Bel-Air opened its gates in 1923, "villa sites" were offered at the grand price of fifty thousand dollars. Stepping-stones, fountains, and wellheads like those in sixteenth-century Italian gardens were duplicated by myriad local sculptors and tile manufacturers, and arranged on residential grounds that looked more like parklands.

The grandest villa in town was silent-film actor Harold Lloyd's, designed by Sumner Spalding, an architect who taught at the University of Southern California. Four years passed before the immense, forty-room Greenacres complex in Benedict Canyon—with eleven acres of gardens and a golf course—was completed in 1929 for $2 million. A. E. Hanson, a nurseryman with big ideas who often collaborated with Neff, designed the landscape. Numerous articles and photographs documented the estate, for Lloyd was intent upon notoriety.

ABOVE: *Jarvis and Marion Barlow House*
LEFT: *Barlow House entry hall*

What is known of Neff's own most impressive villa commission is much more sketchy, due to his casual record keeping. His client was the flamboyant Dr. Walter Jarvis Barlow, who had championed a cure for tuberculosis. A graduate of the Columbia University College of Physicians and Surgeons, Barlow had come to Southern California at the turn of the century after he contracted what was then called consumption or the nervous disease. He recovered after spending so much time outdoors that he appeared to be naturally dark-skinned. Setting out to find a definitive cure for the leading cause of death in America, he purchased property in the foothill community of Sierra Madre, but was unable to convince his neighbors to approve his plans to house victims of the dreaded disease on his land. Instead, he built a sanatorium in remote Chavez Ravine. "The great Barlow Sanatorium," historian John E. Baur wrote, "made Dr. W. Jarvis Barlow a prominent physician and, through his hospital, one of Southern California's most effective philanthropists."[3] For those who could afford to pay dearly for treatment, he built Las Encinas, a deluxe facility in Pasadena.

When downtown commerce began to encroach on their house on Figueroa Street, Barlow and his wife, Marion, decided to build a house on the Sierra Madre parcel. The granddaughter of the founder of Baldwin Locomotive Works, the largest manufacturer of heavy machinery during the Gilded Age, Marion had returned from a trip to Italy with picture books of great country estates.[4] Her ideal, the Villa Collazzi on Lake Como in Certosa, was attributed to Michelangelo. The Pasadena architect she hoped to commission was busy with other projects, but he steered her to the up-and-coming Wallace Neff; because of Neff's training, he said, Neff was capable of imitating Michelangelo and Palladio. Neff's office was crammed with the same oversized picture books Mrs. Barlow had brought home. In fact, he used them so often over the decades

Villa Collazzi, attributed to Michelangelo

that masking tape had to be wrapped around their spines to hold them together. "I'd get all the books available on the job," Neff said, "and study it, read it, study it, and read it until it was really a part of me."[5]

Some would have considered a commission to design a house in the authentic Florentine Renaissance style a coup for a rising architect—including Neff's college professor Ralph Adams Cram, who had taught that all architectural styles had been discovered and had only to be improved upon. Others believed architects must listen to their own muses, not their predecessors'. Neff was sympathetic to the latter view, and it was his unspoken conviction that the house the Barlows wanted to build was too large for twentieth-century Southern California living. Yet he discovered elements in the Villa Collazzi that pleased him, which he would continue to use in house after house.

One important element was the entry. How does an architect prepare visitors for an appreciation of his work? He provides a place protected from the weather, where they can put the world behind them and anticipate the structure ahead. Neff's anteroom, with its glass doors covered in wrought iron, was the inspiration for dozens more. Michelangelo's villa was entered from the base of a U-shaped plan, but visitors approached the Barlows' Villa del Sol d'Oro from the side, where a cast-stone pedimented surround was topped by a canopy of opaque glass evocative of the Jazz Age. Beyond the alcove, guests encountered what was to become a Neff signature—a grand rotunda hall dominated by a staircase suspended without apparent support. Hanging from the elaborate wrought-iron railing was a tasseled Spanish shawl.

An Italian house's patina comes from the pigmentation added to wet stucco, and Neff used the same process.[6] He shied away from dark shades like the burnt-paprika color that home owners in Southern California find so appealing today. The Barlow House nevertheless had more vivid coloring than any other house Neff designed. Its mottled, rusty ocher was selected by Mrs. Barlow, legend has it, from samples of toasted bread.[7]

Neff faithfully reproduced the Renaissance orders. The Villa del Sol d'Oro's carved sandstone windows, with architraves and consoles supporting pediments, involved more substantial and intricate masonry work than those of any other Neff structure. Della Robbia plaques appeared in the numerous alcoves. The aspect of the house most faithful to the Villa Collazzi was the *cortile*, or courtyard, which, as in a traditional Tuscan U-shaped plan, featured an interior courtyard surrounded on three sides by classically cloistered, arcaded porches and open on the fourth to a garden and rectangular pool. The Barlows' Prohibition-era wine cellar was hidden behind a vault door in the basement, where there were also thirteen furnaces that heated the mansion and safes that held Mrs. Barlow's jewels and Dr. Barlow's medicine.

The Italian stone pines, cypress, grapevines, and fruit trees that remain on the site today are remnants of a grand, formal plan executed by an unknown landscape architect. The house was sited as the McNallys' house and Neff's own house were: in front of the commanding Sierra Madre Mountains and overlooking the San Gabriel Valley. Presiding over its shallowly pitched tile roof was a tower Neff, not Michelangelo, had designed.

LOCAL ROYALTY

Like his other Italian influence, Andrea Palladio, Neff tried to adapt the architectural forms of the past to present-day needs. Palladio went back to antiquity, and Neff went back to Palladio, borrowing the master's classical vocabulary. Like Palladio, he favored unpaved courtyards that could set off the structure from the land. Both composed with cross axials to create L-, T-, or U-shaped plans, and both incorporated grand, fifteen-foot ceilings.

The two villas that face one another on the hillside at the intersection of Orlando Road and Cameron Drive in San Marino are the easiest of Neff's houses to find (next to the very visible Neff family home on busy Orange Grove Boulevard), for San Marino's municipal codes prohibit high walls. The house on the northwest corner was designed for Frederick Cole Fairbanks, whose father, Charles, served as vice president under Theodore Roosevelt and ran unsuccessfully against Woodrow Wilson in 1916, with justice Charles Evans Hughes of the U.S. Supreme Court. The Fairbankses, who were from Indianapolis, came to Pasadena on their honeymoon and decided to move west. When it was time for their daughter Cornelia's wedding to Robert Murray Vaillancourt on March 1, 1941, the ceremony was held beneath the house's curved, balustraded terrace, where an ancient oak formed a canopy. "My parents used the house to the hilt," Cornelia said. "But

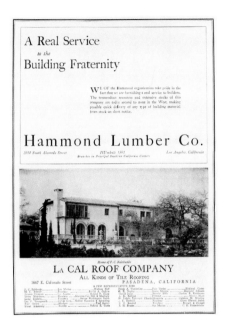

TOP LEFT: *Suppliers like the Hammond Lumber Co. advertised in* Architectural Digest *when the Fairbanks House was published*

TOP RIGHT AND BOTTOM: *Frederick Cole Fairbanks House*

after father died and mother had been an invalid for fifteen years, she sold the house to the son of President Herbert Hoover, Allan Henry Hoover, in 1948."[8]

The 1925 Fairbanks House proves that Neff considered the site before all else. The sloping terrain was bounded by two roads, one flat (Cameron Drive) and the other on a grade (Orlando Road). Neff chose to orient the access to the higher grade on Orlando. There, at the crown of the hill, an auto courtyard was laid and the house—a "handsome and reserved" composition, one critic wrote[9]—was constructed with its front door facing the auto court, not the street. The plan kept the cars and their passengers from being seen from the street, for Neff did not like the specter of an automobile distracting from the vision of the facade.

The other villa, on the northeast corner of the intersection, was commissioned in 1927 by Carroll L. Post, of Post cereals, and his wife, Fannie, who were living nearby in a house Neff had designed for them four years earlier. Set about a hundred feet from the street, the ten-thousand-square-foot structure had a cast-stone entry surround on a par with one of Palladio's grand portals. An anteroom like the entry in the Barlow House prepared the visitor for the grandeur to come.

One block south, around a bend, Neff designed another villa in 1929, this one for Mrs. James Fletcher Skinner, the widow of Sears, Roebuck & Co.'s first merchandise manager.[10] (When Mrs. Skinner moved to Pasadena from Oak Park, Illinois, in 1927, she joined the highest concentration of widows in any city in America—18.2 percent compared to a national average of 11.1 percent. Tax assessors estimated that at the time, 75 percent of the wealth in Pasadena was held by women.) The elaborate interior spaces of the nine-thousand-square-foot Orlando Road house—excess meant to be exclaimed over—suggested that Mrs. Skinner had no intention of living in quiet seclusion. A gilded, stenciled, coffered ceiling in the entry hall was executed by

the same artist who was painting the ceilings of Caltech's Athenaeum faculty club, Giavanni Smeraldi.[11] The house's Palladian-scale, cast-stone entry surround was executed by the artisans at Hamlin and Hood.[12] The vase of fruit in the curve of the broken-scroll pediment above the door was so massive, it stood higher than the ledges of the second-story windows.

Another Italian architect from whom Neff borrowed was Giacomo Barozzi da Vignola, the sixteenth-century author of *Rules of the Five Orders of Architecture* (1562). The concept behind Vignola's hemicycle-shaped Villa Giulia, built for Pope Julius III, worked just as well in the twentieth century, when automobiles, rather than horses, conveyed people to their homes. Neff used its semicircular, elliptical shape in a Pasadena house he designed for Sidney and Lilly Berg, which had an entrance court where an automobile with a generous turning radius could circle without backing up.

The Berg House was commissioned in 1927 by Lilly Anheuser Busch, the widow of the founder of Anheuser Busch Brewing, for her granddaughter Lilly and her granddaughter's new husband, Sidney, the vice president of Blankenhorn Realty.[13] The material Neff selected was nearly impenetrable: gunite concrete. Sprayed over a wood frame, it had a golden hue that made it look as if it had been aged by time and the elements.

Visitors standing at the glass front door could see through the entry rotunda to the lush rear yard, where a pool was poured for young Billy Berg after he was stricken with polio. The elements in the rotunda entry hall—wrought-iron railing on a circular staircase, black-and-white checkered marble floor—were typical of many Neff villas.

Earthquake after earthquake, the Berg House has stood firm. Seventy-some years after it was built, the house has maintained the mellow patina of a centuries-old villa, largely because successive owners have heeded Neff's advice that applying paint over gunite is a waste of time.[14]

THE NEFF FAMILY VILLA

The building that sealed Wallace Neff's image as the master of the villa in the public imagination was one he designed for his parents. In the winter of 1926, as Ed and Nannie were approaching their thirty-fifth wedding anniversary, their daughter, Della, had gone on a tour of the Mediterranean with her cousins Mary and Marion Clow, who, like herself, remained unmarried. When Della returned on April 1, 1927, she discovered that her parents had moved into a new house on Orange Grove Boulevard that bore a resemblance to the grand estates and hotels she had left behind.

Around 1924, Nannie and Ed had moved from their Altadena house to one on Ford Place in Pasadena. All their sons had married except John, and he was about to wed the great-great-granddaughter of the noted banker and lawyer Jackson A. Graves. Ed Neff was laboring at automobile sales in a building Wallace had designed on Lake Avenue, a few blocks north of his Saint Elizabeth Church. Nannie Neff's priorities, after her children, were her church (now Saint Andrew Catholic in Pasadena) and her club.

The Valley Hunt Club had been located on Orange Grove Boulevard since 1908. Across the street was an empty, 200-by-112-foot lot. It was not a large parcel by Orange Grove standards; the boulevard was home to some of California's last remaining battleship-size mansions and was on a par with Park and Fifth avenues in New York. The William Wrigley Mansion to the north occupied an entire block. Every significant, early-twentieth-century, Anglo-Saxon architect in Southern California, from Frederick L. Roehrig to the Greenes, had designed a house there. The Rose Parade continued to take place on Orange Grove. Tradition

Rose garden in the rear yard of the Neffs' house

dies hard in Pasadena, and Orange Grove has always been the fulcrum.

Ed and Nannie bought the lot and commissioned their son to design a house. The villa-style structure he produced represented an effort to create a midsize house in a sea of estates. While its five-dollar-per-square-foot cost was at least two dollars below that of his other villas, the house had elements that appeared in his grandest houses, most notably the entry rotunda with its black-and-white marble floor. Its shallowly pitched roof projected several feet from the walls, shel-

Entrance to the Neff House

The Orange Grove Boulevard house Neff designed for his parents

tering the interior from the afternoon sun, and the second-floor loggia allowed breezes to circulate inside, in an era when air-conditioning was reserved for a few office buildings. Packing ivory-inlaid tables from the smoking room of the old McNally residence, along with carved mahogany pieces they had purchased in prewar Europe, Nannie and Ed moved into their new house on Orange Grove Boulevard. With its circular drive, the house was smartly compact, but there was no mistaking that it was a villa.

Louise and Wallace Neff
with their daughter, Phyllis

CHAPTER TEN

LOUISE

On some Rand McNally Map or Globe, each man can place his finger and say, "Here I was born. At one time this little dot was my World."
—*Sunset Magazine* advertisement (April 1924)

WALLACE NEFF WAS TWENTY-EIGHT years old when he took the plunge that appeases social conventions and became a married man. Not surprisingly, he married a woman from his own social strata. In fact, the couple's parents may have had their union in mind from the moment the two were born.

Wallace Neff's and Louise Up de Graff's family sagas first overlapped in mid-nineteenth-century Chicago, where Rand McNally & Company and Libby, McNeill & Libby were both founded. In 1878, Louise's maternal grandfather, Arthur Albion Libby, filled a can with ice, surrounded it with boneless cuts of beef, and shipped it off in a box, revolutionizing freight transport, for beef had previously been cured by exposing it to the winter air. Libby, his brother Charles, and their partner, Archibald McNeill, became the second organization (after the Wilson Packing Company) to sell compressed meat in cans, and their fortunes were assured.[1]

By the time Libby, McNeill & Libby introduced its metal key, used to open food tins, in 1890, Arthur Libby Sr. had succumbed to exhaustion, brought on by stress and Chicago's miserable air quality.[2] After a year in Europe, he had been persuaded by his son and friends like Andrew McNally that Southern California living was the solution.[3] Libby, his wife, and two of his three daughters, Mabel and Pearl, had headed for Pasadena, first to a Queen Anne–style dwelling on

Orange Grove Boulevard and then, in 1896, to a shingle-style house a few blocks east, designed by Frederick L. Roehrig.

Libby's third daughter, Emma, had married Thaddeus Up de Graff, an up-and-coming ear, nose, and throat doctor, at St. Paul's Universalist Church in Chicago on December 29, 1890, the same year her family moved west.[4] She and her husband followed, settling into Pasadena's social milieu in a Victorian-style house on Lockhaven Street. In January 1893, when she attended Nannie McNally's wedding reception, she was expecting her first child, Louise Eleanor, who was born on July 8. Thaddeus Libby came the next year, on December 1.

Louise's abiding childhood memory was of being conveyed by her father in a pony cart from their home to watch the lamplighter illuminate the gas lights on Orange Grove Boulevard at dusk.[5] Orange Grove became the center of her life. Besides her grandparents, her uncle Arthur and aunt Jeannette lived on the boulevard in a grand, craftsman-style bungalow designed by the Greene brothers. Louise and her friend Della Neff rode up the street in a flower-covered automobile in the 1915 Tournament of Roses, beaming in their own floral regalia—oversized rose-covered bonnets.

The Up de Graffs left Lockhaven for an ivy-covered, mission revival–style house on Columbia Street at

Advertisement for Sunset *magazine, November 1904, for Libby's Food Products, founded by Louise Neff's grandfather, Arthur Libby*

some point during Louise's childhood, and when she was about thirteen, she and her brother were sent to study at Switzerland's Sillig school, where she spent time with Wallace Neff. Later, while visiting Florence, she received orders to return home because of the outbreak of World War I. Back in Pasadena, she volunteered at the Red Cross and the Navy League for the duration of the war.

Louise's brother, Thad, who had also been studying in Switzerland, returned to Pasadena with his sister, and following the war, he worked his way up through the ranks at Libby, McNeill & Libby's Southern California offices. (The company had facilities in Chino and Sunnyvale, where its canning plant was the world's largest when it was built in 1908. Its holdings extended from a pineapple farm in Oahu to a fishing fleet that caught Alaskan salmon.)[6] In 1924, however, he left to capitalize on the land boom. "Mr. Up de Graff has been conspicuously successful in building houses of the highest class, exacting most careful construction and detail, both in design and appointments," the *Pasadena Star-News* reported in 1927.[7] His architect was his new brother-in-law, Wallace Neff.

Neff's draftsmen were under pressure to design houses as quickly as they could, because Up de Graff "sold the houses as fast as Wallace'd draw them," draftsman Clifford Hoskins said. They were not the modest two- and three-bedroom houses of Berkeley Street, but expansive structures that incorporated as many as five varieties of wood in their floorboards.

Neff had also designed a house for Thad and his bride, Dorothy Gray, and another for his in-laws. The latter had been built to replicate the country life of the leisure class in England or in the East: it included a reception room where guests were entertained, a parlor where they waited for the host, a formal dining room, a butler's pantry, a servants' kitchen, and maids' rooms. Photographs of the tall French windows evoke images of Long Island mansions with water views. F. Scott Fitzgerald described a similar house, "broken by a line of French windows…glowing now with reflected gold…ajar and gleaming white against the fresh grass" in *The Great Gatsby*.[8] The night Neff had arrived to ask for Louise's hand, his grasp of the fine points of neoclassical architecture may have been remarked on by his soon-to-be in-laws. They certainly had impressed their prospective son-in-law with their appetite for real estate investment.

Socially minded Pasadena had been informed of the engagement after Neff had escorted Louise to the opening of the 1922–23 season at the Maryland Hotel. "And there was that young architect, Wallace Neff," the hotel's society writer reported, "with his lovely young fiancée, Miss Louise Up de Graff, social favorites in Pasadena. It is hardly fair to remember that this clever young man was a little lad running round the Maryland grounds not a great many years ago."[9]

The pose they struck for the hotel's cameras reveals a couple so similar in appearance and demeanor, they might have been brother and sister. Both were dark-haired, medium-boned, and unsmiling. Neff's eyes were blue; hers, brown. Louise's nose was well-formed, while his protruded slightly beyond prescribed scale and proportion. Six feet tall, 170 pounds, and intense in a wide-breasted tuxedo, Neff had combed every hair with precision. ("A striking-looking man with a quiet voice and a calm, unhurried manner," a woman who knew him observed.)[10] Louise wore a multilayered evening dress with a hint of a waist and plenty of arm coverage, lovely yet conservative for the flapper era. Her only jewelry was a string of pearls and an engagement band. Her wide-set, doe-like eyes peeked out from behind bangs. Her single facial shortcoming was her barely defined chin. Shorter than Neff by a head, she was so demure in repose, it is difficult to imagine an animated Louise Up de Graff. She

had begun a study of Catholicism in preparation for conversion from the Episcopal faith. It was the same effort her future mother-in-law had made a generation before.

MARRIAGE

Surrounded by palms and pink roses, beneath a stenciled, gold-leaf, barrel-vaulted ceiling, they were married by Monsignor John McCarthy at 8:30 p.m. on Thursday, June 21, 1923, in the grand ballroom of the Huntington Hotel. The hillside hotel towered over a neighborhood just beginning to develop, and two Neff houses had been constructed on the hotel's grounds.[11]

Louise wore the same white satin gown her mother had worn when she was married at St. Paul's in Chicago. In her hair were orange blossoms, like the ones her mother-in-law had worn on her wedding day. Neff's sister, Della, was Louise's maid of honor. Helen Holladay, a niece of Henry Huntington, served as a bridesmaid.[12] Thad was Neff's best man, and his three brothers were groomsmen. Mac Blankenhorn, a friend developing Pasadena subdivisions with Neff and Up de Graff, was an usher.

"Mr. and Mrs. Neff are native son and daughter of California," the *Pasadena Star-News* reported, "and the romance which culminated in the ceremony of last evening began in high school days."[13] The couple honeymooned in Cuba, where Neff managed to find time to sketch a building significant to an architect of Mediterranean designs, the Columbus Cathedral. He noted a preponderance of blue-painted wood trim and rustic mahogany doors on Havana's town houses, elegant structures with no glass or screens in their apertures. Shutters were folded out or wrought-iron gates secured to provide protection. Concrete mortar held tile to the roofs. Neff measured doors and windows fastidiously.

111

ABOVE LEFT: *Louise and Della Neff at the Long Beach Pike*
ABOVE RIGHT: *Nannie Neff and her daughter-in-law in Honolulu*
LEFT: *Louise Up de Graff as a Red Cross volunteer during the war*

He also photographed an auto alcove that extended through a two-story building, and within months had used the feature in the Marion-Thomson House. It is not unusual for an architect to be inspired by travel, yet it appears that this trip was one of the rare breaks Neff took from his practice in its early years. Where peers like Austin Whittlesey, Richard Requa, Windsor Soule, Garrett Van Pelt, and Rexford Newcomb went off to Mexico and Spain with cameras and sketchbooks and returned home to publish books and articles, Neff steered clear of endeavors that would take him away from lucrative residential work.

Back in California, he and Louise found a parcel in Altadena in a Frank Meline subdivision called Town and Country.[14] There may have been an agreement to swap architectural services for the land. Not surprisingly, the diminutive house he designed was executed in a Spanish style, albeit with a wood-shake roof. Groomsman Blankenhorn liked it so much, he photographed it for advertisements for his real estate company. Maroon draft curtains hung over the entrance alcove in the manner of Cuban houses. Neff used a towering eucalyptus to establish the axis on which he sited the house. The dignified San Gabriel Mountains were the backdrop.

Altadena was gaining Neffs, but it was about to lose a McNally. By the time Neff's eighty-six-year-old grandmother, Delia McNally, died on January 21, 1924, her home had practically become a civic monument. Christmas Tree Lane was a local tradition: Every year, scores of automobiles with headlights dimmed inched up Santa Rosa Avenue toward the house. Riders exclaimed at the immensity of the deodar cedars lining the street and the beauty of the red, blue, and green lights sparkling in the limbs.

The house was considered an architectural folly, not only for its Queen Anne bric-a-brac, which required vast amounts of paint, but for the rakish smoking room and its dark, mysterious furnishings. After Mrs. McNally's death, "we rattled around the house for a few months," her granddaughter Helen Belford remembered much later, when she was eighty-four, "until we sold it to a couple from New York. He died before they moved in, and his wife sold it to a realtor. The realtor subdivided the five acres. I believe it was the first subdivision of the grand old Altadena estates, and our name was mud."[15]

Two years later, Louise's mother died after an asthma attack.[16] Emma's estate left Louise twenty-five thousand dollars, a figure the family considered disappointing.[17] Her father died thirteen years later. By then, Neff and Louise had three children of their own. The physical resemblance of their youngest, Arthur, to his great-grandfather, Arthur A. Libby, was remarkable.

The Administration Building of the Rancho Santa Ana Botanic Garden in inland Orange County

ADOBE DAYS

Californians claimed a noble history with the missions as landmarks of civilization and worn images of strength.
—Elizabeth McMillian, *California Colonial*

ONLY A HANDFUL of local individuals qualified for membership in the American Society of Landscape Architects when Neff began his career. Some focused on planning college campuses, subdivisions, and civic centers. Many more were proficient in the design of small gardens, and Neff was able to work with such emerging talents as Florence Yoch, Katherine Bashford, and A. E. "Archie" Hanson, and later Ruth Shellhorn, Edward Huntsman-Trout, and Thomas Church.[1] Neff himself was not the outdoorsman or horticulturalist one might have expected from his upbringing on a ranch surrounded by exotic, imported plants and citrus groves. But while his knowledge of plants may have been elementary, his opinions were firmly established and he was able to converse generally on the vegetation of Southern California.

The *Solandra maxima* vine (copa de oro) was a Neff favorite. He had the eye to set a scene with terra-cotta pots in a courtyard or a climbing espalier against a cool, light wall. Where the landscaping of his grandfather's era relied on imported plants like palms and roses, Neff's 1920s gardens were more apt to be composed of native plants with subtle colors that were the natural result of drought. Occasionally a Neff structure would be surrounded by a formal, Renaissance-inspired garden with terraces, parterres, axes, and vistas, but his granite-covered auto courts usually presented deliberately austere approaches to the architectural compositions ahead. He specified a minimal amount of plant material against his buildings so the facades would appear as spare as the entry courtyards. A cypress on either side of the front door was enough embellishment.

One of his clients was an equal to most landscape experts in her knowledge of native California plants—and she carried her obsession to lengths none of the professional designers could afford. Susanna Bixby Bryant began as president of her garden club and ended up overseeing her own botanical garden.

Bixby Bryant, whose girlhood days of riding horseback at Long Beach's Rancho Los Alamitos were documented by her cousin Sarah Bixby Smith in *Adobe Days*, inherited a portion of the ranch from her father, John William Bixby. He also left her half of Rancho Santa Ana, thirty-five miles from Long Beach in the inland Orange County Puente Hills, purchased in 1875 from the widow of Don Bernardo Yorba for nine thousand dollars. While the McNally family holdings in La Mirada were isolated from Los Angeles's growth until after World War II, the Bixby properties were directly in the path of the expansion of Long Beach and later the communities of Downey, Paramount, and Lakewood.[2]

Bixby Bryant found Los Angeles social life insular and stultifying, but Rancho Santa Ana inspired her,

Susanna Bixby Bryant

bringing out her talents as an organizer, equestrian, and horticulturist. Ranch life provided what her daughter called a "lifelong outlet for her superior mind and executive powers."[3] In 1912, she built a bungalow where she and her family could live while planting citrus and cotton and converting pastureland into a plant preserve. The twelve-hundred-foot altitude appeared to be ideal for growing indigenous plants, and the rest matured, her daughter noted, because Bixby Bryant was able to "force reluctant ones to grow by the sheer strength of her will."[4]

By 1925, she had bought out her brother's interest and become the sole owner of the nearly six-thousand-acre ranch. After consulting with leading botanists and landscape architects, she came up with the idea for the Rancho Santa Ana Botanic Garden, which she founded in 1927. One of her motivations seems to have been a desire to honor the ideals of the Mexican Americans who originally settled the land: the sycamore tree, specified in Don Bernardo's will as the origination point for the surveys that established the lines of his rancho,[5] became the botanical garden's symbol, along with the Spanish word *aliso* (sycamore), which appeared throughout the garden's literature.

The Yorba family's adobe hacienda on the property, La Casa de San Antonio, had once been one of the finest in the state,[6] but it had fallen into ruin and was razed in 1927. Apparently in an attempt to respect the traditions of Mexican California, Bixby Bryant hired Wallace Neff to design a new adobe for the gardens and her own personal use. In her employ were men born in Mexico who knew how to construct such buildings.

Neff may have been called an "artist in adobe" in a 1924 magazine story, but he had no more faith in the material than he did in modern architecture. Adobe bricks were produced by pouring a mixture of claylike soil, strengthened with straw or rubble, into wood forms of fourteen by eleven by four inches or larger. To erect a building of more than one story with the sun-dried material was to risk collapse. Adobe melted when it rained (so roofs had to extend beyond the walls to protect them), cracked when temperatures rose or fell, vibrated when the earth moved, and fractured in the wind. Yet the City and County of Los Angeles would grant permits for adobe structures when they were framed with concrete, a material less vulnerable to dampness than wood. House builders of the day promoted the material in *Sunset* magazine and how-to books,[7] and major Southern California resorts, such as La Quinta near Palm Springs, were constructed of adobe.[8]

Neff, who was romantic about design up to a point, was an advocate of reinforced portland-cement plaster. Strenuous testing had proved its durability.[9] Nonetheless, he acquiesced to Bixby Bryant's wishes, designing a three-story adobe structure capped by a tower that appeared to have been inspired by the missions Santa Barbara and San Luis Rey. Workers laid a concrete foundation six inches above grade as a base for the adobe, and windows were framed in metal sash.

When the building was completed in 1927, its towered, arcaded structure looked like a grandiose mission. A vast collection of horticultural volumes and

Wild Flower Display, Assembly Hall, Rancho Santa Ana Botanic Garden, Anaheim, Calif.

TOP: *A portion of the Bixby Bryant holdings in Rancho Santa Ana*
RIGHT: *Exhibition space at the Rancho Santa Ana Botanic Garden*

The Administration Building being demolished in 1952

Bixby Bryant's precise records of plant species filled room after room. A circular stairway led from the twenty-four-by-forty-four-foot reception room to a balcony with panoramic canyon views. Rustic tables sat before a massive, cast-stone fireplace, the image of a sycamore leaf in a panel above the mantel. There was even a mission-like bell in the courtyard to summon guests for meals. The basement herbarium overflowed with seventy-five hundred specimen plants.

Outdoors, seedlings erupted in thousands of concrete pots crafted by the same Mexican laborers who made the adobe. Water was drawn from the Santa Ana River to a two-million-gallon reservoir, where it flowed to the growing fields through thirty miles of galvanized, welded steel pipe. (Water was essential, for in the fall, the Santa Ana winds that blew down from the northeast deserts could dry out everything but the

hearty cactus.) Succulents and bulb gardens, ferns, wildflowers, and penstemons—Bixby Bryant had them all. Her study of the southwestern species of the genus *Cupressus*, the California cypress, was the first of its kind.

Fire did major damage to the garden sometime during World War II,[10] and then, unexpectedly, Bixby Bryant died on October 2, 1946. Her daughter, Susanna Bryant Dakin, suggested converting the horticultural headquarters into a home for wayward women, but her son, Ernest Bryant II, cited escalating taxes as reason to tear it down. The two-foot-thick walls of the Administration Building were being eroded by leaky pipes, and in 1952, Ernest prevailed. When a Fullerton newspaper reported "Son Wrecks Mother's Dream," he was furious.[11] Neff's only known adobe was twenty-five years old when it was razed.

Plants small enough to fit into five-gallon cans were moved to Claremont, twenty miles north, where a new botanical garden was organized on eighty-six acres. Orange County officials purchased a portion of the Bixby Bryant land and created Featherly Regional Park in the late 1960s. Another piece was sold to developers in 1978, and the State of California purchased the San Bernardino County portion in 1985.[12] Today Highway 91, the Riverside Freeway, runs directly through what was once Bixby Bryant's acreage. The craftsman-style headquarters residence, which she built in 1912 near the brow of the Puente Hills, is listed on the National Register of Historic Places and serves as the home of the Yorba Linda Heritage Museum and Historical Society. Surrounding it is a housing development called the Pacific Heritage Bryant Ranch, built in 1997.

CHAPTER TWELVE

ARCHITECT TO THE STARS

In Hollywood, as in Istanbul or Sioux Falls, the rich hasten to express their wealth, and betray
their fitful groping for status, by erecting homes of unnecessary magnitude and splendor.
—Leo C. Rosten, *Hollywood, the Movie Colony, the Movie Makers*

There are several reasons why photoplay corporations are callous, along with the
sufficient one that they are corporations. First, they are engaged in a financial orgy.
—Vachel Lindsay, *The Art of the Moving Picture*

CONTRARY TO CONVENTIONAL WISDOM, entertainment figures did not found Beverly Hills. The first twentieth-century residents were mere doctors and attorneys and land developers. During the days when there were far more empty lots than built ones, the Rodeo Land and Water Company struggled to stay afloat as it developed the town. Streets had been laid out in 1911, about the time young Wallace Neff was skiing down the slopes of the Alps. Empty sidewalks ran along vacant lots and disappeared into open fields. Streetlamps lighted empty streets, and wind blowing across the open spaces discouraged sightseers.

By 1921, when the young realtor George Elkins had just arrived and Neff was designing houses for Frank Meline, the population of Beverly Hills was 700—450 more than in 1914, when residents had voted to incorporate. "It was a tiny little town," Elkins remembered, "with one little market, one little drugstore, and one little hardware store. Most of the area north of Santa Monica Boulevard was in bean fields. In Los Angeles, Beverly Hills was considered too remote and entirely too windy."[1] But for a film star in search of a home off the beaten path, it was ideal, and Elkins eventually made his fortune in real estate by capitalizing on the film community's exodus from Hollywood, where they had gravitated from Edendale, to the east.

With the advent of major film studio enterprises, maps directing fans to film stars' homes began to be printed. Fans bought them from curbside hawkers on Sunset and Hollywood boulevards or picked up complimentary copies at real estate offices. In 1926, realtor George E. Read printed maps keyed with the names of 236 residents, many of them members of the industry that was making Beverly Hills a one-company town. They included Hobart Bosworth, Ruth Clifford, Sidney Franklin, Viola Dana, Allan Crosland, S. George Ullman, Julien Josephson, and Tod Browning.

Despite the proliferation of maps of the stars' homes, there was still a widespread sense of anonymity on the part of film-industry people, and no perceived need for gated communities: "In those days," silent-film actress Eleanor Boardman remembered, "we did not need gates."[2] Zoning regulations separated the city's grand houses from the more modest dwellings of the people who cared for them, with commercial and rail functions allocated to the lots in between. Along the north side of Santa Monica Boulevard land was set aside for public amenities, creating another buffer between the traffic and the large estates.

The population increased 2,486 percent while Will Rogers was honorary mayor during the 1920s, and when the post office became overwhelmed, Rogers lobbied the secretary of the treasury, Andrew Mellon, for a new one: "We are getting an awful lot of mail out here, now, and they are handling it in a tent. It's mostly circulars from Washington with speeches on prosperity, but it makes awful good reading while you are waiting for the foreclosure. It seems you owe us $250,000 to build a post office and they can't get the dough out of you."[3] Rogers got the money, and the architect Ralph C. Flewelling got the commission to build an Italian Renaissance post office.

Flewelling also designed more than a dozen houses in Beverly Hills, and Paul R. Williams, John Byers, J. E. Dolena, Harold Grieve, and Neff's onetime draftsman Douglas Honnold walked away with a number of local residential commissions as well. Honnold was doing especially well, helping MGM's head of set design, Cedric Gibbons, build one of the era's greatest modern mansions for himself and his bride, Dolores del Rio. Gibbons had a sideline designing houses for film-industry executives like Louis B. Mayer, whose Spanish-style beach house was built in Santa Monica in 1924. But as Honnold learned while working on Samuel Goldwyn's house, the construction suffered when it was executed by studio tradespeople accustomed to short-term, overnight building projects. "Much of the place, like the electrical wiring, was very Mickey Mouse," Goldwyn's son later remarked.[4]

Once Frances Marion and Fred Thomson opened their home to their film-industry friends, Neff was able to broaden his practice to include Hollywood clients. Why hire a set decorator (as many in the film industry had been in the habit of doing) if you could afford an architect? Neff, who called women "Miss" or "Missus" long after a first meeting, may not have been much of a filmgoer, but he had the breeding Hollywood aspired to. He was also attentive and willing to finish a project to the finest detail.[5] When Miss Colbert needed her screen doors repaired, he saw to it. When Mrs. Zanuck specified morning glories for her window boxes, he did

not try to talk her into geraniums. And when Mrs. Goetz told him to copy the fence on the Goldwyn beach property, he did exactly that.

FRANCES MARION'S NEIGHBOR

Fred Niblo was a vaudevillian before he began writing screenplays for Louis B. Mayer at his studio on Mission Road, the street in Edendale where the motion picture industry made its transition from infancy to adolescence. In 1924, he received the assignment of a lifetime, when he was sent to Italy to rescue *Ben-Hur* from a profligate director. Cedric Gibbons was the set designer, Harold Grieve was the costume designer, and Ramon Novarro and Francis X. Bushman were the stars. The story of the honorable Jew who defeated a villainous Roman soldier and converted to Christianity was a hugely popular nineteenth-century novel that became the box office smash of 1925, and was the most expensive silent film ever made. On Broadway, it ran for twenty-two months.[6]

The stars of the film were flush with their proceeds. Novarro purchased a Los Feliz–area house of breathtaking originality designed by Frank Lloyd Wright's son Lloyd. Harold Grieve gave up costumes to design houses for entertainers like George Burns and Gracie Allen, Jack Benny, Bing Crosby, and Ernst Lubitsch.[7] Fred Niblo and his wife, the actress Enid Bennett, spent $285,000 on eight acres of Beverly Hills land, the services of Wallace Neff, and a grand house on Angelo Drive near their friends Frances Marion and Fred Thomson. (An early map of the stars' homes shows the Niblo House directly below the Marion-Thomson House.)

Like the oval Circus Maximus in the famous chariot scene of *Ben-Hur*—and like the actual Roman Circus Maximus—the Niblo House was built to resemble a hemicyclic amphitheater. But it was oriented around an auto courtyard instead of a field, like the Marion-Thomson House. Both houses had overhanging tile roofs that shaded patios and protected interiors from the afternoon sun. The style of the flagstone-covered Niblo House was influenced by country villas in the south of France where Henri Matisse might have lived or F. Scott Fitzgerald could have written *Tender Is the Night*.[8] The semicircular plan spread out over the site, from the panoramic views on one side to the auto court on the other. Neff supposedly calculated the turning radius of Niblo's favorite car before determining the circumference of the court. A driver could easily make his way around the well in the touring car of the day without backing up.

A fifty-seven-foot-long auditorium in the basement provided enough space for an Academy of Motion Picture Arts and Sciences awards ceremony. One floor above, the living room was paneled with antique English wood, and the library paneling was executed by George Hunt, one of the foremost furniture makers of the time.[9] A cast-stone mantel was created by a leading Los Angeles artisan. Electric wall heaters—promoted by the manufacturer as a "modern" accessory—were installed in all eight bathrooms.

The construction plans drafted by Neff's staff, now in the archives of the Huntington Library, are infinitely more interesting than today's computer-generated plans. One architect reviewing the archive was struck by their detail: "The geometry of the plan is accompanied by a series of explicit notations describing in detail the process of its layout step by step," Stefanos Polyzoides observed. "The description is evocative of some kind of ancient ritual. Indeed, the foundation plan is given the veneration one might expect to be reserved for monumental Roman works and is drawn with equivalent strength. It expresses a tangible sense of respect for turning the earth, for occupying the ground."[10]

Everything was made to last, except Niblo's show business career. The industry swept him aside when sound was introduced to film, and he was forced to rent the house to Katharine Hepburn, while Nelson Eddy took a lease on the guesthouse.[11] Cary Grant vied with talent agent Jules Stein (whose Music Corporation of America managed the careers of such stars as Bette Davis, Paulette Goddard, Fred Astaire, and Greta Garbo) in a bidding war when the house went on the market in 1940.[12] Stein's version of events seems improbable, yet it reflects the financial climate of the times: "When houses weren't popular in the hills, Niblo had to sell his and he asked $60,000," Stein said. "He turned down my $50,000 offer, and traded the house for a piece of business property. The new owner didn't want the house, however, and offered it to me for $45,000. I bought it for $35,000."[13]

Stein called the estate Misty Mountain, after the marine air that often shrouded it. His wife, Doris, decorated it with antiques from a house they were leaving in Chicago. Decades later, when William Randolph Hearst's beach house was being dismantled, the Steins trucked its classical columns up the hill to their estate and installed them in their glass solarium. "The garden room cost more to build than the entire house was worth," Doris Stein's son Gerald Oppenheimer recalled.[14] Misty Mountain was considered one of the great showplaces in Los Angeles when Rupert Murdoch purchased it from the Steins' estate in 1986 for $5.8 million. In 1998, after Murdoch and his wife, Anna, made improvements, the house went on the market for $19.5 million.[15] Real estate brokers were interviewed by the *New Yorker* and the *Wall Street Journal* to determine just who might buy it. In the end, Anna left and Murdoch kept the house in a divorce settlement.

King Vidor and Eleanor Boardman

A KINGDOM FOR A KING

While Fred Niblo was reconstructing the wonders of Rome on the biggest set in Hollywood history, director King Vidor was restaging the Great War on another MGM lot in what became the most profitable silent film ever made. The realism of Vidor's *The Big Parade* earned him a reputation as a maverick among conformists. Vidor wanted to inform his audience as well as entertain them. Studio chief Louis B. Mayer often preferred less realism, and he prevailed upon Vidor to depict John Gilbert's doughboy character in the film as an uninjured survivor. Vidor reshot the ending to suit Mayer at his own expense, on the condition that Mayer preview the film in both forms. Test audiences favored Vidor's version, in which Gilbert loses a leg, and Mayer acquiesced.

The Big Parade catapulted Gilbert to the top of his profession and established the newly formed Metro-Goldwyn-Mayer as a studio of high-quality productions. Vidor earned twenty-five hundred dollars a week for directing,[16] but he could have profited more if he had agreed to take 20 percent of the film's proceeds, as the original contract specified, for the movie grossed $15 million on a $205,000 investment.[17] Raised in Texas and named for his uncle, King Wallace, King Vidor may have promoted populist stories as a filmmaker, but he was an elitist in reality. He had a taste for premium design in film and in life, as did his fiancée, Eleanor Boardman, who had studied design before becoming a film star.

Vidor's infatuation with Boardman began in the Goldwyn Studios' commissary, when he saw the actress in the lunch line, wearing a pink circus performer's costume.[18] Soon she was starring in *Souls for Sale* and *Wine of Youth*, directed by Vidor. Vidor's wife, Florence, an actress herself, filed for divorce. The situation was fictionalized in F. Scott Fitzgerald's short story "Crazy Sunday." "In his first marriage," Eleanor's character says, "he transferred his mother complex to his wife, you see—and then his sex turned to me. But when we were married the thing repeated itself—he transferred his mother complex to me and all his libido turned toward this other woman."[19]

The couple married on September 8, 1926, an event that had its own dramatic moments. The double-wedding ceremony with John Gilbert and Greta Garbo failed to take place, because Garbo never showed up. The glum Gilbert posed with the wedding party as they gathered at Marion Davies's beach house. His frustration mounting, Gilbert knocked Louis B. Mayer to the floor in one of the bathrooms after Mayer suggested that Gilbert was better off sleeping with the elusive actress without the benefit of a ring.[20] Boardman believed the incident was the beginning of the end of Gilbert's career.[21]

She and Vidor—whom she also called Theodore, but never King—lived near Gilbert on Seabright Drive, until the birth of their first child made it necessary to find larger quarters. "Wallace Neff came to the house for a year before we broke ground on a lot we bought on Tower Road," Boardman said.[22] Plans for a two-story house in Neff's characteristic California-Spanish style were drawn during the months of November and December 1927, as Vidor prepared to shoot *The Crowd*. A. E. Hanson, hard at work on Harold Lloyd's grounds and soon to tackle Pickfair's, was selected as the landscape designer. The land was steep hillside, difficult to build upon without extensive grading, and the fifteen-hundred-foot-long driveway was so narrow, Boardman recalled, that "there were [only] two places where a car could pass."

Vidor's films suggested that pretension was the precursor to moral decay, and certain features of the landscaping could be seen to reflect this idea, such as the use of drought-resistant olive trees in keeping with the austere chaparral surrounding the site. Fully grown olive trees, planted outside the eight-foot-tall living room windows, framed views of the city below.

TOP: *Fully grown olive trees were trucked up Tower Road and planted between the auto court and the entry of the King Vidor House*

LEFT: *Belinda and Tony Vidor with their mother on Easter 1936*

The King Vidor House at the pinnacle of Tower Road

The sewing room became Boardman's favorite place, from which she could escape to the top of one of the exterior staircases, leaving the clutter behind her. From there she could see a birdhouse in a tree at the center of the entry court, and she watched as a dove caught a baby bird before it fell to the ground.

The house was "always too big," she said later, yet "they don't build them the way they used to" remained her sentiment. "You build today and two men walk in with the wall. Ours were eighteen inches thick. The halls were four feet wide. You can't carry a tray in today's halls."[23]

Vidor sent a studio photographer to record the construction. Albums show bottle-glass windows await-ing varnish on the sashes. Piles of bricks and bags of concrete sit below scaffolding running around the tile-roofed, brick-faced house. Carpenters' tables hold planks of Oregon pine, prized for its unknotted appearance, being planed to fill the forty-one-by-twenty-one-foot living room.[24] Three corner fireplaces are ready to be lighted for the first time. Neff considered the austere rooms and their gleaming tile floors so fine an example of his California-Spanish style, he commissioned the architectural photographer he respected most, Padilla Studios, to photograph them and used the images to represent his work. His eye was pleased by the right angles of the steps' risers juxtaposed against the round corner fireplaces and the arched doorways. Arch after arch, room after room, the continuity of forms seen from the entry hall created an illusion of spaciousness beyond the actual square footage.

The relationship between Boardman and Neff was congenial. "He knew I appreciated the quality of his work," she said. "He liked the fact I was so enthusiastic." Asked to describe his demeanor, she said, "He was desperately Catholic." But did she mean that Neff was steadfastly intent upon his work, serious and quiet in nature? Or was her comment a reference to the monastic quality of his buildings? Cary Grant compared the calm and quiet of a Neff house to that of a cloistered retreat. Glass negatives of 1920s-era rooms in Neff houses recall sanctuaries with candles burning in candelabra and dark paintings in gilt frames adorning alcoves. The mystery, pomp, and ceremony of Neff's religion influenced his choice of adornments. Shawls draped over staircases and pianos conveyed the mood of the Kasbah. One house painter remembered Neff as being so intensely devoted to his work when he visited a house under construction that he was unaware of the rain pouring down around him.[25]

Boardman traveled in search of furnishings. In Paris, with F. Scott Fitzgerald and his wife, Zelda, the Vidors visited Sylvia Beech's bookstore and found photographs of the Great War. "War should be shown the way it is," Vidor told them. When Fitzgerald later fictionalized the Tower Road house in "Crazy Sunday," he depicted it as a place "built for great emotional moments."[26]

Unfortunately, those "emotional moments" had degenerated to a level of such unhappiness that the marriage ended in 1932 and the couple battled for custody of their daughters, Belinda and Toni. When the girls were released to Boardman, the three celebrated the Fourth of July by standing on the master bedroom balcony and watching fireworks sent up by the City of Beverly Hills. Boardman never forgot the view they had

of Catalina Island.

She later married another film director, Harry d'Abbadie d'Arrast, and moved to France. Learning that Vidor intended to sell the house at a rock-bottom price, she rushed to Tower Road with an attorney. They finally agreed upon a figure that was acceptable to Boardman, and the house sold. Although Cole Porter took up residence in the guesthouse and Ingrid Bergman lived there later, the house suffered under a succession of owners. One of them, Geoffrey Swaebe, complained to his friend, the architect Caspar Ehmcke, that the plan was one-sided and thus did not "flow."[27] Another owner concerned about heating bills installed dropped ceilings. The inevitable subdivision of the large parcel altered the address from Tower Road to Tower Lane.

GETTING TO THE GOETZES

Boardman considered her tastes superior to those of industry hostesses like Edith Goetz and Irene Selznick. (In her old age, she scorned the two "Mayer girls," as she called them, for selecting "electric buttons that opened windows and everything else you could think of." She had conveniently forgotten that a push of a button released a retractable screen from the ceiling of her Wallace Neff living room.) Wallace Neff may have agreed, but he was not apt to let on to anyone, for Edith Mayer Goetz was as instrumental to his rise in movie circles as her father, Louis B. Mayer, was to MGM's. Neff scribbled the phone numbers of Goetz's friends in pocket date books: LeRoy, Gershwin, M. Hart, H. Goetz, J. Bennett, F. March, Z. Marx, C. Colbert, S. Jaffe, J. Schenck, Adrian. Edith was like another F. Scott Fitzgerald character, the narrator of *The Last Tycoon*. "Though I haven't ever been on the screen," the daughter of the studio executive (who resembles Mayer) laments in the book, "I was brought up in pictures."[28]

LEFT: *The balcony of the King Vidor House master bedroom, overlooking the swimming pool*

RIGHT: *The double-height entry, with a series of arched openings leading to the stairs and the dining room beyond*

Edith Mayer Goetz with her daughters

Edith attended the Vidor-Boardman wedding before serving as Norma Shearer's bridesmaid when the actress married Irving Thalberg. After her father forbade her to enter show business, she began to focus her attention on her dreams. "On a train in the Italian Alps when we were traveling to Rome to shoot *Ben-Hur*," Edith remembered, "I dreamt that the director's wife had became pregnant. When I told my parents, they brushed it off because they knew I didn't have any idea where babies came from. When we got to the hotel, and stood waiting in the lobby, Mrs. Niblo came down the stairs with a very large stomach."[29]

Within a few years, twenty-five-year-old Edith lost her naiveté to a film producer, William Goetz, whose bawdy humor made her sister, Irene, uncomfortable. His standard joke, "whatever Edie wants, Edie gets," was especially unnerving to Irene, and a rivalry begun in childhood intensified. What Edith wanted, she always received from a father who encouraged her to "seek to impress." ("The important question in the Mayer household," Irene observed, was 'How does it look?'")[30] Armed with the name of the architect who had designed Fred Niblo's, King Vidor's and Frances Marion's houses, Edith approached her father. Mayer proceeded to purchase a lot in Bel-Air, underwrite Neff's services, and pay for a house.

Efforts by developers to prohibit property sales to Jews, let alone members of the entertainment industry, had been eviscerated by the Depression, when it became clear that they were among the few who could afford a new house in Los Angeles's fanciest subdivision. Alphonzo Bell was forced to sell all his land holdings, except Bel-Air, to eastern interests and to rescind the restriction against selling to members of the film industry that had excluded Frances Marion and Fred Thomson a half dozen years earlier.[31]

Today the 1932 Goetz House on Saint Pierre Road is overshadowed by a high perimeter wall. Inside, an auto entry courtyard circles around to the front door. Neff designed many provincial country French manors in painted white brick ("cha-a-a-r-ming as a postcard picture," Edith proclaimed in her regally modulated, professionally trained voice), but this particular house wrapped ideas about exaggerated scale and proportion into a conical witch's cap of a peak over the entry. Another exaggeration—a triangular gable so steep no drop of water could remain on its surface for more than an instant—was set off by white tiles running along its edges. To break up a facade that had a minimal number of windows, in typical Neff fashion, small niches were carved out. As if the effect weren't exaggerated enough, a white chimney soared skyward far beyond the triangle and cone. The composition succeeded as storybook cottage while exhibiting Neff's ability to create a bold interplay of shapes penetrated by voids.

All that was missing from the accoutrements of Hollywood wealth inside the house was a screening room, and after Neff designed one for the house in 1933, calling it "the amusement wing," a film industry institution was born. While moguls like Jack Warner viewed rushes in monumental basement screening rooms, the Goetzes showed their movies in a comfortable room they called "the den." "After dinner," the wife of composer Richard Rodgers recalled, "everyone would go into the projection room and a film would

be run."[32] Claudette Colbert, Joan Bennett, and Fredric March asked Neff to design similar rooms for them, where they could show films and relax with family and friends.

Edith claimed one could read "the whole history of Hollywood" from her book of menus.[33] Her long-ago guest lists reveal that screenwriters were not up to her standards, for few were invited. But Edith was ready to impress the rest of Hollywood, along with her sister, who had married David O. Selznick and was entertaining across Summit Drive from Pickfair in a colonial-style house designed by Roland Coate.[34]

Edith insisted on a certain brand of plate heaters for her butler's pantry and a cutting garden to provide flowers for her dinner party centerpieces. Baby Goetzes were cared for by a nurse who monitored them with an intercom from her room next door. The perfectionist's every whim could not be overlooked if Neff wanted his architectural practice to grow.

Pickfair, Beverly Hills

CHAPTER THIRTEEN

PICKFAIR

The house and grounds grew grander with the years and so did the ambition of the Fairbanks.
—Brendan Gill, *The Dream Come True*

Ⓓuring the summer of 1926, Wallace Neff would often drive west on Sunset Boulevard, past the Beverly Hills Hotel, and turn right up Benedict Canyon Drive, steering his Packard into the verdant San Ysidro Canyon and the entrance to Summit Drive. At the base of yet another canyon, he would enter the gates of the estate known as Pickfair. He had met its owners, Mary Pickford and Douglas Fairbanks, at their film studio, United Artists, where "they were all sitting at one table in the building on Santa Monica Boulevard having lunch."[1] They had decided, they told him, to enlarge Pickfair and build a house nearby for Mary's mother. They wanted to remodel their cottage at the beach in Santa Monica as well.

Neff's son Wallace claimed that his father believed the original Pickfair was a candidate for demolition.[2] When Pickfair was finally torn down in 1990, the president of the Beverly Hills Historical Society insisted that "it really wasn't a pretty house," an attitude shared by others who believed that Neff's renovation was no more worth saving than the house he had encountered in 1926. When Neff was asked what he thought of the house, his response—"Pickfair is a good house"—was vague enough to conceal his real opinion.[3] "Good," he had said, after all, not "great." Whatever he believed about the myriad changes he was commissioned to make, he complied with the owners' wishes, as archi-

tects do if they want to earn a living. As a result, Mary Pickford trusted him and went on to underwrite his experiments in low-cost housing during the Depression and the cold war.

The attention Pickford paid to the state of her properties intensified as she became less and less in demand on the screen. But how far she had come: she had arrived in Los Angeles in 1910 with D. W. Griffith's Biograph Company. With a five-dollar-a-day salary, she had found shelter at the Lille rooming house at South Olive and Fifth streets.[4] After she married Owen Moore in 1911, they lived in hotel rooms and eventually moved to a large bungalow on Western Avenue and then to a house on Fremont Place.

Time has made many a silent-film star's overly animated performances appear silly, but not Mary Pickford's. In *The Little Princess* and *Stella Maris*, both written by her friend Frances Marion, one sees how deeply the restrained Pickford immersed herself in characterizations. A diminutive five feet, she had soulful eyes that belied an indomitable spirit. Years of negotiating with directors D. W. Griffith and Adolph Zukor had produced a woman who was a savvy filmmaker in her own right.

In 1915, while still married to Moore, she met Douglas Fairbanks. By March 31, 1920, Pickford and Fairbanks had divorced their mates and the *Los Angeles*

ABOVE: *Before Neff's redesign, Pickfair resembled a Tyrolian country estate*
LEFT: *Frances Marion, left, with Mary Pickford*

Mary Pickford in the Pickfair dining room, on the cover of the Los Angeles Times Home Magazine

Pickfair following the renovations by Neff and Elsie de Wolfe

Times was reporting that "strenuous efforts to keep the news [of the Pickford-Fairbanks wedding] secret for at least another week failed because a telephone leaked." The union that had captivated the public had been legalized.

"This house is yours, Mary," Fairbanks had told her as they sat down to a wedding dinner at Pickfair with the Baptist minister who had united them. "It's my wedding present to you."[5] They had honeymooned in Europe, joined by Frances Marion and Fred Thomson,[6] before returning to the increasingly famous house that had initially been built as a weekend getaway in 1911.[7] "A ramshackle shooting-box," one writer called it, "in the scrub woods high above the hundreds of acres of bean fields."[8]

Fairbanks had bought it and eleven and a half acres on a street that was still nameless on April 22, 1919, for thirty-five thousand dollars.[9] Until then, Beverly Hills had been free of actors. A few years later, Charlie Chaplin built a house several hundred feet away with the help of a crew from his film studio. Fairbanks had used United Artists' talent himself, selecting a set designer named Max Parker to remodel the house for the newlyweds. John C. Austin, a noted civic architect, had helped with the scheme to double the size of the small box to a grand L form.[10] On the short end of the L were a dining room and library. On the long end were the entry hall, living and projection rooms, and the kitchen. Albert, the butler, kept an eye on both wings from his outpost behind the central entry hall. On the second floor were half a dozen bedrooms.

A well had been drilled and a swimming pool poured. With a tennis court and garages for six automobiles, the estate was becoming grander. The architectural style was a Germanic version of the English arts and crafts, which had been used repeatedly by the builders of the earliest houses in Beverly Hills and Los Angeles. From the diamond-paned windows to the bracketed eaves that held steeply pitched, green shingled roofs, it was a local form of mock Tudor.

Babe Ruth, the king of Spain, and Albert Einstein, among others, had begun coming to dinner. Frances Marion noticed that Fairbanks "kowtowed to a duke and a duchess but he'd say, 'why are those people coming?' when some nice ordinary people were expected."[11] Still, Fairbanks maintained his sense of irreverence: "He waited for the right moment to slip out from behind a drapery and apply 'the goose,'" heavyweight champion Jack Dempsey remembered.[12] But Fairbanks's image as a gallant gentleman had become entrenched, and he and his wife were seen as American royalty. "The couple established Hollywood high society," film historian Kevin Thomas wrote, "a social register not of old blood but of new fame, along with the glittering party life that society would enjoy."[13]

By the time the press joined their names to coin the "Pickfair" moniker, the two had come to see the property as too modest for what was expected of them. In 1926, Neff and interior decorator Elsie de Wolfe were put in charge of remaking the house in the French version of Adam style, not unlike the grand lobby of the couple's own United Artists Theater downtown at Ninth and Broadway, with its pastel painted surfaces. Any objections to pretense Neff might have raised in his advocacy of simplicity were rejected, for de Wolfe's clout as an international social arbiter trumped his as a California architect.[14] She knew Louis XVI style when she saw it, for she owned the Villa Trianon at Versailles. Reproductions of the king's furnishings, such as a white grand piano, filled every room at Pickfair but the barroom, where western artwork hung over an authentic nineteenth-century oak bar. Displays of a burgeoning number of collections—French plates, Japanese dolls, Buddhist statues—dictated the format of some of the rooms.

Neff extended the length of the dining room to accommodate additional guests, and added a breakfast

Pickfair interior

room and a pantry. The new square footage also included a subgrade porte cochere. Dormers and balconies were removed from the exterior, exposed rafters were covered, and striped awnings were taken down. Mullioned windows were replaced with delicate, oval-shaped ones. French doors appeared. Twelve-foot-tall Beaux-Arts columns, topped by cupids, bore brass-plated "Pickfair" signs at the curbside entry gates. Quarters for a dozen servants were constructed on the second floor of the now eight-car garage. In the auto court, guests walked through attenuated Ionic columns, under a beaded frieze and broken pediment, and through double doors with leaded-glass windows to the revamped below-grade entry. "A surprisingly narrow stairway leads from the entrance to the main floor above," film historian Arthur Knight noted, "where at once everything is sunny, graceful, and in quiet good taste. The main living room is dominated by a single large portrait of Miss Pickford."[15]

A rare collection of Napoleonic porcelain dinnerware gleamed in mirrored cabinets in the dining room. Gold-embossed leather volumes had been purchased for the bookshelves. Pale green carpet covered the hardwood floors. Everything was ready, on the evening of August 9, 1932, when the International Olympic Committee arrived for dinner during the Summer Olympics. Remodeling expenses had reached sixty thousand dollars,[16] and the only clue to the influ-

ence Neff was able to exert was a pair of overscaled chimneys reigning over the steeply pitched roofs.

The week Franklin Roosevelt declared a bank holiday in his first "fireside chat" in 1933, Pickford's film *Secrets*, written by Frances Marion, was lambasted by the critics and boycotted by the public, who were reluctant to accept the ingenue in an adult role. As if the curtain to her film career were not enough, Pickford was home alone. A break with Fairbanks was headlined on July 2, 1933. Pickfair became hers three years later with a divorce decree. Fairbanks kept their Santa Monica beach house, where he lived with his third wife, Sylvia Ashley. He died there on December 11, 1939, of a coronary thrombosis. Neff stayed in contact until the end, becoming acquainted with Douglas Fairbanks Jr. and his wife, for whom he remodeled a house.

Pickford married Buddy Rogers in 1937, and became increasingly reclusive. On October 11, 1955, she appeared on the cover of the *Los Angeles Times Home Magazine* in a dining room unchanged since the 1932 renovation. Neff remained in touch with her as well, selecting a crew to repair plaster in January 1954, and then in 1961, supervising the installation of a fallout shelter.[17] Pickford had given him a pocket watch engraved "Thank you for Pickfair," which he carried everywhere. When he lost it in his later years, he was despondent,[18] for she had provided him with many projects besides the famous house on the hill.[19]

The entrance to Louise and Wallace Neff's house, flanked by olive trees

CHAPTER FOURTEEN

PUTTING IT TOGETHER

The country club life at the time is something that has not been indulged in since.
—Robert Alexander

ℬETWEEN THEIR HUNDRED MILLION dollars' worth of oil stock, their association with the Teapot Dome furor that rocked the nation during the 1920s, and the unsolved murders in the family's Greystone mansion, Edward and Estelle Doheny were the most talked-about clients Wallace Neff served in his fifty-five-year career.[1] Their constant need to evade public scrutiny while constructing a house here and a monument there provided him with lucrative projects for as long as they lived. He did not have a monopoly on their fervent campaign to build, however. Gordon Kaufmann, Albert C. Martin, Ralph Adams Cram, Stiles O. Clements, and even Frank Lloyd Wright and his son Lloyd won commissions from the Dohenys over the years.[2] But Neff walked off with a major chunk of work for two reasons: he was an avowed Roman Catholic, the faith the Dohenys generously supported, and he had effectively charmed the otherwise implacable Estelle. Neff's command of traditional architectural styles and his circumspection were also appealing.

"Everyone knew Wallace Neff was her favorite," the architect Samuel Lunden said upon the occasion of his retirement testimonial dinner.[3] As a young man, Lunden had supervised the construction of the Edward L. Doheny Jr. Memorial Library at the University of Southern California and, later, the interior decoration of the Doheny-funded St. Vincent's Church,

but with his Scandinavian Protestant reserve and clipped dialect, the blond Lunden never managed to endear himself to the Dohenys the way Neff did with his languid, worldly manner.

Neff proved his loyalty by agreeing to take on such thankless projects as the shoring up of the rickety Victorian-era garages around the Dohenys' Chester Place enclave. He sent Mrs. Doheny roses on her birthday and the largest bottle of Chanel No. 5 available at Christmas. When he was near the seaside resort of Laguna Beach, he stopped to purchase bags of her favorite popcorn, then proceeded to deliver them to her door, forty miles away. He cut a photograph of her from the *Los Angeles Times* and mailed it to her when she was named "Woman of the Year" for her philanthropy in 1954,[4] and he always sent her a personal letter—a rarity for him—once a project was completed.

Nannie Neff took pride in her son's relationship with this woman who used her oil earnings to support Catholic causes. Oil was a commodity that Nannie and nearly everyone else in Los Angeles coveted. Oil fever had been in the air since Edward Doheny had struck California's first significant gusher in 1892, and wildcatters had been drawn to Los Angeles the way gold rushers were to Sutter's Mill. (When the Neffs had lived in La Mirada, the Santa Fe struck a vein on a hillside overlooking the family holdings, and the Neffs had waited in vain for a miracle.)[5] Doheny's public relations machine depicted him as an innocent soul who had wandered into Los Angeles and unwittingly discovered oil. In fact, he shrewdly proceeded to purchase every lease he could at rock-bottom prices. After respectable citizens began tearing up their lawns and gardens with mule trains on the chance that fortune might be hidden beneath their property, a neighborhood association was formed to fight such front-yard blight. Nevertheless, two thousand wells had been drilled before the nineteenth century was over, by which time Doheny controlled most of the oil in the state.[6]

In early 1927, after Doheny had been acquitted of charges that he had conspired to bribe the secretary of the interior for the right to tap California's and Wyoming's naval oil fields, Neff was commissioned to plan a house for Mrs. Doheny's sister, Daysie, and her husband, Crampton Anderson. A site was found on the south side of Sunset Boulevard, just below the Dohenys' getaway estate on a Beverly Hills hillside. Because Sunset Boulevard had been paved by Alphonzo Bell to create a right-of-way to his Bel-Air enclave, the Dohenys could easily travel to their vacation house and the Anderson House.

For the bare knoll on Sunset Boulevard, Neff designed a house heavy with tile ornament, wrought iron, and exterior hand-painted stenciling. One of the workmen described it as the most structurally sound house he had encountered in his career. "The walls were so thick," the painting contractor, Paul Schwenzfeier, recalled, "a man could slide sideways between the outer and inner studs. The plasterers troweled a pure, hard portland cement of white gunite."[7]

His lead subcontractor, Harry Martin, returned to the house sixty years later to recount the yearlong process of painting the house. He described Doheny's brother-in-law, the president of Doheny's Pan-American Petroleum Company, as possessing the same "rough-and-ready" demeanor that Doheny had (although Schwenzfeier recalled a pleasant, well-educated man). Daysie, however, was "insecure" in the presence of her forceful older sister, Martin believed.[8]

"Mr. Neff made regular inspections," Martin said, sometimes with friends in tow: flapper-film star Colleen Moore arrived on Neff's arm one afternoon. Neff was always courteous to the workmen, Martin noticed, unlike his colleague Roland Coate, who didn't welcome suggestions from the work crew.[9] "It wasn't below Wallace Neff to ask a question of a man in overalls. He was a very nice man."

Neff let his construction supervisor, George Young Cannon, put the fear of God into subcontractors like Martin. "He terrified us," Martin recalled. "He carried a stick with a mirror on the end of it to inspect surfaces on doorjambs and surrounds to be sure they were not left unpainted." Martin passed inspection with his laborious, six-step process for staining wood. Surfaces were wetted to raise the grain, primed, stained, covered with benzene and liquid wax, rubbed with rotten stone, and then given a patina with steel wool.[10]

Neff asked one of the painters, Bill Harriman, to create a "Renaissance effect" by hand stenciling and gold leafing the beams on the living room ceiling.[11] The effort would relieve their darkness, Neff said. Harriman spent sixteen weeks lying on his back on scaffolding to comply with Neff's request. He earned a thousand dollars, but not the satisfaction of Mrs. Anderson, who spared no expense to achieve the desired appearance. "It made the wood look dirty," she told Neff, so Harriman started over.[12]

Mr. Anderson's tastes were extravagant too, from the crew's perspective. After specifying that the wrought iron on the outside of the house be painted blue, he changed his mind and decided it should be gold. Then, when the Lindbergh baby was kidnapped, Anderson ordered additional wrought iron bars placed over the windows as a security device. He also "gave up going to prize fights," Martin recalled, "and listened to them on the radio. He hired a Texas gunman to chauffeur his car, and another for Mrs. Anderson."[13] Security measures abounded as the Doheny family gained notoriety, and perhaps in reaction to the pressure, one day a frustrated Mrs. Doheny, unhappy with the progress being made at the Anderson House, threw a hammer at one of the workmen.[14] The Anderson House was everywhere in the architectural press,[15] but the publicity was overshadowed by the news of a possible murder and suicide in the family.

On February 16, 1929, the bodies of Doheny's son, Edward L. Doheny Jr.—"Ned" to his wife, Lucy, and "Dad" to his five children—and his secretary, Hugh Plunkett, were found at the fortresslike, forty-six-thousand-square-foot, Indiana limestone–faced mansion known as Greystone. Police searched in vain for clues, although no formal inquest was ever held. The official verdict of the investigation was that Plunkett, suffering from mental instability, had killed his employer and then turned the gun on himself, although over the years there were rumors of various other scenarios.

Because of the Dohenys' wealth, the crime was a source of ongoing public fascination. Neff's staff buzzed with speculation after word of the deaths reached them in Pasadena, for the draftsmen recalled that the commission to design the house might have been theirs if Gordon Kaufmann hadn't beaten out their proposal. The scale of the final project was so immense that, according to assistants to the landscape architect, truckloads of plants would arrive at the site without any instructions about where they should go and the assistants would be directed to just "put them somewhere." The landscape architect Ralph Cornell recalled, "It was a big job. In fact, I think it was the biggest job at that time in Southern California."[16] ("The

Dohenys wanted gold-plated everything," Neff's draftsman Clifford Hoskins said of the commission that got away. Hoskins believed it would have been the largest residential commission of Neff's career, as it turned out to be for Kaufmann.)[17]

While the police investigated, Ned's stepmother, Estelle Doheny, took action. (After the death of his son, her husband was a "shattered man," historian Margaret Leslie Davis wrote in her biography of Edward Doheny.)[18] Estelle implored Neff to design and build a retreat she and her distraught husband could escape to within six weeks in a valley called Ferndale, in Santa Paula in Ventura County. The site was surrounded by ancient live oaks and had a stream where Doheny could fish. "Neff was extremely hesitant to make such a guarantee, but finally, after much frantic planning, he relented," Davis wrote. "Hundreds of workers were hired to complete the job; they labored forty-two days and nights. Miraculously, they finished the job ahead of schedule."[19]

Santa Paula is half an hour from Rancho Camulos, the Del Valle family estate where Helen Hunt Jackson absorbed the Spanish mores she popularized in her legendary novel *Ramona*. The Dohenys wanted a classic hacienda with an open courtyard, like the one the Del Valles had, with spacious interior corridors that would form the heart of the hacienda and whitewashed brick that would resemble adobe. The construction of a chapel also honored Hispanic values. In keeping with the informal plan, the entry was located under a covered porch that led directly to the U-shaped plan, obviating the need for Neff's customary vestibule. Windows, shutters, and ironwork, painted turquoise, were finished to Neff's approval. The entry gates of stone and iron, however, were executed without his approval, and he ordered them demolished, contributing fifteen thousand dollars of his own to pay for a second set that met his exacting standards.[20]

THE RAZOR KING

Neff had been reluctant to promise the Dohenys a quick turnaround because he had just received a major commission to design a house for King Camp Gillette. Neff was born the same year Gillette invented a disposable razor with a flexible, movable blade, and Gillette's image on the logo had become as recognizable as Washington's on the dollar bill or Betty Crocker's on a box of cake mix. Gillette had moved to California to join the political avant-garde that identified with Upton Sinclair's literature of conscience and Kate Crane-Gartz's left-wing philanthropy, although even in California such beliefs made him something of a pariah. "The razor king explained his idea of making over the American industrial system," Upton Sinclair's wife, Mary, wrote. "He wanted a mammoth enterprise called 'the People's Corporation.'" Addressing his comrades, Gillette perspired and wilted. He was "good, but naive," she concluded.[21] Gillette's ventures into local real estate were not as naive. He invested in a citrus ranch in Tulare County, a parcel overlooking downtown Los Angeles's Pershing Square, 480 desert acres of date and grapefruit groves, a house on Crescent Drive across from the Beverly Hills Hotel (which was sold to Gloria Swanson in 1922), and a house on Newport Harbor.

In 1928, he commissioned Neff to design a ranch in Calabasas, a remote but sizable part of the still-quiet San Fernando Valley. The finished complex was such a picturesque version of an Andalusian village—a rural walled compound that included a master's residence, an overseer's quarters, stables, and cellars, with eucalyptus trees flanking the entry road and ponds, weeping willows, and native oak on the horizon—that editors seized on it as a quintessential example of the Spanish colonial revival. It was published extensively.[22]

The land was as deep in the San Fernando Valley as it could be and still be in Los Angeles County. "We drove miles and miles over the winding roads of Topanga Canyon," screenwriter Salka Viertel wrote of her trip to meet a group of Russian filmmakers for a picnic on the huge sweeping lawn in the 1930s.[23] Except for an adobe owned by an old Californio family named Leonis, residential ranches of this size in the area were few. Six hundred acres extended toward a horizon of mountains, which Paramount and Warner Brothers photographed to stand in for various mountain ranges throughout the world.

Neff called the Gillette project his ideal job because the Gillettes were on a world cruise while it was being built,[24] so he was able to make decisions without taking into account their concerns about cost and design.[25] While the Gillettes visited Bulgaria and Egypt, Neff oversaw a half dozen draftsmen toiling half a year over plot plans, foundation plans, floor plans, elevations, sections, and details. The hard physical labor began with the excavation of the swimming pool. With the excess dirt, the contractor and crew created adobe-like blocks that could be burned on the site and had the longevity of brick.[26]

The entry road wandered past a stable and bunkhouse, up a hill, through an opening in one of the house's exterior walls, and into a motor court covered with local Calabasas stone. All the axes for the roads and structures were drawn from the center of this great circle. Inside the main house, protected from the heat of the sun by two-foot-two-inch-thick walls, case after display case held Gillette's razor-blade collection. Doors were carved in nineteen styles and were made to last, it was hoped, for centuries. A review of the door schedule shows 113 doors in the main house alone. Floors were covered with the best grade tile. Because Gillette's eyes had become sensitive to bright light, his bath was tiled and outfitted in black. The tub was oversize to accommodate his 250-pound frame.

When the Gillettes' ship sailed into Los Angeles Harbor in June 1929, their architect was at the dock to

greet them. The emotional Gillette burst into tears
when he saw the house—tears of sadness as much as
joy. He was not well, and he had begun to plan for his
demise. He had decided to sell fifteen thousand shares
of Gillette stock on margin and hold on to thirty-five
thousand additional shares.[27] After he was talked out of
the sale by his attorney, the stock market crashed and
he lost a fortune. He filed suit against his counsel, but
died in the master suite of the house before the dispute was resolved. He was buried at Forest Lawn
Memorial Park. Creditors sold the estate at the
depressed price of $150,000 to the director of *Anna
Christie*, *National Velvet*, and *The Yearling*, MGM's
Clarence Brown, who put in an airstrip so he could fly
in from the studio in Culver City.[28]

Brown called upon Neff to design a screening
room like the one his acquaintances Edith and William
Goetz had installed in their Bel-Air house. Years later,
in the early 1950s, after hosting numerous MGM Labor
Day picnics at the ranch, Brown sold the compound to
the Claretian order of the Roman Catholic Church and
retired to Palm Desert. He and Neff discussed building
a house on the links of the Tamarisk or Thunderbird
country clubs, but no commission ever materialized.
After the Claretians closed the seminary in the 1980s,
Soka University in Japan purchased the property, only
to find the Santa Monica Mountains Conservancy and
the Mountains Recreation and Conservation Authority
of the State of California watching its every move. What
ensued, the *Los Angeles Times* reported, was "one of the
nastiest and costliest land use battles over the Santa
Monica Mountains in recent history."[29] In the spring of
1996, the conservancy dropped an eminent domain
lawsuit after the school agreed to set aside 375 acres as
public open space and to restrict the height and location of new buildings. The state placed a value of $20
million on the onetime Gillette ranch.

Neff's office on California Street in Pasadena

TOP: *The Neff House as it appeared in architecture magazines*
BOTTOM: *The courtyard of the former Neff House on Orlando Road, after a major remodeling in the early 1990s*

PERSONAL MATTERS

In 1928, Neff and Gillette's contractor, Frederick H. "Fritz" Ruppel, who was known for his work on the restoration of Mission San Juan Capistrano and El Molino Viejo, had formed a partnership to construct a "home building profession center" where they could both do business.[30] The building on California Street in Pasadena was made from Adoblars, a building block Ruppel had invented to create an eighteenth-century adobe appearance with twentieth-century technology and materials. One Adoblar was as large as four bricks and so cumbersome a mason couldn't pick it up.[31]

Neff's staff shared the ground floor of the building with Ruppel's, and the Adoblar Brick Company was on the second floor. A courtyard focused on a well Neff placed off-center instead of, more predictably, mid-axis. Neff's reception room was a lofty space with exposed rafters overhead, Ruppel's Adoblars underfoot, and a rounded corner fireplace. The drafting room, which had almost a dozen skylights, held ten tables to accommodate twenty draftsmen. A vault over seven feet square held blueprints. Another Adoblar structure across the street housed furniture maker George Hunt and decorator Robert Cheesewright. A third brick building, designed by the architect Palmer Sabin, sat next to the Neff-Ruppel office, creating a little cluster of Spanish buildings.

The complex was a half mile west of an internationally known center of scientific research, Caltech, leaps and bounds larger than its Throop College of Technology days when Neff was seeking a college. Visiting lecturer Albert Einstein lodged on South Oakland Avenue one semester, close enough to campus to ride a bike to class, in a French provincial–style cottage Neff had designed for Henriette Stowele in 1924.[32] Clark Millikan, an aeronautical genius and the son of Caltech's president, also lived in a Neff house, on a hillside overlooking the Arroyo Seco Parkway.

The Neff family's own house in Altadena had become inadequate for their needs after a daughter, Phyllis Louise, was born on Christmas Day, 1925. By the time their second child, Wallace Libby, was born on September 12, 1930, the family had settled in a house built on land purchased from the Huntington Land and Improvement Company, directly across Orlando Road from Henry Huntington's compound of gardens, libraries, and art collections. Drawings for "Job #253" were executed in the Neff office in May and June of 1928.[33]

Describing the design as "a distinct credit to the tract and to the neighborhood,"[34] the Improvement Company approved plans for a south-facing house of seventy-three hundred square feet, set back seventy-five feet from the street. Where the dominant feature of Neff's 1924 Bourne House a block north had been the curvilinear staircases that projected from the meandering plan, the distinguishing element of his own house was a second-floor loggia painted turquoise, above a centered front entry. The loggia's deep recess into the gunite was Neff's way of focusing the eye in an otherwise flat expanse. Its vibrant color was as exotic as the wooden latticework Mushrabiyah screen mounted over a second-story window—the one and only projection on the facade, which let in a bit of light.

The fanciful Bourne facade had rambled high and low, but this one appeared rectangular, although the plan was actually a T shape. Both houses hid garages far from street view. The new house showed Neff's continuing desire to unite a formal plan with a vernacular building type, combining classicism and informality. To Neff, it was "a California house," yet many would have called it Italian Lombard.[35]

The austerity of its large, decomposed granite entry courtyard and plain facade was softened by scattered terra-cotta pots filled with geraniums. Two towering cypress trees planted well away from either side of the entry introduced vertical elements that distracted the eye from the vast horizontality of the mass of the house. One of Neff's signature exterior staircases led to a second-floor porch on the rear facade. Although it was based on a Tuscan villa plan, the building was much more informal than Neff's other Italian Renaissance–style houses. The formal gardens with allees and parterres that A. E. Hanson proposed for the rear yard never materialized, for Neff had already made the financial commitment of his life in the house and the office building.[36]

Inside, a seventeen-by-thirty-one-foot living room rose two stories, climaxing in a vaulted ceiling. Neff created a broad view of the backyard before there was such a thing as tempered glass by joining two large pieces of glass with a small central column. The foyer had a straightforward stairway with one landing and risers covered by colorful tiles. Large tiles on the floor extended to adjacent rooms. Paneled wood ceilings contributed to the provincial Italian ambience.

The American Institute of Architects, which granted awards on four occasions during the 1920s, selected the house as the best medium-sized residence in Southern California in 1929. Almost seventy years later, *House Beautiful* featured it in a survey of the century's best domestic designs. "Neff's scheme projected an easy, irresistible charm and a clear appropriateness to its site and climate," the editors commented. "It helps to explain the loyal following Neff was to develop during the decade ahead among movie stars and moguls who found in his luxurious designs their real Hollywood dreams."[37]

CRASHING TO EARTH

The Neffs had borrowed thirty-two thousand dollars from the mortgage banker A. G. Cox at 7 percent interest to underwrite the house, and the balance was due on February 8, 1932.[38] But the bottom fell out of the stock market first, on October 29, 1929. While Neff, who had a dozen houses either on the boards or under construction, had not invested significantly in the stock market, he saw friends, neighbors, and clients lose homes and businesses. Who knows how many prospective clients were lost? His cousin Helen dropped plans to build a getaway Neff had designed for her in Ojai. A. E. Hanson, the landscape architect of many a Neff project, witnessed numerous clients bringing on their own demise: "Everybody had money; everybody spent money, just as though it were water," he wrote. "I was at a project, ready to give the superintendent the weekly payroll checks, when the owner, greatly agitated, said, 'Stop all work! Fire everybody! The stock market has crashed! We're all broke!'"[39]

Los Angeles was filled with paper millionaires who claimed fortunes based on land prices. When the Depression hit and tenants couldn't pay the rent, banks began taking back properties from landlords who could not afford to pay the mortgages. They also began foreclosing on home owners who had purchased their houses with large mortgages that they now could not pay. Dr. John Baer, a Neff client who was a bank president, told the press, "Such a spectacle as occurred will never happen again in this country because the banking and business men realize the frailty of such pyramiding of stock issues based purely on paper and visionary profits." He went on, "Many who thought they could make easy money playing the market have gone back to work, where they should have been in the first place."[40]

More Americans were hungry and ill-fed than ever before in the country's history. "It is a pathetic sight to see the army of hoboes trudging along our highways with all their worldly goods rolled up in a handkerchief," Kate Crane-Gartz wrote to the *Los Angeles Times*.[41] Nine million savings accounts were wiped out by widespread bank failures, eliminating lifelong savings. Stocks fell to a tenth of their 1929 highs. Pasadena's Colorado Street bridge was shut down after more than two dozen despondent residents committed suicide. Department store windows sat empty.

New notions of thrift crept into the drawing rooms of the wealthy, who were now too pinched to hire servants, let alone architects. Matrons gardened and shopped for their own groceries. Country clubs shut down. Grand resort hotels, which had been established at the turn of the century as centers of social life, closed. "You never saw such a state of affairs in San Marino," Emily Bourne lamented.[42]

The grand Pasadena estates that had once conveyed such cachet were now becoming hard to maintain. The immense Barlow villa sold for a paltry $28,566 after Barlow died. Deluxe enclaves like Linda Vista, San Rafael, Annandale, Prospect Park, Prospect Circle, Oak Knoll, and Oakland Avenue went untouched by the construction industry. Neff built one house in the area during the depths of the Depression, in 1935—a French provincial design that was eventually called the Hutchins House after a retired professor from the University of Chicago named Robert Hutchins purchased it around 1953.[43]

Neff said of the Depression, "It wiped out my practice."[44] In fact, it was as much the rise of modern architecture as it was economic uncertainty that decimated his career. The overblown mission style that had provided La Mirada with its nineteenth-century identity had fallen out of favor. The domed and turreted Santa Fe depot, which had been the pride of Los Angeles thirty years before, was now considered an embarrassment.[45] After a giddy decade of designing stately villas and informal haciendas, Neff faced a world suddenly suspicious of tradition; in its place a new "International" style was emerging.

By 1933, Neff, who was employing attorneys to pursue delinquent accounts, was in financial and marital straits. When he and Louise put their house up for auction, their youngest child, Arthur Libby, who had been born on August 31, 1932, was eight months old, young Wallace was three, and Phyllis was eight. On April 16, 1933, a photograph of the house appeared in an advertisement on page ten of the *Los Angeles Times*: "The residence of Wallace Neff," a headline announced. "One of the most desirable properties it has been our privilege to handle . . . An opportunity to get one of Southern California's most famous residences at an exceptional price."

After ten years of marriage, the Neffs were separating. Was there a love triangle? Had financial pressures broken them emotionally? Had he devoted his time to work to the exclusion of his wife's needs? A friend of Neff's put it bluntly: "He was weak for women, what some call 'a chaser.' Pasadena's confines did not suit his artistic nature."[46] Eleanor Boardman had considered Neff a quiet aesthete, so apparently he had not sought a romantic liaison with her, but he had with others.

Louise had lived with his limited presence before their separation because she enjoyed the social opportunities his work provided, like dining at Pickfair or cruising to Catalina Island on the Dohenys' yacht. Like her husband, she was soft-spoken, gentle, and nonconfrontational. She had been raised at a time when women of wealth were expected to marry men of wealth, with no thought to developing skills that would make them self-supporting, and she was unable to compete with the women her husband met in Hollywood, who demanded high salaries and inched their way toward equality with their male colleagues. Her apparent inability to arouse him sexually, his day-to-day interactions with women seeking his architectural expertise, a home made noisy by three youngsters, and his emotional need to work above all else—all aggravated by the uncertainties of the Depression—meant an end to their decade-long union.

At the age of thirty-nine, Neff moved into an apartment in Hollywood. He called home each night and visited on Sunday afternoons. He lived frugally to provide for his family, relying on income from architectural commissions and distributions from his share of the McNally trust.

In her new life, Louise frequented the Valley Hunt Club, where a single socialite could feel comfortable. "She never talked about things as they were," Emily Bourne said. "Once she called to report she was going to Hawaii with Wallace. The truth was he was no longer a family man."[47] Louise kept a bedroom ready for his return and listed their names in social directories as husband and wife for the next forty years.[48] Her difficulty with facing reality would manifest itself in her children's decisions when they were grown.

Divorce was part of a revolution of manners and morals among Neff's generation, a cultural by-product of World War I. Emily Bourne and her husband, Arthur, were themselves divorcing as the Neffs separated. But Louise did not condone divorce because the Roman Catholic Church held fast against it, and she was not going to leave the church. Neff's resentment could be felt at family gatherings, where he would sit in the same silence his parents had exhibited when they were miffed. By the time *Architectural Forum* published a photograph of the Neff House, captioned as "owned by Capton M. Paul," in March 1934, the break in the relationship was irreversible.[49] The magazine headline that had described the house as "a dream that came true" two years earlier was no longer accurate for the Neffs.[50]

Peggy Hamlin was a girl in 1938 when her parents purchased the house. "The beautiful features in his home," she later said, "make me believe Wallace Neff must have had high hopes. Leaving his work behind must surely have been difficult."[51] For much of the remainder of his life, Neff lived in rented apartments and bungalows.

The Sol Wurtzel House, Bel-Air

CHAPTER FIFTEEN

GOING HOLLYWOOD ON A SHOESTRING

The old and the new [architecture] met in the '30s.
—David Gebhard and Harriette von Breton, *Los Angeles in the Thirties*

*I*N NOVEMBER 1933, Wallace Neff gave up his Pasadena office in order to move his architectural practice closer to his Hollywood clientele to the west.[1] He was now no longer residing with his family in a house of his own design, and he was facing an uncertain professional future. Architects lucky enough to find work in the 1930s were apt to receive their paychecks from the federal government or the film industry. (Neff was startled to find one former colleague serving drinks at a party at Pickfair.)[2] Where 246 architects had been employed in Los Angeles in 1923 at the height of the building boom, by 1934 only 164 were still at their drawing boards, and the following year another thirty disappeared from the *Los Angeles City Directory.*[3]

The Long Beach earthquake of March 10, 1933, revived some architectural practices, such as the Albert C. Martin office, which picked up school rebuilding projects and went on to excel in seismic engineering. But Neff's friend Carl Dumbolton, who worked with Gladding McBean, the manufacturer of so many of the ornamental tiles that fell off schools and other buildings during the quake, found that the demand for terra-cotta had evaporated. Neff's trusted draftsman Clifford Hoskins left his employ to build movie sets. George Young Cannon, who considered himself as close to Neff as a brother since their Alpha Tau Omega days at MIT, also quit working for him as the workload began to diminish in the early 1930s. Neff's brothers

John and Bill, who managed his office during the 1920s, had moved to Laguna Beach toward the end of the decade to collaborate with their oldest brother, Andrew, on designing and manufacturing pottery.[4] Neff managed to get some of their first pieces displayed at Bullocks Wilshire in 1929, and the three brothers sold their pottery out of the reception room of Neff's empty office in Pasadena when they came north from the beach.

STAYING AFLOAT

Nothing better demonstrated the importance of the film industry to Neff's practice than the location of his new office in the Hollywood-Western Building.[5] The architect of the building, S. Charles Lee, had made his name designing streamlined movie theaters with flashy marquees and terrazzo paving. The Motion Picture Producers and Distributors of America—the feared Hayes censorship office—was one floor above Neff's office, and Central Casting's switchboard in the building operated twenty-four hours a day.[6] Directly north, in the Los Feliz hills, the film director Dorothy Arzner was building a house so monumental that its Corinthian columns were visible for miles. The back lots of Paramount and Columbia studios were blocks away, and Warner Brothers was just around the corner.

Neff's Hollywood office, located above a produce market

Hollywood had hardly noticed the crash. "Everything they touched," the journalist Leonard Mosley wrote, "provided it had sound effects, turned to gold."[7] Audiences filled theaters down the street and throughout the country. Neff's landlord, the highest paid executive in the country, was Louis B. Mayer, who had commissioned the building.[8] The space was cramped and there was no natural light, but Neff sacrificed for the modest twenty-five dollars a month Mayer charged.

Within two years Neff had put enough away to move to a building a mile west, where the light was abundant. The neighborhood around his new office on Franklin Avenue was a slice of Raymond Chandler's Hollywood. The Spanish-style building was only a decade old, but it already had an air of neglect. The rents were low and the building's maintenance deferred. Above an open-air produce market, down the hall from a dentist's office, Neff settled into a small suite. He stayed for forty years.

The Villa Carlotta in the next block was owned by the same landlady, Elinor Ince, the widow of the film producer Thomas H. Ince. A rumor circulated by the tenants suggested that the flamboyant publisher William Randolph Hearst had given Mrs. Ince the buildings in exchange for her silence about the mystery of her husband's death on Hearst's yacht. In fact, the house had been purchased for $650,000 by Universal Pictures founder Carl Laemmle.[9] The Villa Carlotta was as good an example of Los Angeles's 1920s Mediterranean style as the Chateau Elysee across Franklin was of the city's later infatuation with French chateaux. Because of its proximity to his office, Neff decided the Villa Carlotta was the apartment building for him.

The modesty of his personal habits matched that of his living situation. His closet was filled with suits that were decades old. He would withdraw a mere five,

Marian and Sol Wurtzel on the set of a Tom Mix film

ten, or twenty dollars from the bank and live on it for days at a time. Expenses like insurance, car repairs, film and cameras, child support, gifts, and the occasional trip were underwritten by architectural commissions, income from the McNally trust, and loans from banks, his parents, and even building contractors. He watched his weight, and ate and drank sensibly, subsisting on peanuts, tea, and fruit, and rarely dining at fine restaurants. He always tried to get a full night's sleep, even if he did enjoy nightlife and meeting new people. The tires on his Packard were retreaded to save money, although the car itself had been an indulgence, purchased from Earle C. Anthony in downtown Los Angeles. Neff put on his best face for Hollywood, getting a haircut every two weeks to make sure he was ready to impress potential clients. The strategy must have worked, for Sol Wurtzel, the head of the Fox Film Corporation—and one of the most important clients Neff ever had—commissioned him to design what was arguably the most showstopping house of his career.

Entry portico of the Wurtzel House

The Wurtzel House from the golf course of the Bel-Air Country Club

A PALACE FOR THE KING OF THE B'S

Fox had good years and bad as it made the transition to sound, but Wurtzel, who had worked for the company since 1914 and knew the film business inside and out, had made enough to be able to trade his house in middle-class mid-Wilshire for a grand Bellagio Road villa in upscale Bel-Air, even during the Depression. The new house sat on a lot 270 feet wide at the street and 350 feet deep at one end. The terrazzo floor alone cost $1,285, the marble stairs and entry floors, $675, the stonework, $5,000, and the ornamental ironwork, $2,407.[10] In the best Hollywood tradition, Ben Wurtzel, Sol's brother and Fox's chief of construction, took charge of building the estate.

Adolescent Lillian Wurtzel was overseas at a Parisian boarding school when her parents began planning their new six-figure house. "The house is getting along splendidly," Wurtzel wrote to his daughter at finishing school the day before Christmas in 1931, "and we hope to be in by the middle of April. It's been a long

153

Swimming pool and pergola at the Wurtzel House, added on in 1939

TOP: *The Wurtzel House dining room*

RIGHT: *The projection room on the ground level, which also served as a bar and recreation room*

Double windows in the Wurtzel House living room

tough battle with your mother, but I finally won out, and I think for the first time in the history of building, a house will be erected at the original contract price."[11] The nature of the battles alluded to is unclear, but as the architect, Neff must have been drawn into them. "Neff had to be calm because my mother wasn't," Lillian Wurtzel Semenov said fifty-five years later.[12]

For all his boasting and boorishness, Wurtzel was a puppy compared with his high-strung wife, Marian. Their bigger-is-better ideals resulted in a semicircular structure, 176 feet at its longest point and 50 feet at its deepest, with seventeen rooms and a three-car garage. Like so many of Neff's residences, the construction was wood frame covered by gunite, with a tile roof. "The site is very steep and in the shape of a bowl," Neff was quoted as saying in the *Los Angeles Times,* in a customarily succinct appraisal.[13] "The house was designed to fit the natural contour of the ground. All rooms have at least two exposures opening onto wide loggias and terraces which overlook the gardens."

He had sited it so the entry courtyard was hidden from street view. From the drive up to the east side of the house, visitors arrived at an entrance of cast stone as elaborate as any he had ever devised. Columns holding a broken pediment, an urn in its apex, were topped by Corinthian capitals. If that were not enough, a balustraded balcony protecting a set of amber leaded windows extended over the deep passageway. What could be seen from Bellagio Road was a three-story palazzo with eleven arched, balustraded colonnades on the ground floor alone.

With the lush greens of the Bel-Air Country Club across Bellagio Road for inspiration, Marian painted in oils on the piazza. Her framed work was hung on walls covered with green velvet Belgian linen. Her taste for silver serving pieces had been cultivated in England, where the plummeting value of the pound had served her dollar well. (She had also purchased crystal chandeliers in Murano, Italy, before retrieving Lillian from boarding school.)

Lillian's life in Bel-Air resembled that of royalty. She dined in a sitting room adjoining her bedroom. Servants waited for her to finish and then sent her dishes down to the kitchen in a dumbwaiter. "We had a maid who did nothing but keep the daybeds made," she said.[14] She watched her father's Charlie Chan serials and Shirley Temple films with friends in a theater below the living room.

In January 1937, Lillian was married in the house: she descended the oval staircase to the grand hall, where her fiancé, Dr. Herman Semenov, waited to escort her to the living room. The ceremony was held under a gigantic oil painting executed by her mother's teacher, Alexander Rosenfeld, which depicted Wurtzel and his film stars in Renaissance costume. "They were copied meticulously from art and history books borrowed from 'Research' in the studio library," writer S. N. Behrman claimed.[15]

Shortly thereafter, their grand life began to fall apart. Marian learned that a Fox ingénue was going to have Sol's child, and she fled to Europe to paint.[16] Sol wrote to her in a plea to reunite, "When I walked into the house for the first time, I realized that this was the home for me and why you had built it the way you did."[17] Marian ignored him. While he consoled himself at the Clover Club in Las Vegas, she rented the house to tenants anxious to make an impression, including the likes of Howard Hughes, Pat Boone, and Elvis Presley. By 1955, when Prince Rainier rented the house while waiting for Grace Kelly to give up acting and follow him to Monaco, the Wurtzels had sold it.

MOVING TOWARD EXPERIMENTATION

The Wurtzels had been able to afford a hundred-thousand-dollar house at the beginning of the Depres-sion because so many were escaping their woes every week at the movies.[18] Los Angeles's economy had shrunk 60 percent during the first four years of the decade, and while the president of the Chamber of Commerce blandly dismissed the crisis as "the secession of activity in the building trades,"[19] a third of the nation was living in slums and some had been reduced to sleeping in box-cars and church pews.[20] The federal government instituted a National Housing Act to stimulate con-struction, offering low-cost loans for remodeling and new building, and more than a dozen federal housing agencies sprang up to promote economic recovery.

In the July 15, 1934, *Los Angeles Times,* Neff announced his solution, "America's first completely factory-built house": "These houses are built com-pletely under the personal supervision of my associates and myself," he said, "and they may then be moved by truck to any desired location."[21]

Throughout the 1930s, architects proposed thou-sands of low-cost housing schemes, but most of these mobile homes did not resemble traditional wood-sided houses: Buckminster Fuller attracted the curious at the 1933 Chicago World's Fair with his aluminum Dymaxion House. German architects Walter Gropius and Konrad Wachsmann, who invested thirty years of their lives in their General Panel Corporation before it collapsed in financial ruin in 1948, devised a prefabri-cated house of steel. Fred Keck's air-conditioned Crys-tal House, which one could view for ten cents at the same World's Fair where the Dymaxion House was shown, was made entirely of glass.[22] Neff's premade house, on the other hand, looked like an all-American bungalow. He presented it as conventional, not revolu-tionary, and together with financial backer Mary Pick-ford, came up with the name Honeymoon Cottage. Signs announcing the modest one-story house with its towering brick chimney were erected on a lot at the heavily traveled intersection of Wilshire Boulevard and

BEACH HOUSES

TO SUIT
ANY LOT

$2000. and Up

+

WALLACE NEFF
ARCHITECT

182 E. California Street
PASADENA

ABOVE: *The Honeymoon Cottage*
RIGHT: *Neff's only known advertising, done on behalf of the Honeymoon Cottage*

Rossmore Avenue. The ads depicted a lovely little cottage with a wide, four-step stoop and an entrance surround identical to the one on Gary Cooper's Brentwood house. Dozens of terra-cotta pots surrounded the cottage, concealing the absence of a foundation.

At the February 12, 1935, meeting of the Southern California Chapter of the American Institute of Architects, Neff learned of another venue where he might promote the Honeymoon Cottage.[23] Samuel Lunden, the architect who had supervised the construction of the Doheny Library at USC and was secretary of the Los Angeles Chamber of Commerce's National Housing Committee, was looking for demonstration houses for an exposition called the "Village of Tomorrow," to be held on a twelve-acre lot adjacent to the new Pan-Pacific Auditorium. In addition to Neff's project, two other model houses were selected, one sponsored by the *Los Angeles Times* and the other by a lumber company.

The Honeymoon Cottage was trucked to the site forty-eight hours before the gates opened on May 18, 1935. Traveling west on Beverly Boulevard, the driver of the truck halted east-west traffic while he made a wide left turn onto the Pan-Pacific grounds. Neff, who was usually the most conscientious of architects, still had not appeared twelve hours before the opening (for reasons that remain unknown), and Lunden rushed to the site and found a painter at work in the living room, panicking because the paint was not drying. A fire had been lighted in the fireplace, which had been solely for display, and the marble floor underneath had begun buckling. Lunden stayed with the project throughout the night. Fifteen minutes before the governor of California appeared to cut the ribbon, a truck pulled up and dumped a length of white picket fence. Lunden set it up around the cottage. "The last bit of mortar was swept off the stoop of Neff's house," Lunden recalled.

"I'd been up all night."[24] When Neff showed up at the May meeting of the American Institute of Architects, the normally taciturn Lunden lambasted him.[25]

Lunden had clout with the architectural community and the government that Neff lacked, yet even he could not conjure up buyers. The Honeymoon Cottage cost hundreds of dollars more than the experimental houses the federal government was building, which included three quarters of an acre of land. When Neff said that he "was possessed by the thought that there should be a demand for small homes of real charm within the reach of people of limited means,"[26] he revealed how little he knew about the take-home earnings of the American working class. In the midst of the Depression, even the lucky ones who had a job made an average of less than twenty-six dollars a week.[27]

After thousands of fairgoers had seen the mobile cottage, Neff sold the prototype.[28] In the meantime, a second Honeymoon Cottage had been trucked south to another exposition at a new residential subdivision, Lakewood Village, a "semi-sustaining garden community" between Los Angeles and Long Beach.[29] The selling agent hoped Neff's name would attract interest, but there was none. Neff later conceded that the steel-reinforced brick chimneys and six-inch-thick redwood walls had catapulted the price to nearly three thousand dollars—way beyond affordability for the thousands who walked through the models. His dream of reducing the price to a thousand dollars after enough units had been sold was not to be.

Neff was in a predicament similar to the one his father and grandfather had experienced during the financially troubled 1890s, when they had tried to sell land to a middle class that could ill afford to invest. Experimental housing was a risky business, and Neff had lost several thousand dollars of his own money, plus that much of his investors'. Now he considered

getting the government involved, for Uncle Sam was paying for a dozen new projects in Los Angeles, as a result of the 1937 Housing Act, which had created the U.S. Housing Authority. Many of the projects housed defense workers employed at plants gearing up to send supplies to America's allies fighting the Nazis. Pueblo del Rio was the first such project in Los Angeles—400 units for 1,350 people, designed by the architect Paul Williams in southeast Los Angeles. Baldwin Hills Village, another development built with Federal Housing Association funding, was designed by Reginald Johnson, two other architects, and the master of site planning, Clarence S. Stein. Johnson, once as staid and predictable as an architect could be, had taken up Fabian Socialism. "He got involved politically," his son, Joe, recalled, "and it had a big effect on him." With its 275 apartments facing open parkland, it was Johnson's "proudest achievement," his son believed.[30]

Neff kept in touch with such colleagues, hoping he too could win a public housing commission, as work was so scarce he was barely able to pay his bills. But the free time allowed him to pursue a housing idea that was as different from Baldwin Hills as a jet is from a propeller plane, an idea that was as much an engineering project as an architectural one.[31] It was an unparalleled time for experimentation in Los Angeles, but as architectural historian David Gebhard has pointed out, "Such points in history are always delicate and short-lived."[32]

Darryl Zanuck's stables in the San Fernando Valley

< *CHAPTER SIXTEEN* >

COSTARRING THE EUROPEAN PROVINCIAL
AND THE AMERICAN COLONIAL REVIVALS

My father did not like mansions.
—Darrylin Zanuck

Low-cost housing was obviously not what film industry leaders commissioned for their expensive oceanfront and hilltop parcels. For their needs, Wallace Neff defied the Depression during the second half of the 1930s with one debonair period-revival house after another on the west side of Los Angeles. Near the intersection of Beverly Glen and Sunset boulevards, south of Bel-Air's east gate, Robert Brigham and his family lived in a white-brick, French Norman–revival house effusive with geranium-filled window boxes and low, white-brick perimeter walls, which Neff designed in 1936.[1] The roof was so steep, and the chimneys at either end so high, it brought to mind cottages in Disney's recently released film, *Snow White and the Seven Dwarfs*.[2] Orange terra-cotta tile on the ridges of the brown shingle roof made it look even more whimsical, for it created the kind of heavy outline a child adds to a picture with a crayon. The house was the antithesis of modernism's gleaming austerity.

Neff usually did not believe that his houses required architectural theatricality, even the ones he designed for clients in show business.[3] But now, being loose with scale and proportion was a way for him to distinguish his provincial cottages from the myriad other French- and English-influenced houses popping up all over town. "It was a time," one of his draftsmen recalled, "when Wallace Neff was intrigued by the

Bavarian style."[4] It was also a time, the scholar Leo Rosten wrote, when Hollywood was "in search of cultural stability. The movie people have learned to snicker at Byzantine portals and Moorish patios. The houses are...characterized by a harmony which was absent in the gilded mausoleums with which the original children of fortune expressed their sudden wealth."[5]

The demise of the Spanish-colonial style was inevitable, for developers had transformed the landscape of agriculture and chaparral into more neighborhoods of Spanish colonial–revival schools and open-air markets than public taste allowed. Developers like the dynastic Janss family took pains to imitate Neff's style, but his ability to create whimsical structures that adhered to hard-and-fast principles of scale and proportion was beyond their contractor-designers. Historian Kevin Starr described their efforts as "sales-oriented pastoralism" and "a way of dressing up tract housing with pseudo-romance."[6] Spanish design was suffering from overkill, and the period revivalists had moved on to another period.

As early as 1926, the actor-turned-decorator William Haines had remodeled his Spanish-style house into what was becoming known as Hollywood regency.[7] In 1935, Jack and Ann Warner had erased the Spanish aesthetic from their mansion in favor of the new Hollywood regency style.[8] And Neff eliminated the

TOP: *The Reisch House*
BOTTOM: *Liesel and Walter Reisch with business manager Noel Singer, kneeling, and Neff, standing on left*

Spanish elements from A. K. Bourne's Glendora ranch to create an American federal–revival estate in 1936, while simultaneously remodeling Louis B. Mayer's Spanish house to reflect the colonial-revival style.[9] For the film community, the demise of one style in favor of another was simply an opportunity to one-up each other once again.

By 1936, Neff had gotten so busy, he often had to schedule visits to five sites during a period of three hours in a single afternoon. This frenetic schedule was possible because the sites were in such close proximity. And the proximity was important to the insular film colony, especially émigrés like Austrian Walter Reisch, who had been a screenwriter in England. (Santa Monica, Pacific Palisades, and Bel-Air were attracting a number of Eastern European artists who had fled Nazi persecution. Being with one another made the cultural adjustment easier.) Reisch and his wife, Liesel, had set sail on the maiden voyage of the *S.S. Normandie* on May 29, 1935.[10] Reisch's business manager, Noel Singer, recommended Neff to the newly arrived Reisches. "We met him at our new site in Bel-Air," Liesel Reisch recalled, "a block from Ernst Lubitsch. Neff said to me, 'What kind of house do you want?'"[11]

The Reisches commissioned a stucco chalet so straightforward in its vernacular, it might have been designed for a Swiss farmer. Only the swimming pool and the courtyard filled with automobiles distinguished it from the humble cottages of Reisch's homeland. "We argued with him about how many windows to put in the second floor," Liesel said, "but he prevailed, and the upstairs was always dark because there were so few."[12]

Neff planned the dimensions of the rooms around the Reisches' furnishings, such as an antique wardrobe for church robes and religious objects, which had been converted into a bookcase, and a dining set made by a man Neff called "an old Pasadena carpenter."[13] Liesel held out for additional closets. Costs escalated, and the anticipated twenty-five-thousand-dollar budget climbed to sixty thousand dollars.

Neff's appointment books from this period reveal a clientele as star-studded as that of any time in his career. Cary Grant and Barbara Hutton called to request Tyrolean-style alterations to George Miller's former house. "The house is fine as it is," Neff insisted. Grant, who was tightfisted with his and Hutton's money, became an admirer. He also gained an appreciation for architecture. "What he cared about were his houses," Grant said, "right down to the lowest lock and smallest hinge. He never imposed any opinion on any person or subject except as it related to architecture."[14]

Joan Bennett also lived in a Neff house, as the WPA pointed out in its guide to California. "It is a two-story white painted brick mansion of Norman design surmounted by two large chimneys," the guide reported, quite accurately.[15] The hundred-thousand-dollar, 12,557-square-foot house was built at a cost of eight dollars a square foot. Builder William Warmington cited the house in an advertisement: "Depression?" it read. "Not with such a list of satisfied owners recommending their builder."[16]

Bennett's memoirs called it her "dream house on Mapleton Drive."[17] She regaled guests with the reaction of a building inspector who questioned the soundness of Neff's fireplace flues, which traveled horizontally before being routed vertically. In fact, she should have been more concerned about the electrical system, for on May 1, 1943, a fire caused by faulty wiring destroyed a third of the house. Bennett and her film-producer husband, Walter Wagner, were captured on the front page of the *Los Angeles Times* standing in their pajamas on a lawn filled with children and furniture. "Actress Witnesses Blaze Resulting in $175,000 Damage," the headline read.[18] War-scarce materials were not available to repair the structure for another year.

At the same time he was working with Bennett, Neff was also meeting with Claudette Colbert to discuss remodeling her house. The residence had been designed by Lloyd Wright in 1935 for Colbert and her husband, Joel Pressman, the doctor who had cured her sinus problems and won her heart. The star of *It Happened One Night* complained that she had requested "a Georgian house" from Wright but was given "a Roman bath."[19] Neff converted two bedrooms into a what Colbert called a "playroom" for screening films.[20] Neff's pleasure at winning the commission was not shared by William Warmington, the building contractor, who was annoyed that the actress insisted that he wait for her to wake up in the morning before beginning work. Instead of starting at seven o'clock, the crew had to begin at ten. "It wasn't an easy job," his son, Ed Warmington, remembered fifty years later.[21]

Neff's penchant for steep roofs and soaring chimneys was evident in the house he designed for Dr. Stanley Imerman on Beverly Hills's star-filled Tower Road (where the actor Jack Lemmon later lived for decades, until his death). The ski-slope silhouette, outlined with white ridge tiles, created the appearance of a house that was all roof.

The next hilltop over from the Imerman House, Fredric March and Florence Eldridge had commissioned Neff to design a grand French Norman–revival cottage on Ridgedale Drive. He was so thorough that his specifications for the building materials and details filled a hundred single-spaced pages. Eldridge took a year off from acting in 1934 to put the house plans together, while her husband appeared in six films. He could earn a hundred thousand dollars for a few weeks of work, which he did in *We Live Again*. "I enjoyed working with Mr. Neff enormously," Eldridge later commented. "In addition to having great taste and talent, he was always gentle and serene and responsive to any ideas I had to offer. For instance,

TOP: *The March House, Beverly Hills*
LEFT: *Screening room added to the March House while it was under construction*

when the house was in construction, I had a sudden brainstorm that required a rather major change of plan, and he immediately accepted it with enthusiasm."[22]

Eldridge's last-minute brainstorm resulted in a screening room, and it was there that *The Spanish Earth* was screened in 1937 to help the Republican civilian effort in the Spanish civil war.[23] Actors Rhea Perlman and Danny DeVito, who later bought the house, sold it in 2001 to another thespian couple, Jennifer Aniston and Brad Pitt.

OUR HOUSE WAS EXTRAORDINARY

A half mile west, Neff designed a New Orleans colonial-style house in 1937 for Sam and Mildred Jaffe, a couple with especially deep roots in the film industry. At twenty-two, Jaffe had relocated to Los Angeles from New York and gone to work managing production for Paramount. By the time he was twenty-eight, he was supervising fifty-two films a year and had negotiated the purchase of the studio's famed location on Melrose Avenue. When he contacted Neff, he was earning his living as a theatrical agent and raising three daughters with his wife.

The seven-thousand-square-foot, fifty-thousand-dollar house Neff created for the family had its cross axis in the entry hall, a formal arrangement he had used a decade before in villa plans. "There were many ordinary houses on the street—Fred Astaire's house... William Wyler's... Mary Pickford's," Jaffe said at the age of ninety-two, recalling the house on San Ysidro Road. "Our house was extraordinary. Neff did everything he could to accommodate our social lives. The dining room was like a ballroom. In the entry hall, he devised a door which slid back into the wall to block off the stairs to soundproof the second floor so the children could sleep."[24] Jaffe even enthused about how Neff hid

TOP: *Naomi, Barbara, Mildred, and Judith Jaffe in Beverly Hills, 1945*
BOTTOM: *Naomi and Judith Jaffe watching sister Barbara on the diving board at the Jaffe House*

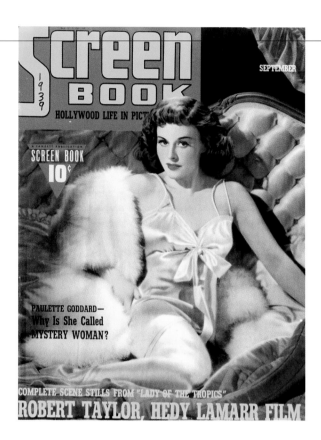

Actress–cover girl Paulette Goddard, with whom Neff had a close relationship

the garage underground to avoid detracting from the facade: "I have looked throughout the United States and I have never found a New Orleans colonial home like ours," he said. "We should never have sold it."

Soon after they moved in, Jaffe received a phone call from Buddy Rogers, who lived a block away in Pickfair with his new wife, Mary Pickford. "Mary has been admiring your house," Rogers said. "She thinks it will increase the value of our property. Can we come over?" That the new house down the bend from the best-known house in America could "increase its value" was a stretch, yet apparently Pickford was as curious as anyone to learn how her neighbors lived.

Charlie Chaplin and his wife, Paulette Goddard, also ventured out from their home around the corner to have a look. Impressed, Goddard called Neff in

August 1938 to discuss alterations to the exterior of Breakaway House, the name their house had acquired after Chaplin's carpenters from the film studio built it on the cheap.[25] Neff knew Chaplin through King Vidor and a ski club they both belonged to, but he had never met the actress. As Chaplin started work on *The Great Dictator*, which would star his wife and mock Adolf Hitler, Goddard and her friend and decorator Sylvia Fairbanks began selecting carpets, wallpaper, curtains, and furnishings for a transformation of the main floor and two second-floor bedrooms, in anticipation of the improved facade.[26]

Neff proposed a neo-Georgian scheme, engulfing the entry in six neoclassical columns topped by a balustrade, in the popular Hollywood regency style. Chaplin turned Neff's plan down. It may be that he found it ostentatious, or that his social conscience prevailed over his wife's spendthrift nature. Perhaps he was content with the Mediterranean style of the exterior, or maybe he sensed that his wife's interest in the architect extended beyond that of a professional relationship. So often that was Goddard's tendency: she was a vital woman with great enthusiasms, and her sexual exploits were legion by the time she was thirty-five. (A tryst with the director Anatole Litvak under a table at Ciro's nightclub inspired a scene in the 1975 film *Shampoo*.) While it never actually became romantic, the relationship between the actress and the architect lasted several years. They skied in Reno and the San Bernardino Mountains, where she encouraged film producer Joseph Schenck to develop a ski resort and hire Neff to design it. She also introduced Neff to her theatrical agent, Myron Selznick, who was interviewing architects for an office on Wilshire Boulevard, and to Diego Rivera, the politically radical painter, who may have been another object of her affections.[27] (Rivera's modern house and studio, by the architect Juan O'Gorman, was the kind of flat-roofed design that repelled

Neff.) The Neff-Goddard relationship came to an end sometime in 1942, after her divorce from Chaplin became final, but Neff relived its particulars over drafting boards with his associates for years.

A UNIQUE (IF NOT ECCENTRIC) LIFESTYLE

By the mid-1930s, Neff's life had become more focused on work than ever. He rented apartments for a year at a time, holding on to the high-ceilinged, windowless, one-room studio in the Villa Carlotta as a place where he could escape for afternoon catnaps. (It had a bed that folded into the wall and a sofa supported by concrete blocks. There was also a hot plate, where he could brew his favorite Lapsang souchong tea; peanut butter was kept on the shelf and avocados on the counter.)[28] He tracked his weight, which fluctuated between 173 and 188 pounds. He wore the same two-button suits for decades, splurging on a white sports coat when he sat for a portrait in which he looked like a cross between John Gilbert and Ramon Novarro. His ties were devoid of design or pattern. He continued to account for every transaction in black pocket-size appointment books. At Christmas in 1936, he noted having given five dollar bills to his children. Flowers, fruit, perfume, or whiskey went to clients, and bottles of Lanvin's Arpege to Louise.[29]

Every January he projected earnings for the year ahead. Anticipating $273,000 worth of construction in 1937, he estimated $27,300 in fees and $12,000 in "earned profit."[30] The same little black book showed morning appointments, with afternoons devoted to inspecting building sites. It also revealed numerous overdrafts from his bank. "He always complained that money was tight," his friend Irving Gellman recalled.[31]

In 1938, the delineator Frank Jamison came to see Neff at his office to show him renderings he had done for a presentation Neff was making to the husband-and-wife actors Robert Taylor and Barbara Stanwyck.

"He had good days and bad," Jamison remarked. "I could see the tension. The man had an artistic temperament. He would change a design many times, even if it was not a major commission."[32] Jamison witnessed Neff's pique at his avant-garde competition. Spotting one of his draftsmen perusing *Architectural Forum* with a picture of Frank Lloyd Wright on the cover, Neff grabbed it and threw it on the floor. "They are crazy!" he shouted.[33] Wright's sharp lines and angles put him in a league with Neutra and the International style in Neff's mind. Philosophies of architecture and the glorification of the architect made Neff suspicious. There was nothing theoretical about his approach.

Many of the movie executives who were his clients shared his mistrust of design dogmas, which may explain his enduring relationship with the film industry. The chairman of a corporation that employed thousands, Darryl Zanuck wanted nothing of industrial materials in his living room. He made no bones about having worked hard to reach his position, and he wanted to put those days behind him. For Zanuck, Neff created a house similar to one he was designing just next door for the difficult Edith Mayer Goetz. He must have felt absolutely certain that that particular plan was the best one for a narrow oceanfront lot. But he was taking a chance.

MOGUL RIVALRY

On a Thursday in November 1935, Neff had driven his twelve-cylinder Packard Deluxe road coupe to the Saint Pierre Road house he had designed for Edith and William Goetz to discuss designing another house for them at the beach in Santa Monica. The following afternoon at four thirty, he had appeared in Beverly Hills to discuss a beach house for Virginia Zanuck and the exacting Darryl, as a landscape architect and an interior decorator sat in on the meeting. Neff continued to meet regularly with Mrs. Goetz and Mrs. Zanuck over the next couple of years, moving from a one o'clock appointment with one to a two thirty appointment with the other.

What he did not reveal to these women, who were competing with one another to be seen as the best hostess, was that they were about to receive the same floor plan in the same beach enclave on the same stretch of Pacific Coast Highway. It seemed perfectly logical to Neff, after he discovered that the dimensions of the parcels were exactly the same: on oceanfront lots, building vertically provided sorely needed space. Neff designed both houses to rise three stories. The plans were L-shaped, with servants' quarters above the garages on the long leg of the L. The adjoining living and dining room space had a broad view of the water in the foot of the L. A screen could be dropped from the ceiling to divide the living space on the south from the dining space on the north. Framed art on the south wall flipped back on hinges to reveal a projector.

Neff's notes reveal that his clients were equally exacting in specifying the fine points: Etna venetian blinds, soundproofing in the adults' bedrooms, covered electrical outlets in the children's bedrooms. Jacks for telephones were installed in almost every room. Virginia Zanuck wanted a tie rack of a specific make in her husband's bathroom, while Edith Goetz wanted soundproofing in the butler's pantry to maintain the flawless ambience of her dinner parties. "Copy Goldwyn, Pickford fence," Neff wrote in his vest-pocket notebook, a clear acknowledgment that he was not above stealing a good idea.

The two families, who paid nearly fifty thousand dollars each, became aware that they were building neck and neck when the contractor, Carl G. Johnson, was seen at both construction sites. Zanuck's work began on January 14, 1937, followed by Goetz's on February 23.[34] Work continued into the summer after John-

son's son gave up his summer vacation to assist his father. The race was on.

It seemed as if all the stars in Hollywood lived in Santa Monica. Goldwyn, Lasky, Mayer, Carmel Myers, Pickford and Fairbanks, and Shearer and Thalberg all called the beach home. The crush also included renters like Cary Grant, Myron Selznick, Paulette Goddard, Anita Loos, Constance Bennett, Harry Warner, William Wyler, Loretta Young, Van Johnson, Keenan Wynn, and Mervyn LeRoy. Marion Davies and William Randolph Hearst's mansion extended for an entire block on Ocean Front Walk. Most lots were 30 feet wide and 180 feet deep, so long and narrow that two had to be combined to build a good-sized house.

Zanuck had four lots, one of which already had a modest beach house on it; the rest were reserved for his children's play. (His son Richard launched model airplanes in the sand.) Zanuck was as driven and megalomaniacal as any other movie mogul, barking orders at the top of his voice, which some compared to the rat-a-tat-tat of a machine gun. The influence he exerted on the films of 20th Century Pictures was as all-encompassing as Louis B. Mayer's at MGM, and his role in developing Vitaphone, which brought sound to motion pictures, had secured his place in the film firmament.

William Goetz, next door, was considered by some "a gentle man of taste, erudition and manners,"[35] but he was never able to escape the stigma of nepotism, because his father-in-law, Louis B. Mayer, had used his influence with his business associates Joseph and Nicholas Schenck to get him a position at 20th Century Pictures. (One of Goetz's first jobs was assisting Sol Wurtzel, the Neff client and Fox producer.) Building contractor Carl Johnson was trapped between these two driven competitors. "Zanuck told Dad to work overtime so he could beat Goetz, and Goetz told him to do the same," Carl Johnson's son remembered. "We were putting in ten-hour days, seven days a week."[36]

The Zanucks moved in a month before the Goetzes. When young Darrylin Zanuck, who liked to dive into the swimming pool from the roof of the house, went over to play with the Goetz girls, she recognized that the houses had the same plan and told her mother. Soon Richard Zanuck heard his mother complain to a friend on the telephone, "Edie Goetz stole my floor plan!"[37]

"I can't remember their house," Edith later insisted, but she knew enough about it to declare that "it was not of any period. Our house was of a period."[38] She had chosen the Cape Cod style, she told dinner guests, because it reminded her of her Boston birthplace. She was determined to be considered a blue blood, although no one on Beacon Street had antiques culled from MGM's property department like she said.

The Goetz and Zanuck houses were embellished with variations on the American colonial style. Where there were dormers on the roof of the Goetz House, there were none on the Zanuck roof. The Zanuck House had wide wood siding and a cedar shingle roof, while the Goetz House had narrow wood siding and an asphalt shingle roof. Shutters adorned all the Goetz House windows, while the Zanuck House had few. Both houses had window boxes, which held Neff's favored red geraniums.

Where the Zanucks had a badminton court and a swimming pool on the beach side, the Goetzes had grass. The Zanucks had a bar; the Goetzes didn't. Zanuck stored alcohol in a basement stockroom below the barroom. Goetz collected books; Zanuck collected clothes. (Zanuck's sleek dressing room had compartments for belts and drawers for socks, and a Dunhill humidor for his trademark cigars. "Everything had to revolve around his dressing room," Fox set designer Walter Scott remembered.)[39]

When the Wurtzels were invited to dinner at the

Zanucks', young Lillian was surprised to find modest rooms and low ceilings: ceiling heights were eight feet in the main rooms compared with ten and a half feet in the Wurtzel House. The Zanucks, who were diminutive in size, would not have wanted high ceilings that would have made them appear even shorter. They were, however, sure enough of themselves not to fall for the bigger-is-better Hollywood mentality.

Eventually, though, they decided that the dining room was not imposing enough. Neff was brought back, evidently forgiven, to help create a room with a grand table and wallpaper that depicted George Washington crossing the Delaware. A bay window, with glass bent into a semicircle, provided an additional foot in dimension. Then the Goetzes decided that their dining room was too modest, and Neff made similar changes to their house.

When the Goetzes finally decided to sell both Neff-designed houses and build a new house in Holmby Hills, Edith Goetz kept a photo album of the beach house. "The charm of this house," she mused as she looked at it years later. "I remember reading *Gone With The Wind* on the living room sofa."[40]

DOWN IN THE VALLEY

Zanuck kept polo ponies at the Uplifters Club in the Rustic Canyon area of Santa Monica. After he decided he needed stables of his own, he began looking for property in the San Fernando Valley. The valley had been rural until five Los Angeles developers had formed the Los Angeles Farming and Milling Company in 1910 and civilization had followed. Farmers raising dry crops were followed by citrus growers, then film industry ranchers, then developers. Edward Everett Horton lived at Belly Acres, a mile from the Clark Gable ranch in Encino. Hal Wallis and Louise Fazenda operated a ranch in Van Nuys. Feeling confi-

TOP: *Draftsman Frank Jamison's rendering of a house*
for Darryl and Virginia Zanuck
RIGHT: *Tack room at Darryl Zanuck's stables*

dent that he could maintain fifty-five acres, Zanuck bought a parcel in the Santa Monica Mountain foothills. Neff wrote directions to the site on the inside cover of his July 1937 date book: "Zanuck property—Sepulveda to Ventura Blvd.—turn left—go about a mile will see large yellow arrow on right says 'Raenford School for Boys.' This street is Havenhurst. Turn left, drive to end of road, then turn right into property."[41]

Working for the first time with the architect Roland Coate, Neff designed a horse breeder's dream, a complex that included a stable, hay barn, stud barn, riding ring, and caretaker's house. Zanuck called it Ric-Su-Dar Farms after his children, Richard, Susan, and Darrylin. "Once Zanuck decided what style he wanted," his equestrian caretaker, Bob Adler, remembered, "I helped with details like what hardware to put on the double Dutch doors. Each door had a brass strip on the bottom to keep the horses from chewing the wood. Every stick of lumber was hand sawed. One man on the construction crew did nothing but file saws. Darryl spared no expense for his horses."[42]

Zanuck's tack room at the center of the stable had a stall shower, two Murphy beds, a couch, two green leather chairs, and a stained glass window depicting polo ponies. Saddles and bits were mounted on wall brackets. A rack held the polo mallets. A blanket monogrammed "D. F. Z." hung from a bar. "Every Friday was brass day," Adler recalled. "We had thirteen grooms for fifty-six head of horses. The electric flycatchers were so effective, you never knew there was a horse on the grounds. You could eat off the floor. Movie people like Walt Disney couldn't play polo for sour apples, but they came anyhow."[43]

"David Selznick and Douglas Fairbanks sat under a tree with us kids eating hamburgers which Daddy prepared," Darrylin said. "He pitched a tent for me to nap in while he rode. We had honeycombs to eat and

a bomb shelter to explore. I had a wonderful childhood."[44]

While Zanuck was serving in the Second World War, cows and sheep joined the horses. After he returned, he made *In Old Kentucky* and *Straight, Place, and Show* at the ranch, but he decided against building the house he had commissioned Neff to design. He later gave up horses after a polo accident sent him to the hospital, and the ranch was sold for $175,000 in the mid-1950s ("peanuts," Darrylin Zanuck scoffed).[45] The stables were dismantled and moved to Buellton in the Santa Ynez Valley a hundred miles northwest.

In the postwar era, the San Fernando Valley mushroomed, and film personalities got caught in the crossfire of eminent domain. Hal Wallis and Louise Fazenda were forced to sell to a school district so a junior high school could be built, and they moved to a house Neff had designed for Joan Bennett on Mapleton Drive. Edgar Rice Burroughs's estate was subdivided and the community of Tarzana was born. Orange groves, dairy farms, and Edward Everett Horton's Belly Acres farm all had to make way for the Ventura and San Diego freeways.

Richard Zanuck, who decided to seek out the site of his boyhood ranch one afternoon in 1984, found out just how much of the original valley remained. Trying to re-create the old route from memory, he encountered one residential subdivision after another and became completely lost. Frustrated, he gave up and returned to the beach house in Santa Monica where he still lived, nearly fifty years after it had been constructed in the great rivalry between moguls. The old San Fernando Valley, he concluded, was gone forever.[46]

Draftsman Caspar Ehmcke and Wallace Neff in the San Gorgonio Mountains

CHAPTER SEVENTEEN

FIGHTING BACK

If you asked me whether Neff likes Modern or not, I would say that he likes it so long as it is traditional.
—Mark Daniels, *Architect and Engineer* (January 1941)

Nᴏʀᴛʜ ᴏꜰ ᴛʜᴇ ɢᴏᴇᴛᴢ ʙᴇᴀᴄʜ ʜᴏᴜꜱᴇ, construction crews converged on a piece of land being carved up as a building lot in 1937. Albert Lewin, Irving Thalberg's scout at MGM for screenplays like *Mutiny on the Bounty* and *The Good Earth*, had begun building a house for his family in the same long, narrow configuration as the Goetz and Zanuck beachfront properties, with enough room for a two-car garage at the street. But there the resemblance to Neff's work ended, as Lewin was erecting a streamlined, flat-roofed, glass-enclosed house.

Beneath the bands of metal cornice, vertically mounted, factory-made windows—what modernists were calling curtain walls—wrapped neatly around the house. The unobtrusive entrance was on the side. A circular bay on the ground floor was capped by an aluminum-sheathed balcony on the second floor. Lewin's architect was Richard Neutra, who said of his style, "The frame was the house; the house was the frame."[1] Now, more than a decade after his Lovell House in Los Feliz had become a beacon for modernism, Neutra's ideals had progressed as far as the Pacific.

The schism between modernist and historically based architectural philosophies was epitomized by this beach scene, where contemporary met traditional head on. The tension became evident to a twenty-nine-year-old refugee from Nazi Germany, Caspar Ehmcke, who had witnessed a similar friction in Munich. "They were deadly enemies," he said of the modernists and traditionalists. "The Fuhrer hated modern architecture."[2]

For his part, Ehmcke, who was of partial Jewish extraction, was proficient in both styles and associated with both camps. He set sail from Germany with a letter of recommendation from Neff's long-ago employer Fritz Norkaner, and another from an architect named Frick, a friend of Richard Neutra's wife, Dione. Neutra wrote to Ehmcke, telling him to get a room at the Rosslyn Hotel in downtown Los Angeles upon arriving. After following Neutra's suggestion, Ehmcke lit out from the hotel for Neutra's office in Silverlake. He was convinced, after Neutra's encouraging letters, that the father of Los Angeles's avant-garde would hire him. He knew Neutra himself had been taken on by Frank Lloyd Wright when he came to Chicago from Austria in 1923. And Gordon Kaufmann, an architect of both period-revival and modern styles, had given Neutra one of his first jobs.[3]

"I told Neutra I worked with Otto Haesler, the great advocate of industrialization of housing," Ehmcke remembered. "I told him I'd worked as a carpenter in a truss company. Neutra said, 'You need an education,' and I told him, 'I have an education.' I'd attended technical school in Stuttgart at the Werkbund, where my father was a leading designer."[4]

Richard Neutra on the grounds of the Lovell House in Los Feliz

Neutra offered Ehmcke work as a draftsman in exchange for room and board. "There would be nothing but the glory of working for him," Ehmcke said he realized, as it became clear that the traditional European-style architectural apprenticeship was alive in Los Angeles. "I told him I didn't come to America to work for nothing. I said, as if it were an incentive to hire me, 'I have an introduction to Wallace Neff,'" said Ehmcke, who then pulled out Norkaner's letter. "'If you want to draw Spanish houses,' Neutra scoffed, 'work for him.'"[5]

Although Neff and Neutra were contemporaries and were both widely accepted in architectural circles, they were as different in their outlooks as John Singer Sargent and Pablo Picasso. What they did agree upon— that Germany's 35-millimeter Leica was the best camera

and that gunite was the ideal building material—were minor harmonious notes in a rivalry that never subsided, at least on Neff's side.

Neutra had not come to America to build houses like his Bavarian ancestors' cottages. Antique furniture, hand-hooked rugs, and stone fireplaces were old-country remnants not fit for Neutra's twentieth century, the era of the airplane and the automobile. The jumble of period-revival architecture on Los Angeles's streets was Hollywood's fault, Neutra wrote.[6] He assiduously avoided the picturesque in favor of the functional, influencing the architectural establishment to eschew historical sources.

Ehmcke left Neutra and drove four miles west through the hills to Neff's office in Hollywood. Neff, he discovered, was looking for an architect who knew how to put warmth—or *gemütlichkeit*, as it was called in German—into a drawing. "'I will have something very soon,' Wallace told me," Ehmcke recalled, and he was employed within a few weeks. Ehmcke added what he called that "cozy feeling" to Neff's elevations, and a rendering of a chalet he executed soon after he was hired received Neff's praise.[7]

"You wouldn't put a wooden bench against a wall of glass," Neff said to Ehmcke, as he showed the German a rendering of a design he was proposing for a house on Tower Road in Beverly Hills. When Ehmcke pressed him to explain his preferences in design, Neff said with characteristic brevity, "I like all the old styles." Neff grumbled when he noticed Ehmcke reading a magazine that depicted Neutra's work. Neutra, Neff sniffed, had not understood the properties of concrete when he built the Lovell House.

In Neff's mind, the austere house had no affinity to Los Angeles's geography. Glass facades left him as cold as interiors of chrome, magnesite, glass brick, Monel, and plastic. Modern buildings looked thin, and they left one wondering where the entrance was. Neff's preoccupation with accenting a building's entry by creating a void in a stucco wall had become one of his trademarks. Nothing in his training or his privileged upbringing encouraged him to sympathize with modernism and its contempt for the past. He took Ehmcke to the construction sites of the Joan Bennett, Darryl Zanuck, and William and Edith Goetz houses to demonstrate how it was possible to adapt traditional styles to accommodate contemporary needs.

THE RISE OF MODERNISM

The modern era began in Europe as the nineteenth century gave way to the twentieth and Vienna's Secessionists abandoned the academic approach to design. Walter Gropius's Fagus Factory, designed in steel and glass, advanced the movement in 1911. After World War I, his philosophy drove the Dessau Bauhaus, where he and his followers, who had become disillusioned with the postwar economy, set out to free Germany from traditional political and social structures. In 1933, the Bauhaus was silenced by the Gestapo, which regarded its ideas as un-German, and many of Gropius's followers made their way to America, where they discovered an eager audience at Harvard's Graduate School of Design. Gropius, Mies van der Rohe, and Marcel Breuer all instilled American students with their philosophies, while their crisp buildings rose side by side with traditional Ivy League Gothic-style buildings on the campus. The modernists' contempt for architectural history extended to its study, and Gropius saw to it that the subject was dropped from Harvard's curriculum.[8]

By the early 1930s, the Austro-German Americans Neutra and Rudolph Schindler led the local avant-garde in Los Angeles, winning film industry clients like Albert Lewin, the filmmaker Josef von Sternberg, and the actress Anna Sten. Even politically conservative Walt Disney abandoned the Spanish-style studio

he had built at the height of the Mediterranean vogue to erect a sleek new studio with the talents of a modern architect. Disney was attracted to modernism, for it was in keeping with a deeply ingrained American puritanical streak.

California Arts & Architecture, the magazine that had once featured Neff's Goetz House, dropped the word California from its title after the publisher decided it limited the work the magazine could cover. It became known as *Arts & Architecture*, aligning itself with the International style, and architects like Neutra began to win more clients from such magazine coverage of their work than from word of mouth.[9]

American taste had blossomed in the 1920s with the creation of cultural institutions like the Museum of Modern Art in New York and the Hollywood Bowl in Los Angeles, and now MoMA's exhibition on the International style, which opened in early 1932, promised to be to architecture what Frederick Jackson Turner's 1893 paper on the American frontier had been to the study of American history.[10] The exhibition arrived in Los Angeles on July 23, 1932, where it was displayed at the Bullocks Wilshire department store. If they had been carrying binoculars, visitors might have looked out the windows of the store to Griffith Park's hills and seen the same Lovell House that was depicted on paper and in models in the store; on the hillside it looked as new and as exotic as it did in the show. (Some neighbors nevertheless considered it a terrible eyesore, according to Lucille Terry Hobart, who grew up directly below it on Aberdeen Avenue in a traditional Spanish house.)[11]

Betty and Morton Topper, who purchased the Lovell House much later, in 1960, noticed that a crowd of people usually accompanied Neutra whenever he visited. They recalled that Neutra seemed far more interested in the structure than in observing any social niceties and that he apparently considered their house his own.[12] "Can't you control your children?" he would

Wallace Neff, circa 1939, wearing one of his signature sports jackets

ask when he had an editor in tow and toys obliterated the architectural order. Fiercely ambitious, he was constantly pressing the Toppers to allow one more photograph or one more guest to tour the house, although showmanship and a book, *Survival Through Design*, published in 1954, had brought him the fame he sought. Neff remained unimpressed, despite Neutra's presence on the covers of magazines like *Time* and the *Saturday Review*.

Ehmcke, for his part, learned to leave his magazines at home.[13] "Neff paid $35 a week, which was enough until I had a family," he said. "The office was messy compared with the stuffy German offices I'd worked in. There were half-nude calendars [*sic*] on the walls. Wallace would come to the office early, give us instructions, then leave around nine for the day. He came back at five to check our work. He put his earnings into creating the drawings. He was very, very thorough, but he was just [barely] making a living."[14]

Neff could not offer him a raise, so Ehmcke eventually found work designing signs for Bullocks. They remained friendly for the rest of their lives, seeing one

another at restaurants, if not at professional meetings. ("You want to see a group of frustrated men," Ehmcke said, "go to an AIA meeting. They all want to be Welton Beckets. You can only have so many stars.")[15]

RECREATION

Like many of Los Angeles's architects, Neff indulged his abiding passion for photography at Morgan's Camera Shop on Sunset Boulevard in Hollywood, where he purchased German-made Leicas. When he was low on funds, he placed his cameras on consignment at the shop, which had been designed by Rudolph Schindler. "He was modest," the owner, Gilbert Morgan, recalled of Neff, "but he told me no one could tell him how to build with concrete."[16]

For the most part, Neff chose the least expensive forms of recreation he could find, given the hole in his paycheck that modernism was helping to create. He frequented clubs like the Cocoanut Grove, but skipped meals. He also visited public attractions like the Griffith Observatory, where he arrived breathless from joyriding up Vermont Avenue. But what really satisfied his taste for high-speed adventure was a sport just coming into vogue in America, which he had excelled at in his youth—skiing.

In Southern California, skiing took place on mounts Waterman in Snow Valley in the San Bernardino Mountains and San Gorgonio, which separated the San Bernardinos from the San Jacinto Mountains and towered 11,499 feet high. Caspar Ehmcke shared Neff's love of skiing, although he was younger and more active. Neff "did a lot of standing around," Ehmcke said, recalling a trip when he, Neff, and Neff's secretary, Florence Didier, crowded into Neff's two-seat Packard and headed for San Gorgonio.

Mounts Waterman and Gorgonio had cabins adequate for changing a pair of skis, but no place luxuri-

Draftsman Carl Oscar Borg's rendering of a ski lodge in Sun Valley, Idaho, for W. Averell Harriman

ous enough to call a resort. That was no deterrent to skiers Neff knew who had second homes in the mountains, or to his brother Bill, who helped organize the Southern Skis social club in 1939. After asking Neff to drum up support for the club in the film community, he sent out letters to film industry people on paper embossed with a design Neff had conceived.[17] King Vidor, Joan Bennett, Edith and William Goetz, Darryl and Virginia Zanuck, Amelita Galli-Curci, Paulette Goddard, and Claudette Colbert and her husband, Joel Pressman, all signed on. Goddard also showed the film producer and land developer Joseph Schenck a presentation drawing Ehmcke had done of a lodge for Snow Valley, hoping for his patronage. She told Hedda Hopper the project would be ready in time for Christmas in

1938, but the plans were canceled when no backers materialized.[18]

But resorts were being built. At the base of the San Bernardinos, where a spring produced pristine mineral water, the Arrowhead Springs Corporation sold the newspaper and nightclub impresario Billy Wilkerson land for a casino and hotel around 1937. Neff, Gordon Kaufmann, and Paul Williams were selected as the architects. Striking modern buildings designed by Kaufmann and Williams were completed, but Wilkerson's operation was shut down for gaming violations before Neff's design could be constructed.[19] Two years later, Neff proposed another design for a resort known as Sky Lodge in Lake Tahoe, also supported by Paulette Goddard, but it too went unrealized.[20]

The one ski lodge he designed that was built was commissioned by W. Averell Harriman of the railroad Harrimans. Neff's Sun Valley Lodge in Idaho became the first destination ski resort in the United States.[21] After witnessing the success of the Canadian Pacific Railroad's resorts in Banff and Lake Louise, Harriman dreamed of a ski resort that would be accessible only by his Union Pacific Railroad. He and an Austrian ski instructor scouted western locations, including Mount Waterman, which is probably where they met Neff. One by one, they eliminated potential sites as too high, too windy, too near a city, or too far from the Union Pacific.[22] Ketchum, Idaho, home to 270 people and great herds of sheep, emerged at the top of the list. "It contains more delightful features for a winter sports center than any other place I have seen in the United States, Switzerland, or Austria," the ski scout wrote to Harriman, who made his first visit in January 1936.[23] "I can remember vividly getting off the train car and putting on my skis and skiing into Sun Valley on powder snow," Harriman said.[24] Sold on its potential, he purchased the forty-three-hundred-acre Bass Ranch.[25] His plan was to open the new resort in time for the Christmas season in 1936.

Neff conceived a three-story lodge in a double-Y configuration, with slightly pitched roofs on all the wings, except at the very ends of the building. There he drew roofs that swooped down two stories, like steep mountain slopes, anchoring the long, horizontal building to the valley. Historians mistakenly credited Gilbert Stanley Underwood, an accomplished resort designer, with designing the lodge. Underwood was accustomed to overseeing the construction of large hotels, and Neff was not in a position to do such work, for it would have meant leaving Los Angeles and living in the most rustic of conditions. (The muscular young men who laid the foundation and poured the concrete structure were housed in Union Pacific boxcars.) Underwood's office actually worked from Neff's renderings to execute the working drawings, squaring the pitch of the roofs that Neff had sloped. The lodge took on a more institutional appearance, which, in Ehmcke's eyes, lacked the character of Neff's design, although its wood-formed, painted concrete was a material Neff would have chosen. On December 21, 1936, with workmen exiting out the back as guests entered at the front, the 220-room, $1.5 million hotel opened.[26] Not even a year had passed since Harriman had paid his first visit to the valley. Neff was finally able to visit the resort that winter on a trip on the Union Pacific with Claudette Colbert and her husband. (Ehmcke read an item in a newspaper that referred to Neff, in the Colbert party, as "an unknown man." "We laughed about it in the office," he recalled.)[27] Neff returned to Sun Valley to ski for the next several years.

The taste for such design—which Neutra would have called schmaltz—faded after the rise of Nazi Germany. But to this day, Neff's original conceptual drawing for the resort hangs in the manager's office there.[28] In Neff's own office, Caspar Ehmcke's rendering for a San Gorgonio lodge was displayed on the wall for decades. Its hues reminded draftsman Harry Balthazar of the green smocks he and his coworkers wore in "the Pasadena years," as Neff had begun calling the 1920s.[29]

CHAPTER EIGHTEEN

THE DIVA, THE CAR DEALER,
AND THE DOHENY LIBRARY

Working in the Churrigueresque style, the architect who hesitates is lost.
—Brendan Gill, *The Dream Come True*

WALLACE NEFF'S FAVORITE CLIENT was Amelita Galli-Curci, an opera singer appealing for her lack of artistic temperament, not to mention the revenue her residential commissions provided.[1] Neff appealed equally to her: his worldliness, his physical resemblance to her husband, the pianist and composer Homer Samuels, and his enjoyment of skiing made him not only an architect in her mind, but an artist. His appreciation of her talent and his brother's involvement in Pasadena opera also helped his cause. He designed at least four houses for Lita, as he and her friends called the singer.[2]

Italian by birth, with an aquiline nose, finely arched brows, blue eyes, and a diminutive stature, Galli-Curci became the outstanding coloratura of her generation after making her American debut at the Auditorium in Chicago in 1916.[3] She appeared at the Hollywood Bowl in 1923, soon after it opened, moving west permanently in 1930 after purchasing a lot on the magnificent Palos Verdes peninsula, southwest of Los Angeles. Neff's plans for the site were exhibited at the Architects' Building and printed in the real estate-conscious *Los Angeles Times*, but the house was never built. Perhaps Galli-Curci decided that Palos Verdes was too far from the heart of Los Angeles's cultural life. Six long Depression years later, the couple managed to sell the land and focused their attention on a parcel in

one of the Los Angeles enclaves that had sprung up overnight during the 1920s.

The Janss Investment Corporation had created the Westwood community from the proverbial bean field, then promoted it relentlessly with newspaper ads illustrated with the same romantic vision of womanhood that Andrew McNally had used in his advertising for La Mirada. The Janss woman, however, wore a headband inscribed with the word "education," an allusion to the land the company had donated to the nearby University of California at Los Angeles. The company issued press releases to the local papers whenever a celebrity bought a parcel in Westwood, and Galli-Curci's 1936 purchase got plenty of ink. "Madame states," one newspaper account read, "that she selected the site because of the sweeping view, which includes the buildings and spires of the University of California at Los Angeles, as well as the distant mountains and sunsets."[4]

Galli-Curci's household was modest by the standards of Neff's other clients, with room only for the soprano and her husband, a grand piano, a servant, and one guest, although she did request a Romeo-and-Juliet balcony where she could look down on the university's Italian Lombard–style buildings. She called the house *Il Gio* (the Little Gem) and insisted on having a pair of wrought-iron gates, which she said were sixteenth-century Venetian, installed at the entry. From

ABOVE: *Galli-Curci House in La Jolla*
LEFT: *Wallace Neff with Amelita Galli-Curci*

outside the gates, visitors glimpsed a bust of the opera singer, cast in stone, on a brick walkway. To the right was a guest wing, to the left, the main house, and in the distance, a Florence Yoch–designed garden.

Shallowly pitched tile roofs were topped by a towering chimney, far from the fireplace it vented, but placed where Neff felt it suited the balance and scale of the elevations. As he had done with the fireplaces in Joan Bennett's house, Neff designed a flue that ran horizontally, then vertically. The "elbowing" of chimney flues, press releases explained, allowed the chimney to pierce the roof at the design's focal point.[5] Terra-cotta pots from the kilns Neff's brothers operated in Laguna Beach sat on plinths in the courtyards, which held bougainvillea and olive trees. Common morning glories wired to stucco walls grew into hanging gardens within a year. The garden walls and enclosed patios served as outdoor living rooms as effectively as they had in many other Neff designs.

In the summer of 1938, as the opera singer prepared for an appearance at Los Angeles's Philharmonic Auditorium, the Southern California Chapter of the American Institute of Architects held its first awards ceremony in four years and presented Neff with an honor award for the Galli-Curci House. The style was Italian in honor of the singer, Neff told the assembled guests, who included Galli-Curci and the craftsman who executed the woodwork, George Hunt. As in Neff's other pared down Mediterranean assemblages, it was the composition of solids and voids that made the house exceptional. The following year, the AIA included it in the book *Residential Architecture in Southern California*. With his E. L. Doheny Ranch House and Orlando Road House also featured in the book, Neff received more recognition than any other architect, including the modernists.[6]

After UCLA grew into a sprawling campus, and cars and students invaded the hillside, Galli-Curci and Samuels took their sixteenth-century Venetian gates and headed for Rancho Santa Fe in North San Diego County. There, after World War II, Neff designed a courtyard house for them, with a facade stripped of all openings but an entry and one window. The hostess ultimately found the windowless kitchen too gloomy and the location too hot in the summer, and the couple began searching for another San Diego County property. At the age of eighty, Galli-Curci commissioned a house overlooking the Pacific. With its courtyard plan, shallow gabled roof, and austere facade, it turned out to be one of the best examples of what Neff could accomplish while modernism held sway. "The one in Westwood was too cool at night; the one in Rancho Santa Fe too hot in the days; the one in La Jolla was perfect," Galli-Curci wrote to Neff in 1963, but within months, she was dead.[7]

THE BEST ADDRESS IN TOWN

The ubiquitous Janss Investment Corporation sold another lot about the time Galli-Curci came to Westwood, this one on Sunset Boulevard, on the northern boundary of the Los Angeles Country Club. (Today the location is one that evokes status, stability, and Billy Wilder movies, but in 1939 it did not have quite the same cachet. Still, it was sited well enough that some members of the Janss family built their own houses on nearby lots.) The clients were Mr. and Mrs. Henry Foster Haldemann, country club regulars. Haldemann had been a car dealer since he was eighteen and was opening a showroom in nearby Beverly Hills. His wife, Katherine, later estimated that because of his work they moved thirty-five or forty times during seven decades of marriage. "We seldom went to Pasadena," she recalled, "until Santa Anita Racetrack opened on Christmas Day in 1934, and we drove through the area on our way to the track. I found the homes perfectly stunning. I did a search to find the name of the architect of one, and it was 'Neff.' It turned out that his office was directly across the street from our apartment in the Chateau Elysee."[8]

The Haldemanns wanted "something different," they told Neff, although they preferred a Mediterranean style. By now, it was impossible for Neff to ignore modern architecture, since even mainstream publications covered it. In 1940, for instance, *House & Garden* ran a story entitled "Tell Me, What Is Modern Architecture?"[9] As Neff's houses started to reflect some of the tenets of Southern California modernism, they began providing more access to the out-of-doors. The Haldemann decor used Asian artifacts to create what was becoming known as the Gumps look, after the store where the art was sold. The structure itself was horizontal, with a low, pitched roof, and was described as "modernized Mediterranean."[10] The dusty-pink stucco facade was punctuated with blue-shuttered fanlights.

Wallace Neff and client Katherine Haldemann, photographed as part of a Janss Investment Corporation publicity campaign

Under Florence Yoch's direction, palms and tropical plants contributed to the languid feeling of the grounds. Fully grown trees were brought in to shield the house from the street, for the frontage on Sunset Boulevard extended 513 feet. The lot was very deep as well, and nearly a hundred feet separated the house from the road. A forecourt was paved with black macadam and planned around a signature Neff fountain. The Haldemanns paid Yoch four thousand dollars to design the grounds and another four thousand to purchase the plants, and they employed three full-time groundsmen to keep up the three-acre lot.[11]

They stayed until 1946, and then Judy Garland and Vincente Minnelli lived there for several years before Charles H. Babcock purchased the house and made alterations under Neff's guidance. By the late 1980s, the shopping center mogul Stanley Black had renovated

the grounds, placing life-size sculptures of a house painter, a policeman, and gawking tourists by J. Seward Johnson Jr. outside a high perimeter wall. The patio with its fifteen-foot-high columns—inspired by Neff's widely praised Edward L. Doheny Memorial Library—was razed, and now the house no longer bears any resemblance to Neff's original design.

THE DOHENY LIBRARY

Considered by some to be Neff's best work, the Edward L. Doheny Memorial Library is still standing, although it has been threatened by encroaching development. In 2004, the Archdiocese of Los Angeles closed the undergraduate facility of St. John's Seminary, the campus where the library is located, and sold sixty acres to Shea Homes, a residential developer.[12] But the library's

ABOVE: *The Haldemann House, one of Wallace Neff's favorite projects*
RIGHT: *Interior of the Haldemann House, decorated by Charles Ray Glass*

Building contractor J. V. McNeil, center, with Estelle Doheny at the construction site of the Edward L. Doheny Memorial Library on the campus of St. John's Seminary in Camarillo, California

The Edward L. Doheny Memorial Library under construction, with Wallace Neff's Packard in the foreground

history has long been a complicated one, as its planning and development were fraught with difficulties from the beginning.

During her husband's Teapot Dome trials, Estelle Doheny had become interested in collecting rare books. The stress of the litigation, coupled with that of her stepson's murder and her husband's physical illness (Doheny was incapable of speech toward the end of his life, after suffering a number of strokes), drove her to find a distraction. Her husband's lawyer, Frank J. Hogan, collected Elizabethan literature, and he was initially her guide, but by 1935 she had become one of the leading bibliophiles in Los Angeles.[13] Medieval and Counter-Reformation writing by monks skilled in the art of calligraphy and illumination had become her passion.

Father William Ward, a priest who knew her well, was convinced that she invested with divine guidance. "She felt every dollar she had was a talent from God," he said.[14] She may have lacked academic credentials, but she was a "Papal Countess," a title Pope Pius XII bestowed upon her in 1939. It "pleased and surprised her," her secretary, Lucille Miller, said, yet "she never used it," contrary to the claims of her biographers.[15]

Around 1937, Mrs. Doheny approached the president of USC, Rufus von Kleinsmid, to request a home for her books at the Doheny Library, which had been dedicated to the memory of her stepson. Caught between the interests of the library and the influence of the Methodist Church, Von Kleinsmid demurred that the shelves were intended for books the students could use. Historian Kevin Starr has observed that as Roman Catholics, the Dohenys frequently met resistance to their projects in a culture dominated by Protestants, but that with the help of Archbishop John J. Cantwell, they were able to fight ostracism with generosity.[16] If that is so, Wallace Neff's talents were often a means to their ends.

A better place for the books, Archbishop Cantwell convinced Mrs. Doheny, was a seminary the Roman Catholic Church was building in Camarillo, halfway between Los Angeles and Santa Barbara, on land donated by Juan E. Camarillo. A building dedicated to her husband, who had died two years before, could house her collection.[17] With funds from an earlier Doheny donation, the architect Ross Montgomery had already begun a campus plan for St. John's Seminary. Now he reworked the plan to accommodate the Edward L. Doheny Memorial Library.[18] Neff won the commission over the eager Samuel Lunden, whose proposal did not impress Mrs. Doheny.

When Neff came to call at her house on Chester Place to discuss the plans, Mrs. Doheny would receive him in her office in the morning or in the front hall in the afternoon. Her sitting room, he noticed, was furnished with a small, rather shabby floral sofa, where the telephone was close to her left hand.[19] Neff knew the Chester Place house steal beam by steal beam, for after the Long Beach earthquake of March 10, 1933, which measured 6.3 on the Richter scale, he oversaw a $150,000 seismic structural renovation. Stylized, ornate, and ostentatious, the house was so large that thirty-seven servants were needed to staff it in Doheny style.[20]

Bronze fixtures had replaced Victorian-style bubble lamps during Neff's renovation, and a glass canopy and wrought iron had been introduced at the entry. Cast-stone lions had also been added at the door. Inside, a baronial oak fireplace had been eliminated in favor of an ornate French rococo mantel. Layers of plaster Adam-style detail decorated walls that had once been covered in dark paneled wood. "The cracks in the plaster were so severe," Neff told a student, "that it was necessary to replaster a major portion of the walls and ceilings."[21] While they were at it, they had applied 24-karat gold leaf to the new plaster ceilings.

Getting the steel beams through the structure without destroying it was the greatest challenge, Neff told the student.[22] Heavy wood doors separating the rooms off the great hall were placed on sliding tracks on the renovated parquet floors. Of greatest significance to Neff's architectural future were the rooms on the third floor that contained Mrs. Doheny's books. By the time he came to discuss the library commission at Camarillo, fifty-four hundred volumes had consumed all the available space.

It would have been like Mrs. Doheny to express a preference for an architectural style, but it appears she did not, for Neff collected photographs of library buildings in a variety of styles. At the 20th Century Fox research library, the Allied Architects Library on Wilshire Boulevard, and the Los Angeles Public Library, he studied images of the J. P. Morgan Library in New York City, the Folger Library in Washington, D.C., the Stanford University Library in Palo Alto, and the William Andrews Clark Library in Los Angeles. After formulating a concept, he contacted Myron Hunt's office for a recommendation for a craftsman who could execute wrought-iron grillwork. He was referred to Clarence Donaldson.

Neff's plan favored drama, contrast, and simplicity, in service of the style that was still imbued in his imagination, Spanish colonial revival. "The main body of the building is coral in color," he noted in his one written account of the library. "The stonework, columns, cornices and trim are white. Iron grilles and sash are dark green."[23]

At a budget of four hundred thousand dollars, it was as costly a building as he executed until 1962, but he was not given carte blanche. Ideas about bronze doors were scrapped in favor of less costly oak doors, and antique bronze doorknobs were jettisoned for knobs that could hold up under student use.

A silver safe from Mrs. Doheny's Chester Place house was eventually moved to the library in Camar-

The Edward L. Doheny House of Studies for Vincentian Seminarians at Catholic University in Washington, D.C.

illo, along with the Steinway piano her husband had given her on her birthday in 1904, her paintings, and her other artwork, because the remote location seemed a safe haven. "Of all her public buildings," Lucille Miller commented, "Camarillo was the most personal. It had her husband's name on it, not his son's. Because it would hold her own possessions, she wanted it to be a beautiful building."[24]

PULLING OUT ALL THE STOPS

Neff's design featured a crucifix on the highest point of the library. It also incorporated ornate cast stone, which imparted an ecclesiastical aura. Other ornament included the coats of arms of the individuals closely associated with the building—the Dohenys, Pope Pius XII, and Archbishop Cantwell. The Spanish baroque treatment of the cast-stone entry portal, set against Neff's customary unadorned gunite and mounted above brick steps, bestowed a strength and monumentality that the diminutive building did not possess in square footage. If Neff ever created an homage to the California missions, this was it.

Admirers compared the library to the centuries-old baptistery of the Cathedral of Mexico City, but it also recalled his 1924 California Security Loan Corporation Building, where plain wall surfaces were offset by the ornament of a cast-stone portal. The bank building, however, competed with structures on either side, while the Doheny library sat on a hill, facing a rectangular formal garden, with open land all around. Neff wrote a note to remind himself: "Cornerstone ceremony, May 23, 1940."[25] The building was completed on the first day of August. By dedication day, every bishop in America, it seemed, was on the road to Camarillo. They "swept in procession through Neff's arched and columned loggias," Kevin Starr wrote, "past sun splashed walls and Churrigueresque portals, in a triumphalist swirl of magenta choir capes and cassocks that operatically confirmed, had there been any doubt, the strong presence of the Roman Catholic Church in Protestant Los Angeles."[26]

Today Camarillo is no longer the outpost it was in 1939, the Edward Doheny Library is no longer the visual focus of the St. John's campus, and the books and artwork that Estelle Doheny assembled are gone. Twenty-five years after her death, the pending auction of her Gutenberg Bible and the rest of her collection by the archdiocese was announced on the front page of the *Los Angeles Times*.[27] Twenty-four million dollars' worth of books were dispersed in a half dozen auctions. Letters signed by Mark Twain and Edgar Allan Poe went on the block with woodcuts by Albrecht Dürer, Currier & Ives lithographs, Brussels tapestries, paperweights, and fans. The terms of her will allowed for the sale.

THE FINAL DAYS

The last Neff-Doheny project was a cloistered retreat for nuns called the Monastery of the Angels. When it was erected in 1948 in the pared-down Spanish colonial–revival style architects had to resort to after World War II, when craftspeople were hard to find, the Hollywood neighborhood where it stood was safe and desirable. By the 1980s, it was "dingy," the *Los Angeles Times* reported, "a cluster of frightened homes and firetrap clapboard. The monastery hides behind barbed wire, barred windows, buzzered doors and an ungodly guard dog."[28] ("It's a reminder that there's another world," Mother Mary Thomas told the reporter. "It stands as a beacon to God.")

Neff continued to consult on modifications to Doheny properties, earning nearly twenty-five thousand dollars in 1951.[29] On August 2, 1944, as Estelle Doheny worshipped in the Chester Place chapel on her sixty-ninth birthday, she suffered a hemorrhage that destroyed the sight in her left eye. Glaucoma in her right eye led to the loss of her remaining eyesight. In 1948, she sold her quarter-interest in three California oil fields for $43 million.[30] When she died in 1957 at eighty-eight, she was buried with her husband's remains in a mausoleum at the Calvary Cemetery in Whittier. Neff's proposal for a mausoleum was rejected—by whom, it is unclear—and Ross Montgomery, the architect who planned the campus of the Camarillo seminary, designed the memorial.

Airforms at the Pineapple Beach Club, St. Thomas, Virgin Islands

< CHAPTER NINETEEN >

THE BUBBLE HOUSE

The absolute absence of girders, columns, and jigsaw trusses startles the imagination.
—Airform Construction fact sheet (1970)

WALLACE NEFF HIT UPON the idea of designing a dome-shaped house sometime during 1934, while he stood at the bathroom sink shaving. "A soap bubble appeared and it held firm against my finger," he later said, "and it came to me, 'Build with air.'"[1] When an influential friend eventually presented the idea to wartime Washington officials, Neff found himself treated as an innovator with a remarkable invention.

The concept of building with air was just being explored in the 1930s, and Neff had a material that was original to the concept. As an engineer in the San Pedro shipyards during the First World War, he had built ships with pneumatically sprayed lightweight concrete. Later he used lightweight gunite to construct the Saint Elizabeth Church and grand estates like the Bourne and Berg houses in San Marino. He liked gunite's ability to harden quickly and form a strong protective layer, and he boasted that no other architect—including Richard Neutra—knew more about the material's properties.

From that moment at the sink, Neff never stopped pursuing acceptance for his idea. Ultimately, he must have hoped it would bring him the financial rewards his conventional residential structures had not. And he expressed aloud on dozens of occasions his belief that the dome house represented the pinnacle of his achievement. Nothing made him prouder.[2]

Neff's invention was unorthodox as a dwelling, for it had no right angles. His fondness for circular forms was evident in his earliest designs, where round rooms created inviting hideaways, and several of his houses were designed to conform to a semicircle. When he first devised the new dome-shaped house, he called it the Rondel, before hitting upon the more euphonious Airform. Sometimes he also called it the Bubble House. And when he designed a double version, which linked two Airforms, he dubbed it the Maidenform. He needed all the humor he could muster to help him face the criticism, for the Airform was ridiculed more often than it was praised. In his own defense, he wrote, "The exterior curved surfaces of [my] Airform buildings may look odd at first sight. However, when one realizes the advantages gained by their shape, what might have appeared odd becomes beautiful."[3]

Despite Neff's claims, the dome house form was not entirely new: it had first appeared on Southern California's horizon as a Native American dwelling called a wikiup, which to today's eye looks like an inverted basket.[4] Later, in the 1920s, when it became fashionable for buildings to mimic the shape of the products sold inside, a stucco igloo on Pico Boulevard was built to sell ice cream.[5]

Neff's own concept initially called for a collapsible, umbrella-like metal structure finished with gunite.[6]

189

Upon consideration, however, he decided that a structure that made use of its shape to carry stress was sturdier than one that depended on metal, steel, or wood, which could bend or distort. The Airform construction process began with a half sphere of rubberized nylon secured to a circular concrete floor with metal anchors. Once the balloon membrane had been tied down and braced for expansion, it could be filled with enough pressurized air to exceed the atmospheric pressure. Door and window frames could then be installed, and lightweight cement could be applied with a spray gun to a thickness of one inch. The air pressure inside had to be kept constant for twenty-four hours, until the concrete had hardened and the structure had gained enough strength to support itself. (The insertion of insulation material came later, in future Airforms.) Heavy wire mesh was laid over the concrete, then covered with pumice and foaming agents. After the form had been deflated and removed, a final coat of gunite was sprayed over the structure. Hundreds of Airforms could be built with just one rubber form. The only other equipment required was a blower, a compressor, and a spray gun.

"Reinforced concrete is known the world over for its resistance to fire, the ravages of war and the elements," Neff wrote in his notebooks as he contemplated proceeding with his research.[7] All he needed was financial assistance, for without it, he could do little but dream.

TRIAL AND ERROR

King Vidor's appetite for experimentation made him a prime candidate to become an investor. In 1937, he had founded the Directors Guild of America as he embarked on his third marriage and his second Wallace Neff–designed house.[8] He wanted to keep the budget as low as possible, he told Neff as they staked out sites for barns and chicken coops on a hilltop in Beverly Hills. Vidor had persuaded himself that redwood siding and shake roofing would result in a humble structure, for he wanted to demonstrate financial restraint. Nevertheless, his daughter Suzanne marveled at the size of the dressing rooms and closets in the new house. Built-in refrigerators and a walk-in pantry could hold enough provisions to feed every household on the hillside.

While Vidor and others stockpiled provisions and planted victory gardens, business leaders swarmed through Washington, D.C., in search of support for their war-industry schemes. Neff was in the capital during much of 1940 and 1941, preparing for the construction of the Doheny House of Studies at Catholic University. King Vidor was also in Washington, arranging a trip to Russia as an unofficial ambassador for the State Department. Over drinks, the two discussed Neff's scheme for building dome houses. The film director had friends from Hollywood who knew their way through the government maze and he offered to ask them to present the idea to various elected officials. "Spurred on by a war effort behind us," Vidor told his main contact, 20th Century Fox executive Robert Goldstein, "I would overcome each obstacle as it is presented and not move on to another one too quickly. If you know the house should be F.H.A. approved, don't let up until this has been done. If any man interferes, he is holding up the defeat of the enemy. If you can't get to see the right men, let me know and I'll send telegrams."[9]

Vidor telegrammed Jesse Jones, the secretary of commerce and longtime chairman of the Reconstruction Finance Corporation, the all-powerful agency created by Congress in 1932 to provide emergency funding to financial and industrial institutions. Jones, who was the federal loan administrator in charge of thirty-nine bureaus and agencies, including the RFC, and later seven gigantic wartime corporations, was said to have facilitated more loans than any other person in recorded history.[10] Wartime housing was just one of his responsibilities. Any American manufacturer who wanted government support during the war years had to deal with him.

The idea of developing fireproof housing with Neff's rubber form and a pneumatic air supply appealed to Jones, who ordered the Defense Housing Corporation, a subsidiary of the RFC, to construct ten Airforms in varying configurations. "Frankly," Jones wrote to Vidor on February 2, 1941, "I am not sure but what he has found the solution of low cost housing."[11] Jones also gave Neff the name of a Washington patent attorney, J. Harold Kilcoyne, who showered him with so much encouragement that the architect relied on him for the duration of his work on the Airform.[12] And while Jones's operatives searched for building sites and the National Bureau of Standards studied the thermal properties of Airform walls, the Goodyear Tire & Rubber Company in Akron, Ohio, began to manufacture the forms. Engineers had begun experimenting with a two-ply tire fabric, devising balloon forms in barrel and oblong shapes to complement Neff's original igloo shape. The vice president in charge of sales, Jack Linforth, approached one of his best customers to see whether he was interested in investing.[13] Henry Ford, who had purchased millions of Goodyear tires over the years, considered Linforth's proposal to house autoworkers in rural Ford plants in Airforms, but eventually decided against it.

While he was staying at the Mayflower Hotel in Washington, D.C., Neff corresponded with engineers at the Blue Diamond Plaster Company in Los Angeles, an organization he entrusted with doing a thorough study of the Airform's structural properties, in preparation for the manufacturing process. He also talked with Mary Pickford, who contacted him at his hotel when she was a guest at the White House. Among other things, he filled her in on the Airform project. (Pickford, who had invested in the Honeymoon Cottage, remained interested in the progress of his experimental work.) A site known as Horseshoe Hill, just outside Washington, D.C., near Falls Church, Virginia, had been selected, he told Pickford, and the Case Construction Company of San Pedro, California, would begin building the Airforms soon. Pickford agreed to take charge of decorating them.[14]

On October 20, 1941, the highly anticipated balloon form arrived from Akron. The following week, Neff wrote "first balloon shell" in his pocket notebook to commemorate the day it was inflated and sprayed with gunite.[15] Twenty-nine hours later, the form was removed from the shell. By October 30, the finished Airform was ready to be painted and furnished. Soon a village of Airforms—all of them just over twenty-three feet wide and almost twelve feet tall—was in place. Several had a double-dome configuration, with living quarters on one side and sleeping on the other. Generals, admirals, and even Jesse Jones himself came to inspect them, with the press at their heels.

"Similarly shaped houses have been lived in for years by Eskimos," *Architectural Forum* reported.[16] "The federal government is blowing up houses," the *Catholic Digest* wrote. "Mobs of people have come out to watch a radical departure in construction. Under the fine old trees, a mushroom village has sprouted. Its shells of gunite cost less than $3,000 each. It is fire-proof, bomb-splinter proof, and best of all, uses almost no critical materials."[17] *Life* sent one of its most accomplished photographers, Alfred Eisenstaedt, along with a writer who was apparently unimpressed with Neff's architectural output. "Wallace Neff has long designed pseudo this and that homes for movie tycoons," he reported. "It was one of them who interceded with Jesse Jones to get government funds for Neff's housing scheme."[18] Capitalizing on the coverage, Goodyear underwrote a two-page advertisement in *Newsweek*. "By repeating this process," the text accompanying a photo of a Falls Church Airform read, "a snug, warm and weather-tight home of four or more rooms can be quickly built."[19]

Jones greeted Neff before March of Time newsreel cameras and posed for the *Washington Post*, wielding the flat end of an axe to demonstrate the strength of an Airform's gunite. "My bank in Houston would consider a project of this kind a safe investment," he said.[20]

But with the national exposure came journalists, like *Life*'s writer, who raised tough issues. "To be commercially successful," *Architectural Forum* warned, "prefabricated houses must suit consumer tastes, and the public is not interested in igloo houses."[21] The Japanese attack on Pearl Harbor in December, however, made such aesthetic concerns seem petty, as war was imminent.

In February 1942, Jones commissioned two more Airforms to study the speed and economy of constructing a smaller version. Even in Washington's sleet and snow, they were completed down to the carpeting in eight days. The following month, though, a "housing shake-up," as Neff called it,[22] resulted in a reorganization of the Federal Loan Agency: Jones, Neff's biggest champion, who had once overseen multiple agencies, was now only responsible for the RFC, as part of his duties as secretary of commerce. Housing had become the province of someone named Blandford, whom Neff did not know.[23] He was unable to get another audience in Washington until the war was over.

He consoled himself by writing an article on the process of creating an Airform for the 1943 *Book of Knowledge* encyclopedia.[24] The chance to see his byline next to those of Nelson Rockefeller and J. Edgar Hoover was heady stuff. It must have infuriated him to discover that the credit had been given to "Walter Neff." (To make matters worse, the following year, *Double*

Indemnity's box-office success meant that for years to come, people would introduce him by that name, which was that of the film's villain.)

With the government limiting its involvement in the Airform project, Neff began searching for prospective partners. He scribbled ideas on Airform uses in notebooks—houses; powder magazines to hold explosives; evacuation huts; trailers; gas, water, and oil tanks; boats, barracks, and hangers; barns and garages. After mulling it over, King Vidor finally agreed to make an investment, although he apparently had some reservations, for he wrote to one of his lobbyists that "the patent is not worth anything unless some profit is made . . . That is the story of a thousand patents."[25] Their partnership was short-lived. Following its three-month duration, Vidor was unable to collect six thousand dollars Neff owed him. Neff's debts were mounting, as he struggled to pay his patent attorney as well.

Goodyear alone remained a war-era Airform promoter, one with enough clout to get an audience with the elusive Blandford. The chairman, Paul J. Litchfield, authorized the manufacture of synthetic rubber Airform grain-storage bins. Subterranean models were used to store gunpowder. Litchfield's connections in Washington were strong, and he convinced the federal Defense Plant Corporation to lease land from Goodyear's Southwest Cotton Company at Litchfield Park, west of Phoenix, Arizona, to build a defense plant.[26] In 1942, Airforms were erected there to house army personnel. Goodyear also had the financial resources to hire one of Neff's favorite photographers, Maynard Parker, to shoot them.

BACK IN CALIFORNIA
In the early 1940s, Los Angeles seemed like the ideal place for an inventor with an idea for inexpensive housing. Between 1930 and 1940, when the city added a

quarter of a million inhabitants, its growth was second only to that of New York.[27] Demand for defense-worker housing led developers to brag that "it wasn't a question of selling the houses, it was just a matter of getting them up."[28] Communities like Mar Vista and North Hollywood were created almost overnight to house the workers who manufactured some of the fifty thousand warplanes President Roosevelt had called for building in the "great arsenal of democracy."[29]

With his debts hovering in the five figures, Neff courted the war industries.[30] Bathing-suit manufacturer Cole of California, which was in the parachute business during the war, underwrote the construction of a small Airform to serve as a bomb shelter for its employees. Instead of rubber, it was made of cotton and muslin. "We need houses quickly," Neff told the *Los Angeles Times*, "and this way we can make them out of materials that are not needed as badly as what we call critical materials, such as nails, wire, lumber for studding, and shingles."[31]

The largest Airform ever built, sponsored by Cole of California, nearly did not make it to completion, because it collapsed twice during construction. *Engineering News Record* reported "a crash that shook the surrounding neighborhood."[32] The thirty-two-foot-high, hundred-foot-diameter dome, meant to serve as a laundry room, was three times as large as the average Airform, and its size increased the risk of distortion and movement.

Neff faulted the contractor for spraying the concrete from the bottom up instead of the top down. "At no time did the structure collapse," he declared after the dome was finally built. "The cause of our trouble has been traced to one source. The air-proofing compound rotted the canvas form, preventing the maintaining of the required air pressure of 1 ½ ounces per square inch. A new form was built and performed perfectly. Due to the difficulty of analyzing the stresses in a dome where

large openings are cut out, the City Building Department required a load test before issuing the final permit."[33] The structure withstood a forty-seven-ton load.[34]

The president of Loyola University wrote to Neff the day he read of the catastrophe, telling him that the school, which had planned to build a village of Airform houses, would still move forward with them. In fact, the only Airforms erected in Los Angeles during the war years were for Loyola and Cole of California. Neff blamed the press coverage of the dome collapse for his inability to find backers.

To compensate for the perceived aesthetic limitations of the domes, Neff designed a form that was less igloo-like, flattening the roof and creating more floor space. In his continuing search for benefactors, he wrote to Henry J. Kaiser after he met the steel industrialist in a restaurant. Kaiser was making a fortune building suburban subdivisions, and he was so highly regarded in Southern California that he had been selected by the American Broadcasting Company to give a radio speech on the crisis in postwar housing on New Year's Day in 1946. He may have been a visionary, but unfortunately there was no land in his scheme for a subdivision of Airforms.

Neff tried to sell military decision makers on his grand dream of creating military bases made from pneumatic forms, and he succeeded in receiving approval from the air force, army, navy, and army corps of engineers.[35] He also hired professional publicists to circulate a 1949 report by the Army Corps of Engineers[36] that concluded that Airforms were relatively quick and inexpensive to construct and could be made of noncritical materials.[37] The promotional materials neglected to mention what the army did not find so appealing—the shape of the dome, a perceived inefficiency in the use of floor space, and unattractive interior concrete walls.

In other countries, however, aesthetic concerns

had not stopped progress. Neff traveled to Rio de Janeiro in 1947 to watch Airforms being built in poor neighborhoods and to Cairo in 1949 to receive a proclamation from Egypt's King Farouk for a housing project erected in the king's troubled country. Workers building the Benguela Railroad, Angola's only connection to the South African railway network, were housed in Airforms built in 1949. The next year, a mining company in South Africa built Airforms to house its workers—quite a step up, Neff told people, from the huts they had been living in. (He sent the photographs to *Life*.) Neff added officers' housing in Karachi, Pakistan, to his resumé in 1953, and five-hundred-ton grain-storage Airform depots in Amman, Jordan, in 1954. In 1956, the *New York Times* reported on massive, 73,600-gallon Airform wine vats built by the Portuguese government.[38] (Neff claimed that French chemists had pronounced that wine stored in gunite vats was superior to wine stored more conventionally.) American financier Daniel Ludwig considered building Airforms in the Bahamas to store provisions for his fleet of ships the following year, and *Time* published Airform houses built for noncommissioned officers of the French army in Senegal, French West Africa, in 1958.[39] (Twelve hundred were constructed in all.)[40]

Mexico could not top the thousand Airforms the Brazilian government had bought near Rio de Janeiro, but it had made a start: in 1947, a Mexico City school composed of seven Airforms was painted by muralist Diego Rivera, and around the same time, a twenty-nine-foot-wide pneumatic form was constructed to house a bar and restaurant on the Avenue Insurgentes. Because Airforms built in Mexico had an unusually large number of windows, they were well lighted and looked more modern than any Airforms previously constructed. Perhaps it was no coincidence that it was in Mexico that Neff finally came to terms with modernism. He became friendly with Manuel Reachi, a the-

atrical agent who managed the career of the acclaimed comedian Don Mario Moreno ("Cantinflas"). Reachi and Neff discussed building an Airform that would meld conventional and pneumatic construction, but Reachi failed to follow through with promised Airform ventures in the Caribbean, Mexico, and Venezuela.

By 1953, such frustrations, and the expense of patent renewals, led Neff to lease his world licensing rights for five thousand dollars a year to the Eastern United Company in New York, which had built the Airforms in Pakistan.[41] Under the new venture, which was called the Airform International Construction Corporation, an architect considered to be a leader of the second generation of the International style redesigned the Airform. Neff was convinced that his long-awaited financial breakthrough had finally come.

NEW SHAPES AND NEW DISAPPOINTMENTS

Eliot Noyes had labored as a draftsman for Walter Gropius and Marcel Breuer after studying under them at Harvard.[42] In 1940, on Gropius's recommendation, he had become director of the department of industrial design at the Museum of Modern Art and seven years later had gone into private practice as an architect, designing gas stations and office buildings. His cylindrical Mobil Oil pump was used at nineteen thousand gas stations.[43] Noyes was also responsible for the design of the IBM Selectric typewriter, still admired half a century later, and IBM's 1964 aerospace headquarters in the Westchester district of Los Angeles.

He had an eye for simple, unpretentious forms, and his prototype for a revised Airform structure was praised by *Time*: "Beautiful Bubbles," the magazine called it.[44] Sliced open at the sides to let in light and air, the form expanded. By flattening the top of the

Airform village in West Africa, where local crews of five men could build a house in two days

The largest Airform ever built, in Vernon, California: thirty-two feet tall and a hundred feet in diameter

One of several Airforms constructed by the Goodyear Tire & Rubber Company near Phoenix, Arizona, in 1943

bubble, Noyes created a profile that was more in keeping with that of a conventional, flat-roofed house. The sixty-foot-long dwelling was influenced by the work of Italy's Pier Luigi Nervi, who was at the height of his fame and had used the ideas of Neff and others to create breathtaking public buildings throughout the world. The sculptural qualities of the Noyes Airform put it in a league with designs by Louis Kahn and Eero Saarinen.

In 1954, two Noyes-designed bubble houses were built in Hobe Sound, Florida, twenty miles north of Palm Beach. As it had been in Washington, D.C., in 1941, the hope was that the publicity the construction generated would bring new commissions. For several months in 1954, Noyes and Airform International met with a Minneapolis school district to formulate a plan to build bubble-shaped schools. In the end, however, the district decided against it.

The following year, Neff terminated his agreement with Airform International Construction, which was now insolvent,[45] and leased the rights to a man he referred to in his records as simply "Waterval." His relationship with Waterval was even less rewarding (Neff was never able to collect the ten-thousand-dollar fee owed to him),[46] and subsequent partnerships yielded equally unsatisfying results.

By the end of Dwight Eisenhower's presidency in 1960, Washington, D.C., had become so densely populated that the original Airform village in Falls Church appeared to be doomed; there was talk of building a new residential or commercial project on the large site. Worried, Neff wrote to *Architectural Forum* that he had conducted an informal poll of Falls Church residents and that the majority wanted to continue living in their Airform dwellings. The residents formed an association, but they were only able to fight off the development for a short time, and the following year the project was demolished.[47] John Elliott, Neff's friend and one of his investors, went to Falls Church to witness the destruction. "The crane operator was amazed at their strength," he later told Neff. "Jackhammers had to be used to break the concrete after a crane with a steel ball simply bounced off the surface."[48]

PASADENA AIRFORM

Neff's efforts to preserve the village in Washington, D.C., may have been in vain, but two Airforms closer to home promised him a better chance at immortality. In 1946, his mother had finally provided financial support, for two of her sons were lobbying for an Airform. Three-quarters of the sixteen-thousand-dollar cost of the Airform built on Los Robles Avenue in Pasadena had been underwritten by Nannie Neff. The remainder had come from Andrew Neff, the intended occupant.

Blowing up a structure with air in a quiet residential community of period-revival houses had been as unprecedented as the erection of Neutra's steel-framed Lovell House on a Griffith Park hillside in 1929. "There was a lot of objection to our building it at first," Neff recalled. "They said it wouldn't hold up, that it would ruin the neighborhood."[49]

The *Pasadena Star-News* had dispatched a reporter to cover the event, and the paper had not been disappointed. Neff had been experimenting with proportions of sand and water, because a new method of steel-bar reinforcement merited, he felt, a heavier mix. Reporter, architect, and spectators had stood by in shock as the Airform collapsed.[50] Back at the drawing board, a Caltech engineer had come up with a variation on the formula, and after another collapse, the Airform had gone up successfully. Eleven tons of sand—thirty pounds per square foot of dome—had been mounted in a load test ordered by the city.

"On the morning of the following day," John Elliott said, Neff told him with "distinct pleasure" that "the collapsed form was removed and the concrete dome was found to have actually risen in spite of the substantial weight of the load test."[51] In fact, the Caltech test had found that the center of the dome had fallen .022 inches, but it had risen .025 inches after the temperature in the room increased by twenty degrees. The city issued a certificate of occupancy.

The dome was thirty-two feet wide, forty-two feet long, twelve feet high, an inch and a half thick at the top, and three inches thick at the base. (Neff said that its windows, which were on the east, were a modern touch, and in fact, the structure did have the feeling of a streamline moderne apartment.) In the spring of 1947, the cover of the *Los Angeles Times Home Magazine* had displayed the house's rose-colored walls and chartreuse-and-white floral draperies under the headline "Outwitting Mars."[52]

Because Neff had reshaped the structure into an elliptical form, the dome did not bear as close a resemblance to an igloo as those in the village in Washington did. But try as he might to make the Airform appear more conventional, it "did not fit in with the way people wanted to live," his associate engineer George Brandow remarked.[53] Andrew Neff did what he could to appease neighbors, planting a hedge around the house. It was not an easy sell when it went on the market decades later, in 1982. And when the second owner wanted to sell it in 1991, he had to wait years for a buyer to materialize (despite bizarre claims made in the sales literature that Elvis Presley and Mahatma Gandhi had both come to see the structure).[54] "This place is a wonder of modern science," the owner, Randy Nerenberg, said with pride in 1985, after putting fifty thousand dollars into improvements. "I am emotionally attached to it. It was a trick to replaster these curved walls."[55]

"It is small," his wife, Marilyn, complained several years later, after their first child was born, "and we need a dehumidifier to remove the moisture which gets trapped inside the house and creates condensation on the walls."[56]

Around the same time Neff's mother financed the Bubble House in Pasadena, there had been talk of building Airform gasoline-storage tanks for the Atlantic Richfield Company, but it had proved to be just that. However, Neff had managed to persuade Mrs. Thomas Ince, his landlady, to underwrite an experimental Airform on a hill in South Pasadena, where tastes ran to the same styles as those in Pasadena. Louise Neff and Phyllis, young Wallace, and Arthur lived in the dome from about 1948 to 1955. After the grown children moved out, Louise had it to herself.

Neff continued to believe that the Airform was an essential part of the body of his work, but he acknowledged that it was also an engineering feat, and as such, it eventually became obsolete. (One of his draftsmen observed, "When you design something that is always the same, that is mass production. It is not architecture.")[57] By the mid-1960s, he had allowed his Airform patents in Costa Rica, Pakistan, Jordan, Cuba, Indonesia, Nicaragua, and Spain to lapse, although he renewed the patents in Mexico, Italy, Syria, Tunisia, Egypt, Portugal, Israel, Venezuela, and Japan.

Monitoring patents for seven configurations of Airforms in more than a dozen countries was time-consuming and expensive. In some nations, if a construction project was not in the works, the patent automatically expired. In others, where there was a project for which he was to earn ten cents in royalties per square foot of floor area, it was impossible to determine just how many structures had been built. "A patent isn't [worth] much unless you have four or five patents on one subject to make it worthwhile," Neff admitted years later. "The minute you start, of course, somebody is trying to swipe what you've got. A patent lawyer once told me, 'Don't worry about patents. That's the mistake everybody makes. They try to patent so fast, nobody else can do it. If

LEFT: *Interior of Andrew Neff's Airform in Pasadena*
BOTTOM: *Interior of a Goodyear-funded Airform in Litchfield Park, Arizona*

you have something good, why, go out and sell it.'"[58]

By 1969, when all the patents but one had expired and Airforms were only being built in two countries, Neff received a letter from J. Harold Kilcoyne, the patent attorney he had retained early on. Kilcoyne kindly suggested that the Airform had served its purpose during the years in which the concrete shell structure was coming into vogue. It was his diplomatic way of conveying the idea that the Airform was one for the books.

Much later, after pneumatic architecture had become interesting to scholars, Neff was considered an influential figure,[59] although the noted engineering historian Mario Salvadori gave an Italian architect credit for the most economical and ingenious pneumatic building method, in which reinforcing bars and concrete were installed before the structure was inflated.[60] The Bini dome, which varied from twenty-five to three hundred feet in span, was built in twenty-three countries, yet like Neff, its inventor, Dr. Dante Bini, found that America was reluctant to embrace it.

"I always thought people would come rushing in by the thousands to buy [Airform] houses," Neff remarked in a 1977 interview, "but it never happened."[61] His chuckle put to rest any question of bitterness. Apparently he had made his peace with the fate of the Airform.

The 1935 Garner House in San Marino, remodeled in 1953 for another Neff client, Robert Hutchins

< CHAPTER TWENTY >

WE MOVED THERE BECAUSE
YOU COULD SMELL ORANGE BLOSSOMS

It was big and still, one of those white elephants crazy movie people built in the crazy twenties.
—William Holden, *Sunset Boulevard*

It had been the residence of a famous star of the silent films and it was one of those enormous, neo-Spanish
haciendas that had successfully extracted from Spanish architecture all that was ugly and depressing.
—Alan Jay Lerner

$\mathcal{B}$Y 1950, THE GOLDEN ERA of the American film industry was over, and so, it appeared to some, was the golden era of Wallace Neff. Gone were the film industry titans like Louis B. Mayer and Darryl F. Zanuck who had helped build the architect's reputation. Billy Wilder immortalized the public distaste for the pretentious period-revival mansions so many of the stars had lived in when he set *Sunset Boulevard* in a 1920s-era, Mediterranean-style behemoth. "It was one of those big houses in the ten thousand block of Sunset," William Holden intoned in the voice-over. The house in the film was actually on Wilshire Boulevard, but it appeared to be on the same block of Sunset as Neff's grand Haldemann House.

King Vidor came face-to-face with the widespread disdain for period revivalism when he set out to film a television documentary at Marion Davies's old estate and discovered that its Spanish elements had all been removed. "There was literally nothing left to photograph," he lamented.[1]

Nineteen-fifties architects and clients saw the old mansions as caverns of gloom that epitomized a bygone, materialistic era. The desire for steel and glass (among those who could afford architects) or ranch style (by those who moved to suburbia) put Neff's estates, and thus his reputation, on the line. One after another, the Bourne, Barlow, Culver, Gillette, Post,

Petitfils, and Pickfair estates were demolished to make way for freeways, subdivided, or donated to religious or educational institutions. The once grand Up de Graff House in Altadena was ignominiously converted into an apartment building. Updating Estelle Doheny's aging properties helped to keep Neff's practice afloat (although her 410-acre ranch on the western boundary of the city had been sold to developers for $6 million, for Los Angeles was experiencing a building boom on a par with those of the 1880s and 1920s).

Astute Los Angeles home owners turned to the *Los Angeles Times Home Magazine*, which avoided the breathy celebrities-and-recipes format of other Sunday magazines in favor of lifestyle and design advice. Esther McCoy's July 19, 1953, article on residential architecture, for instance, explored the careers of Richard Neutra, the Greene brothers, Frank Lloyd Wright, and Rudolph Schindler. An advocate of Southern California's modernists, McCoy wore blinders when it came to the subject of period-revival architecture. Scorning "picture book Spanish" architects, she announced in her article that she was relieved that "the Spanish fever had abated" but was perturbed that Spanish houses still stood on city streets and hillsides, their "bowed picture windows framed with canvas draperies of no earthly use."[2]

With most of the period-revival architects

deceased and unable to defend themselves, and Californians content to embrace the good life as seen through floor-to-ceiling plate-glass windows, McCoy's architectural authority went unchallenged. In 1965, two gregarious young college professors who worshipped her every word inherited her mantle: David Gebhard and Robert Winter published *A Guide to Architecture in Southern California*, which took up where McCoy left off in glorifying modern design at the expense of period revivalism.[3] Forty of Richard Neutra's projects rated inclusion in the guide, while Wallace Neff rated only three (none of which were Airforms, despite their inventiveness and ties to modernism).

The growing disregard for his accomplishments concerned Neff, but his dwindling commissions were a more pressing concern. "Wallace was not building houses at the rate he had before the war," his friend John Elliott remarked, "and he may have thought of himself as becoming passé."[4] He needed a comeback as dramatic as Gloria Swanson's in landing the *Sunset Boulevard* role.

Neff did the only thing he could think to do, producing and distributing a three-page mimeographed leaflet describing himself as "one of the few native architects practicing in the Los Angeles area" and "born on the McNally Ranch." Just as important, to his mind, was being the grandson of Andrew McNally, "one of the early settlers here from Chicago, Illinois."[5] He began his list of clients with Douglas Fairbanks Sr., Fairbanks's son Douglas Jr., and Mark Pickford—actors, he need not have pointed out, of another day. In between allusions to the nineteenth century and movie-star mansions was mention of the Airform. "Wallace Neff is the inventor of the AIRFORM system of Pneumatic construction," the fourth paragraph began. "AIRFORM houses have been built in over fifteen foreign countries. Mr. Neff is a director and Chairman of the Board of Pneumatic International, Inc."

Neff had also begun devoting his time to entering competitions for buildings on college campuses. Just after the war, he had submitted a scheme for Loyola Law School that was free of ornament and decidedly modern.[6] It was not chosen. At Pomona College in Claremont, he had won the competition to design a gym and an addition to the student union in 1950,[7] and in a show of good politics, had written to the president saying he was anxious to design other projects at Pomona.

Resurrecting his Spanish idiom to fit pared-down schemes, he had won competitions to design the Sullivan and Huesman residence halls at Loyola University in 1948, as well as a three-hundred-thousand-dollar gymnasium, which the school claimed was the largest in the Western Athletic Conference.[8] The dormitories had none of the elements that have provided scale and texture in Mediterranean design since the Renaissance—ironwork, light fixtures, or cast stone—but they were appealing because of their semicircular chapels. To make the buildings appear less institutional, Neff had added faux chimneys, overcoming the limited budget to create the best postwar buildings on the campus.

School construction was booming in the San Fernando Valley by the mid-1950s. Appearing before the Los Angeles Board of Education in 1957, Neff sought the commission to design a school in Van Nuys with his draftsman Peter Liszt. "We got the job!" he exclaimed to draftsman Henry Wesley later that year, and they went to work designing an elementary school on Bassett Street.[9]

As it became clear that Neff could adapt to the new preference for casual outdoor living and open floor plans, residential commissions once again began to come his way. His postwar style resembled what David Gebhard called "soft modernism."[10] The one-story structures maintained a closer connection with their

Bassett Street Elementary School

surroundings than his grand 1920s estates had. Glass opened the interiors to natural light, walls came down, and orange-and-yellow partitions went up. Bright Mexican colors were brushed over beams. Neutra's modernist insistence on a house-garden pavilion in which the outdoors became an extension of the dwelling entered Neff's vocabulary, and he used sliding-glass doors as often in remodeling his older residences as he did in new projects. Asked to describe the style, he called it "Spanish contemporary."[11]

It was difficult for Neff to make a profit on a commission because he was so detail-oriented that he repeatedly sent draftsmen back to the boards. "He was never in a rush," his draftsman Jorge de Mattos observed. "We even drew details in full size."[12]

"If he got an idea in his head," John Elliott said, "you couldn't tell him it was impractical."[13]

He sent out his correspondence in longhand when he could not find a sufficiently attractive young woman to type his documents. In 1955, he hired a lovely coed from Immaculate Heart College who had answered his classified ad to do part-time work. She described the office as "a spare little place with a few nice antique chairs," adding that "the great excitement of each day was Conrad Hilton's telephone call announcing he was coming by in his Cadillac convertible to take Mr. Neff to lunch. They practiced their Spanish at El Coyote on Beverly Boulevard when they weren't having lunch at the Brown Derby in Los Feliz."[14]

The young woman, Gloria Ricci Lothrop, went on to become a leading California historian. Her impression of an office in dire need of dusting was shared by the dry cleaner on the ground floor, Irwin Gellman, who remembered seeing the Marx brothers trudging up the stairs to Neff's second-floor office, which didn't even have a doorman. "I said to Wallace, 'Why don't you get an office on the ground floor, or move to a building with an elevator?' Gellman recalled. "But he never tried to impress anyone with who he was. Franklin Avenue remained his headquarters."[15]

The striptease artist Lili St. Cyr was apparently undeterred by the modest office, arriving with a retinue of male bodyguards to enlist Neff's architectural talents. She admired his new Chandler House on the perimeter of the Wilshire Country Club, she told him, and she wanted one like it in the Hollywood Hills. Explaining that it was not a house for a hillside site, Neff added politely that he could not accommodate any new clients for five years. His son Arthur later speculated that St. Cyr's career of exposing more of herself than was considered decent had made her persona non grata with his father. "He didn't take a job unless he liked the people," De Mattos confirmed, noting that Neff had also turned away the singer Ricky Nelson and his young wife, even though it would have meant a good commission. He was aging, and his tolerance for the young and the unorthodox was decreasing. He also rejected prospective clients with dreams of updating the kitchens and bathrooms of the grand houses he

Living room, Robert Hutchins House

had designed thirty years earlier, sending them to Clifford Hoskins, who had helped design them in the first place. Others who wanted ornate houses with mansard roofs were referred to another former draftsman, Caspar Ehmcke, who was making a name for himself as a residential architect.

For the more esteemed rich and famous—in his eyes, anyway—Neff took on the smallest of projects, in the hope that larger commissions would follow. He installed a vault in Conrad Hilton's corporate office and remodeled the office of tire scion Leonard Firestone.[16] The retired chancellor of the University of Chicago, Robert Hutchins, bought Neff's 1935 Garner House in 1954, and the architect and academic were seen cruising through San Marino, scrutinizing new construction as they planned to remodel Hutchins's house. Stopping at a Virginia Road construction site, they discovered that a structural engineer Neff often consulted, George Brandow, had chosen another architect, Calvin Straub, to design his own house.[17] The post-and-beam structure epitomized a new stylistic movement in Pasadena and was a reminder to Neff that younger architects were winning the commissions that were no longer offered to him because of his age.

Movie-theater architect S. Charles Lee sent Neff three clients during the 1950s, including one whose ties to the Chicago underworld might have scared Neff if the client had not redeemed his reputation with philanthropy. Neff's draftsmen claimed that the slate on the exterior of the 1953 John and Rella Factor House was installed to shield the family from stray bullets. It was a good story, but in truth the predominant material was glass.

Art collector Anna Bing Arnold complained that Neff "did not express any originality" when he designed a house for her and her husband, Aerol, in Beverly Hills in 1957, but it could be that she resented his lack of enthusiasm for contemporary art.[18] Draftsmen in

Neff's office believed he lost interest in the project after she expressed dissatisfaction with it. "I think he enjoyed every house," Peter Liszt said, "but if the relationship with the client soured, everything soured."[19]

In 1954, the Southern California Chapter of the American Institute of Architects presented Neff with an honor award for a project with the same shallowly pitched gable roof and towering chimney he had been using on houses since the beginning of his career. The Myrtle Hornstein House also used the slatted-eave configuration that modernist architects favored. (The *Los Angeles Examiner* described its appearance as "Swiss Modern.")[20] Always savvy to the publicity an award could provide, Neff sent photographs of the house to editors of various national publications.

After *Time* magazine published its favorable review of the Noyes Airform prototype in 1953, Neff's confidence soared and he actually attended the national conference of the AIA in Minneapolis in June of 1955. He had another reason to attend as well: his design of a chapel for a Jesuit retreat in Azusa, east of Pasadena, was being recognized with an AIA award of merit.[21] Using the balustraded cornice of a building on the expansive grounds as his inspiration, Neff had designed a thirty-by-forty-foot, white-brick-faced structure capped with its own balustrade and a crucifix. Inside, dark beams twenty-five feet above the nave reflected the glow of light fixtures. Altar appointments were made of the same dark, oiled wood, except for a gilded figure of Christ on a golden oak cross. Manresa, as the chapel was called, was built with funds donated by Conrad Hilton. Architects win awards on the strength of the photographs of their buildings, and Neff had been able to recruit one of the best to photograph Manresa—his friend Shirley Burden. The image that helped Neff capture the award was of Manresa's double entry doors and the round window overhead with a dove enfolded in a cut-glass sunburst.

The following year, when the AIA notified Neff that he had been nominated to become a fellow of the organization, he responded that he would attend "with great pleasure" when the organization convened at the Biltmore Hotel in Los Angeles on the evening of May 17, 1956.[22] He accepted with the dignified shyness he displayed before crowds, yet his pride was apparent.

Another ecclesiastical project presented itself around the same time, and while it only offered him a modest three-thousand-dollar fee, it provided the opportunity to collaborate with one of California's finest visual artists, the multifaceted Millard Sheets. Sheets had become as well known as a regional artist as Neff had as a regional architect. The public knew Sheets for his mosaic murals on Home Savings and Loan branch banks, and collectors sought his watercolors of Depression-era Los Angeles, which evoked the desultory mood of the time as effectively as Edward Hopper's work had on the East Coast.

It was Sheets's mosaic skills that were sought for the Precious Blood Catholic Church in Los Angeles's Westlake neighborhood. Built in the Italian Romanesque style in 1926 with funds from the Forthmann family, it was unusually austere for a Catholic church. The Forthmanns lived a block away in a Tudor-style house Neff had designed for them a quarter of a century before, when the area was quietly residential. Since then, Los Angeles's population boom had changed the area from a neighborhood of single-family houses to one dominated by apartment buildings.

The commission to remodel the church was one of the few in his career where Neff found himself limited to making engineering and structural decisions, for the intent was to focus congregants' attention on Sheets's gilt murals and the tile mosaics executed by Venetian artisans. The J. V. McNeil Construction Company, which had built Neff's Doheny Library and had worked frequently with the archdiocese, oversaw

Manresa, a chapel for a Jesuit retreat in Azusa, honored with an American Institute of Architects award of merit

the project.[23] Neff's structural engineer George E. Brandow also participated. The Forthmanns had made a fortune producing White King soap, so they could afford the best.

After the church was completed, Sheets left on a study tour of Japan with a group of students that happened to include a Neff client, Groucho Marx's new wife. Young Eden Hartford Marx, an aspiring artist, hoped to avoid comparisons with Groucho's former wives by commissioning a new house, thereby removing him from the place where his previous wives had resided.

ONE LAUGH AFTER ANOTHER

Neff had met Groucho's brother Herbert in the 1930s, when Herbert was considered the handsomest and least funny member of the family. His stage names, Zeppo and Blando, were meant to convey his humorlessness. When it became clear that Zeppo was a better businessman than performer, he left the act to manage his siblings' careers. By the time Groucho and Eden were in the market for a house, Zeppo was seeking a "sexy" new residence for his own family.[24] Gummo Marx, aka Milton, was also shopping for houses, in both Los Angeles and Palm Springs. Harpo (Arthur or Adolph) wanted one in the desert. Chico (Leonard) was so hooked on cards that his wife was afraid to build a house, for fear Chico would lose it at the tables.[25]

Gummo and Zeppo took it upon themselves to negotiate a deal with an architect to design new houses for all of them (except the undependable Chico), and somehow, they found their way to Neff's office on Franklin Avenue. Mrs. Harpo (Susan) Marx had another architect in mind, but after Neff agreed to a discounted rate for multiple commissions, she went along with the rest of them. "It didn't matter to me," she said thirty years later, laughing. "Gummo and Zeppo were great

TOP: *The Groucho Marx House, Trousdale Estates, 1956*
BOTTOM: *Master bedroom at the Groucho Marx House*

Living room, Groucho Marx House

people to manage the family's direction."[26]

Harpo wanted to build in the desert where he intended to retire and play golf, but Thunderbird, the only country club there, would not accept Jews. "Golfers were pouring into the desert," his wife recalled. "When we learned that Lou Halper [a developer who was investing in land throughout Riverside County] was building a club called Tamarisk that accepted Jews, we waited until the perimeter roads were graded before purchasing eight acres opposite the fourteenth hole."

They asked Neff for a ranch-style house spacious enough to accommodate a harp, a growing collection of fine art, four boisterous children, golf carts, and a room with a curved bar. "We sank our own well and reveled in the purity of the water after the doctored water of the city," Susan Marx said. "We 'city folk' adapted instantly to country life. Each child had a horse, and Harpo had more dogs running around than he ever dreamed of. Mr. Neff gave us exactly what we wanted."[27]

At a party convened to show off El Rancho Harpo in 1956, rain trickled down a soffit and onto the dining room table. Groucho was upset, despite his brother's insistence that the building contractor was to blame, and when he returned to Los Angeles he took it upon himself to confront the architect. When Groucho arrived, Neff demonstrated how rain drains from the roof of a house into gutters and down spouts, with fascia board and projecting eaves protecting the structure. Adjustments were being made, Neff said. Finally Groucho began making jokes—"he said he had been brought up in the gutter," Neff recalled, "so more gutters wouldn't bother him"—and the architect was relieved.[28]

Neff announced publicly that working with Groucho had provided one laugh after another, but his draftsmen resented the high-handedness of the star of *You Bet Your Life*. Groucho hired the least costly of four contractors and balked at paying a 10 percent architect's commission amounting to $11,800. Neff agreed to take a thousand dollars off his fee. There wasn't a secretary in the office half the time, anyway, he rationalized. The draftsmen, pinched time-wise already because of the secretarial work that inevitably fell to them, took their revenge on Eden and the rest of the Marx wives. When one of them called and introduced herself as Mrs. Marx, the draftsman who had answered the phone would respond, "Which Mrs. Marx?" Then he would put the unsuspecting woman on hold and he and the other draftsmen, who considered themselves comedians, would burst out laughing. Had he known, Neff would have squelched the practice.

In 1956, Groucho and Eden built in Trousdale Estates on the site of the former Doheny ranch, where the developer Paul W. Trousdale had carved 539 lots for a subdivision. Their house had the same configuration as the rest of the houses Neff built for the Marx brothers: radiating from a core that housed the living and dining room were wings that held bedrooms, a garage, and a kitchen. (Calvin Straub had used this pinwheel scheme for the Brandow House, and Neff may have found it to his liking when he dropped by the construction site.)

Groucho's house epitomized the aesthetic of Los Angeles's Westside in the 1950s, where there were as many Greco-Roman houses with crushed rock roofs as there were Hawaiian-French houses shielded by banana trees. The facade, with its curved terra-cotta painted white and laid up in a screen effect, may have appeared costly, but it wasn't, and the two Chryslers in the open carport had been provided by the sponsor of Groucho's television show.

The house's imitation stone walls and hanging globe lights are once again in vogue, but because the house has a flat roof—and therefore flat ceilings—it has none of the warmth of Harpo's, with its gable roof. Harpo's plan has a definite axis, and the balance and

The Eaton House in Hope Ranch, north of Santa Barbara

exposed living room ceiling beams provide a peace Groucho's house lacks, for Neff was not inspired when asked to design a flat roof, regardless of whether the client was a celebrity.

FAMILY MATTERS

Whenever Neff could use the Spanish idiom he enjoyed so much, his work benefited. While providing his design review talents to the Forest Lawn Memorial-Parks & Mortuaries at the Hill of Sinai, where he judged competition entries for new chapels and mausoleums, he discovered that the son of the founder was seeking an architect for a Spanish-style house. Roy Eaton was retiring from his position as vice president in charge of maintenance and construction to move with his wife, Dorothy, to the Hope Ranch residential development north of Santa Barbara. The house Neff designed in early 1962 proved to be the finest of his late career. It was enlivened by brightly painted walls and large expanses of floor-to-ceiling glass.

Nannie Neff, who died in 1959 at the age of ninety-five

By the spring of 1962, however, family matters began to take precedence over professional ones. Neff's parents had long since died, his mother in 1959 at the age of ninety-five.[29] Survived by five children and four grandchildren, she had been generous with them all, although Neff, his son Arthur believed, had received the lion's share of her affection. Edwin Neff's earlier death in 1943, at the age of eighty-three, had been reported in an editorial in the *Pasadena Star-News.* ("Warmhearted," the paper had described him, "the oldest living former president of the Pasadena Tournament of Roses.")[30]

Neff's brother Bill died in his sleep on April 24, 1962, not long after he attended the dedication of La Mirada's Andrew McNally Junior High School. (Neff had visited him at Whittier's Presbyterian Hospital just before his heart gave out at the age of fifty-eight.) And John Neff died twelve years later, separated from his wife and estranged from his family. His daughter, Naneen Boot, was Neff's only niece, and there were no nephews. Adelia "Della" Neff, Neff's sister, had lived demurely at her mother's side, and for her devotion and unblemished behavior she was granted the right to live the rest of her life in the beautiful house on Orange Grove.[31]

Neff's wife, Louise, held on to her title as Mrs. Wallace Neff.[32] Raising their three children with her husband's limited presence, she was as firm as her nonconfrontational nature allowed. If there was any issue that united the estranged couple, it was concern for the future of their daughter, Phyllis, who had suffered emotional damage after the death of a suitor in the Battle of the Bulge. She had finished a course in decorative arts offered by the New York School of Interior Design in 1952, but had not pursued a career, and her use of alcohol had become worrisome.[33] (Nannie Neff tried to keep the key to her liquor cabinet on a string around her neck, even when family members came to call; Neff's consumption was always judicious, but two of his three brothers were known imbibers.)[34] Phyllis had been persuaded to work in her father's architectural office in 1955, in the hope that the discipline of a routine would improve her morale. When she decided to have a rhinoplasty the same year, her father had given his wholehearted support, for she had, after all, inherited his proboscis. Following surgery, bruised but minus the bandages, Phyllis had met him at Scandia, where he asked one of his draftsmen who was dining with them to tell her how nice she looked.[35] A short time later, she moved to San Francisco and then to Honolulu, where her expenses were paid by Aunt Della and the family. On March 23, 1962, less than a year after settling in Honolulu, Phyllis Neff died from complications of alcoholism, at thirty-seven.[36]

The emotional toll on her father was evident to his clients Rosalinde and Arthur Gilbert, who were building a house in Beverly Hills's Coldwater Canyon. In fact, Rosalinde Gilbert expressed the opinion that in the aftermath of Phyllis's death, the Gilberts did not receive the full extent of Neff's talents. "Mr. Neff could not supervise the construction of our house because he was brokenhearted about the death of his daughter, whose body he had to claim in Hawaii, and then the death of his brother," she said. "He did not want [to be paid] for what he had done for us, but my husband insisted."[37]

In a quest for peace and fulfillment, Neff tried to distance himself from work with Spanish lessons, photography, and travel. He studied Judaism and Buddhism and began meditating. He contacted friends like Garrett Van Pelt, an architect who had not designed a building in twenty years. (Suddenly Van Pelt found the AIA at his doorstep, urging him to apply for a fellowship, at Neff's suggestion.) Around this time, two writing projects became as important to Neff as his Airform. One was a thesis on scale and proportion in

Phyllis Neff with her father, circa 1955

the built environment. The other was his own personal account of his career.

Neff's picture as it appeared on the dust jacket of his 1964 book, Architecture of Southern California

RAND MCNALLY REDUX

Neff's first cousin Harry Clow had become an executive at Rand McNally in Chicago after he finished college. Like his grandfather before him, Clow headed for California once Chicago's temperatures dropped in the winter months. He and his wife would journey to La Quinta Resort in Palm Springs, then on to Pasadena for the Tournament of Roses. They usually called on Nannie Neff, who served them tea sandwiches from a three-tiered tray, while they all speculated on the choice of flowers for the Rand McNally float that was inevitably entered in the parade. When it passed by the house early on New Year's Day, the assembled Neffs and Clows watched from the second-story loggia.

Another of Nannie's nephews, Andrew McNally III, had assumed the presidency of Rand McNally in 1948. He was attentive to her as well, for not even his father, Andrew II, could remember the founders of Rand McNally the way Nannie could. Familial goodwill could vanish as quickly as profits, however, a discovery Neff made when he journeyed to Illinois in an attempt to persuade his cousins to publish a book documenting his body of work.

From Neff's perspective, there was no question that Rand McNally was the appropriate publisher for such a book. In the executive offices in Skokie, where Rand McNally had been based since leaving downtown Chicago in 1952, Neff's proposition was considered and found wanting. It would be unprecedented for Rand McNally to publish a book on architecture, Clow and McNally insisted, and a run of a thousand hardcover volumes documenting buildings in California was too small a job for their phalanx of presses. Travel was their specialty: they printed millions of airline tickets

each year, along with maps and atlases and (still, after all these years) train tickets. They also published general-interest books, such as Thor Heyerdahl's 1947 best seller *Kon-Tiki*, but architecture was too narrow a category to provide a market.

Nonetheless, a deal was struck: Rand McNally would provide printing capabilities and access to paper and binding, but Neff was obliged to pay for everything—the research, design, printing, distribution, and marketing. "He thought he could produce it cheaper with us than with anyone else," Clow said.[38] Neff, who didn't want to pay for a graphic designer, even laid out the pages himself. The dust jacket showed the design he loved most, the Airform, in "Neff blue" watercolor. Never one to belabor a point, he reduced the output of a forty-four-year career to a seven-paragraph, one-page introduction, and then filled 144 pages with black-and-white photographs and details from construction documents.

He called it *Architecture of Southern California*, an inclusive sounding title that paid homage to the architects he believed had come to California with Father Junipero Serra in 1769.[39] In fact, Neff's assumption that the Spanish had brought their own architects was inaccurate. (The colonizers had no professional architectural knowledge and were unable to recruit skilled craftsmen, which accounts, architectural historian

WE MOVED THERE BECAUSE YOU COULD SMELL ORANGE BLOSSOMS

Harold Kirker claims, for the plain surfaces of the missions and their abstract character.)[40]

To protect his clients' privacy, Neff withheld their addresses. Photographs were identified with cryptic captions such as "John Factor, Beverly Hills" and "Oval staircase, Mrs. M. Osburn, Los Angeles." Construction dates were also omitted. Celebrated residents who lived in Neff designs were portrayed as the original owners. Thus, Neff was able to take credit for designing the houses of Barbara Hutton, Cary Grant, Red Skelton, and Jules Stein.

Neff arranged for Julius Shulman to photograph Harry and Elsa Kunin's ten-year-old house in Holmby Hills while the Kunins were away, without obtaining their permission. When Mrs. Kunin learned that they had entered her house, she threatened to sue Neff unless he agreed to remove her name from the book.[41] It was not the reaction an artist expected from a patron. Yet those images proved to be the best the book had to offer. Over the years, his architectural and photo files had bounced from Pasadena to his Hollywood office with a minimal amount of care, and according to his son Arthur, a fire in a garage of the house where Louise and the children lived was responsible for the loss of many of the plans from the 1920s, so the selection Neff had to choose from was limited.

Despite the poor presentation of all but the Shulman photos and the limited text, the book was notable because it depicted the portion of his architectural output that Neff hoped to be remembered for. The single villa-style structure—Sol and Marian Wurtzel's grand house—was outnumbered by many more modest houses that bore Neff's beloved shallow front gable. Judging from its prevalence in the photographs, this roofline, which peaked in the center like a mountain and wandered into the horizon like the plains, was his favored architectural profile (after that of the Airform, of course). It was the form he alluded to in the fore-

word when he described Southern California as having "long, sweeping, seemingly unbound lines, flowing to conform to the surrounding terrain."[42] And it was the form he used in his 1930s Honeymoon Cottage.

Photographs of 1920s-era houses for the King C. Gillettes, the A. K. Bournes, and Frances Marion and Fred Thomson, and Neff's own house on Orlando Road were numerous. He also selected the 1930s houses of Henry Haldemann, George Miller, Joan Bennett, Robert Garner, and King Vidor, but he seemed happiest with his postwar work, and of all his clients, with Amelita Galli-Curci. All three of her built commissions were depicted, revealing a common informality of plan and an austerity of detail. And in a move that must have driven the modernists crazy, ducks and sheep were airbrushed into the photographs of the forecourts of the most rural Galli-Curci houses.

Neff borrowed $14,155.36 from First Western Bank and Trust to pay for a run of a thousand copies. Yet as he continued to make changes, production costs escalated so much that the actual cost was three times higher than originally estimated.[43] Since the book retailed for $14.95, he lost money with each copy that went to press. Another 750 copies were printed in a second run, but Neff chose to overlook invoices from Chicago seeking $4,377.52 for their production. "Overdue" stamped in red on bills made no difference. Neff responded to his exasperated cousins with a letter that suggested that the publishing trade expected more of him than the building trades. Andrew McNally III eventually forgave his cousin's debt, conceding that the cost to produce the book was a bargain for the quality that resulted.

A mildly favorable review appeared in the *Los Angeles Times Home Magazine*.[44] "It bears a misleading title," the magazine said, "yet it is a very good book of its kind. Neff's work spans four decades, from Spanish houses of Rancho Santa Fe to the frankly palatial Schondube [Wurtzel] home in Bel-Air, then to the concrete 'igloos,' and finally to the crisp, terse design of the Hummel house." (The latter, built in Reno, Nevada, showed Neff was capable of the most austere, flat-roofed profile.)

OBSERVATIONS ON
SCALE AND PROPORTION

The book's paucity of text can be attributed to Neff's pragmatic attitude about the creative process. Residential architects should not reveal their reasoning, he felt, for it would betray their relationship with their benefactors—the clients. If there was a topic he wanted to ponder in his advancing years, however, it was the role of scale and proportion in his work. His eye for the two had become so sensitive that he had whisked a new 1958 Cadillac Eldorado coupe to a body shop so the fins could be removed. (They were distracting to the overall design, he thought.) Now it was time to teach the layman how to see.

Neff spent nearly ten years seeking a publisher for his manuscript on scale and proportion. It was first displayed in public as part of an exhibition on the hobbies of Los Angeles architects, which ran from 1958 to 1962 at the city's new Building Exhibition Center. There, sharing a case with Richard Neutra's paintings and Ralph Crosby's toy trick shotgun, was a *Biological Age in Art and Nature* typescript. "Unusual hobbies include Wallace Neff's study of head proportions to determine real biological age, as well as suitability of marital or love partners," Barbara Hansen reported in the December 20, 1961, *Los Angeles Herald & Express*.

Neff's theories had been theretofore unexplored, he claimed, and as an architect trained in anatomy and life drawing, he believed he possessed unique insights. He wrote, "Artists and architects create in their own body proportions, for man creates in his own image. This tendency should be recognized and controlled

when doing work for a client, as it is the client to whom the work should be pleasing first."[45]

On page 2, his "law of age and growth in nature" posited that "everything young and undeveloped has relatively large parts in relation to the whole (large scale). As age progresses, these same parts become relatively smaller in relation to the whole (small scale). This is a very profound and significant law."

"Attraction by Proportion," on page 8, asserted that there was "sufficient evidence to indicate the existence of an unrecognized natural force, the 'pull' that draws certain people together." A photograph of the Duke and Duchess of Windsor illustrated his belief that as married couples grew older and the skin of their faces tightened, the similar skull proportions that had originally drawn them together were revealed. A sketch of a southwest mission illustrated the counterintuitive principle he had used in the Saint Elizabeth Church and the Doheny library: "Large scale is correct for a small building."

Since Leonardo da Vinci, architects had been studying the human body. Da Vinci had described the ideal human figure as proportioned to fit within the perfect shapes of the square and circle. Neff's manuscript, however, contained even more sweeping generalizations, and he was unable to attract editorial support.

Nevertheless, the human skull continued to be a source of fascination for him, and he pursued the study of it on his own, examining the skull collection of one of the instructors at the USC School of Dentistry. Anytime there was an opportunity to test his theory, he did, approaching strangers in restaurants to see if he could guess a person's age just by looking at his or her head.

Cary Grant, among others, watched in amazement: "Once at Romanoff's I introduced him to someone," Grant recalled, "and I'll be darned if he didn't guess right."[46] What the subjects thought of the line of questioning is lost to time.

A MUDDY POSTWAR LANDSCAPE

While Los Angeles sliced its downtown into piles of urban renewal dirt during the 1960s, erecting a baseball stadium on a hillside after the low-income housing proposed for the site was rejected by politicians as communistic, Pasadena had a juggling act of its own balancing old and new. After the war, its commercial hub had moved, forsaking Colorado Boulevard, where Neff had begun his practice, for South Lake Avenue, where Bullocks Pasadena responded to consumer demand for vast parking facilities. The California Street district of Spanish buildings that included Neff's onetime office remained intact until the 1960s, when an oil company purchased Palmer Sabin's building, demolished it, and erected a service station in its place.

A historic preservation movement sprang to life in Pasadena after officials granted permission to raze some of the oldest commercial buildings on Colorado Boulevard in the mid-1970s. The Neffs had watched the Arroyo Seco Parkway deliver traffic to Orange Grove Boulevard since it was completed in 1940. Twenty-some years later, the State Highway Commission reached an agreement with city fathers to build a freeway running east-west through the community, demolishing bungalow tract after bungalow tract to make way for Interstate 210. In 1983, Pasadena gained its first spot on the National Register of Historic Places with the designation of the Prospect Park residential district, where Neff's earliest work was still standing.

The freeway system, for better or worse, had also brought rural La Mirada into the fold of urban Los Angeles. With railroads having fallen victim to trucks and automobiles, construction of the Santa Ana Freeway had begun near downtown Los Angeles on October 1, 1946, reaching as far south as Santa Ana six years later. Exits to Imperial Highway and Rosecrans Avenue had put the McNally ranch olive groves just twenty minutes from downtown. Land developers got off the freeway and headed for homesteads where escalating property taxes were killing profits for people like the McNally heirs.

LAND CONVERSION AND INFRASTRUCTURE CONSTRUCTION

William Neff and his wife, Mina, had moved into the old McNally house in La Mirada in 1940, after the death of longtime manager Robert McGill. Bill spent as much time hunting and fishing as he did monitoring the balance sheets, an activity at which he was sometimes joined by his brother John. While their brother Andrew flew his private plane, Bill took aerial photos of the ranch to keep track of the status of the groves. There was income from land leased out to hay and grain farmers and from Standard Oil's explorations. "Standard Oil tried and tried [to find oil]," Neff's cousin Helen Belford reported, "and oil leases paid the taxes for quite awhile," but generally La Mirada was a losing proposition on the books.[47]

The population had held steady at three hundred decade after decade, as the Neffs and their Chicago kin essentially bided their time, waiting for the right offer. But by the 1950s, suburbia was encroaching. "The increasing flow of people brought a need for new roads, schools, fire and police services, and other county-supplied services," La Mirada historian Bob Camp wrote.[48] At the ranch's doorstep, a 120-acre residential subdivision at Rosecrans Avenue and Studebaker Road was being constructed under the eye of developer Milton Kaufman in 1951, and two other developments of two thousand houses each followed. By the early 1950s, quintessential Los Angeles developers like Mark Taper, Louis Boyar, and Ben Weingart were building their fortunes and 17,500 houses in Lakewood Park to the north, where Neff's Honeymoon Cottage had been on display years before.[49]

Earthmovers swarmed over Orange County to the south, creating city blocks at the back door of the McNally groves.[50] Veterans with federally backed loans stood ready to build, and developers like Harold Shaw drove around La Mirada, buoyed by the awareness that McNally's heirs were burdened with skyrocketing taxes. The pressure to convert agricultural land to nonagricultural use was as intense here as it was elsewhere in Southern California. After a year and a half of negotiations with McNally's heirs, Shaw's offer was accepted. In 1951, all parties agreed to $4 million for 2,218 acres.

La Mirada historian Bob Camp wrote, "This was not to be a piece-meal subdivision of Andrew McNally's $115,000 investment! It would be a gigantic cash sale, unprecedented in the history of subdivision real estate transactions."[51] Helen Belford joined Neff and his siblings at Gibson, Dunn & Crutcher's law offices to sign the documents. "The cousins gathered," she recalled, "and proceeds were divided equally among Belfords, Clows, McNallys, and Neffs."[52]

The heirs retained ten acres along Route 39 in hopes that the government might widen the road or oil might spring forth. Ten acres were also held around the house where Neff had been born, where one of the first flame (or bottle) trees introduced in California burst with clusters of pink-and-red flowers every summer.

Issues of land-use planning were not part of the agreement. If the developer wanted to raze the olive trees, so be it. The provision of amenities such as parks and streets was also left to Shaw's discretion. Bill Neff expressed only one wish on the family's behalf: that the Shaw Development Company name the community La Mirada.

Shaw doubled his investment two years later, after Louis M. Halper (the developer who had enticed the Marx brothers to build at the Tamarisk Country Club in Rancho Mirage) bought 2,100 acres for $8 million. Ten thousand housing starts materialized under Halper in La Mirada over the next seven years. The groves were leveled, and olive trees were planted in the front yards of the new tract houses. "One day in the middle fifties," Los Angeles county supervisor John Anson Ford wrote in his memoir, "a Los Angeles subdivider stood up before the Supervisors and made a statement that shocked the roomful of spectators, as well as the Supervisors, into a realization of what was happening in Los Angeles County. 'Throughout the entire year just past,' he said, 'an average of 1,000 trees per day have been uprooted from Los Angeles orchards to make way for subdivisions.' The county that had once boasted of its miles of fragrant orange orchards and shady English walnut groves had lost its agricultural pre-eminence."[53]

Still, the Los Angeles Times found "big crowds" at the unveiling of "Parkwood Estates Mutual Homes" in La Mirada in August 1957.[54] South of the La Mirada depot, dirt flew in the late 1950s to make way for a La Mirada shopping center and an Orbach's department store. Biola College, previously known as the Bible Institute of Los Angeles and located in the heart of the city, purchased 150 acres for a campus in La Mirada in 1955.

You could pick up a xeroxed map of the area at the Valley View Farms Drive-In Dairy ("where your milk dollar buys more").[55] Printed by the developer of La Mirada Woods, a "once in a blue moon" community,[56] the map revealed subdivisions riddled with cul de sacs to eliminate through-traffic; the grid of streets that put humanity in face-to-face contact had been deemed unsuitable. Cinder-block perimeter walls kept out noise and intrusions. "The featureless private floating world of Southern California," as architect Charles Moore would later call it,[57] came to be, and the idea of a public realm and a definable downtown went by the wayside. Who could argue when veterans could purchase a house with hardwood floors, three bedrooms, a family room, and various other amenities for fifteen thousand dollars with nothing down? The American dream was available and affordable.

On January 13, 1959, days before Nannie Neff died, 67.3 percent of La Mirada's citizens voted to incorporate. On March 15, 1960, nineteen miles northwest, in the Los Angeles Civic Center, the County Board of Supervisors certified Mirada Hills as the sixty-eighth city in the county. And on November 8, 1960, 80 percent of the voters selected the name "La Mirada" over "Mirada Hills."

The andro-sphinxes that had once guarded the entrance to the Neffs' house had been stored in the citrus packing house for so long that no one noticed when an intruder removed them. After La Mirada Road was renamed Beach Boulevard and the general delivery post office moved out, the Santa Fe tore down the depot. "Old LAM Railroad Depot Leveled for 'Progress,'" the *Lamplighter* reported on October 10, 1962. The schoolhouse of Neff's youth had been razed in 1955, and the vacant packing house had gone up in flames in 1959, the same year the olive plant, with its magnificent arched portal entry, was leveled. In the summer of 1963, the *Lamplighter* began a series known as the "Saga of a Land Called La Mirada," while its sports page reported the wins and losses of William N. Neff High School's athletic teams. La Mirada seemed to have everything but a main street.

Ralph Chandler House, Hancock Park

CHAPTER TWENTY-ONE

FATHER OF THE SHOWCASE HOUSE

Los Angeles' history has been one continuous real estate enterprise, with land speculation a driving force for its never-ending growth.
—David Brodsly, *L.A. Freeway, An Appreciative Essay*

$\mathcal{M}$ODERN ARCHITECTURE'S DESCENT into ignominy in the late 1960s and early 1970s coincided with Dr. Henry E. Singleton's rise into the economic stratosphere. Singleton's genius had put him at the forefront of the military industrial complex during the Eisenhower era, after he invented a navigational system to guide long-range missiles and became the man to know at Litton Industries in Beverly Hills. Hoping to make a fortune of his own, the forty-four-year-old engineer cofounded Teledyne Incorporated in Los Angeles in 1960, to build computers that would guide military and commercial aircrafts' exploration of space.

Around this time, he and his wife, Caroline, bought a lot on Mulholland Drive high over Bel-Air. Richard Neutra was chosen as the architect of the house that would shield the five Singleton children from the curious, allowing the family to bask in the beauty of the landscape. The result was so dramatic that Julius Shulman's photographs were published far and wide, in spite of Singleton's aversion to publicity. The black-and-white images perfectly depicted the contrast between the stark materials Neutra favored and the natural surroundings.

On November 6, 1961, a bulldozer not far below the house backfired and started a fire that burned six thousand acres and destroyed $25 million in property. The Singleton House was spared, but the vegetation surrounding it was destroyed.[1] One family left homeless, the Burton Fletchers, turned to Neff to design a new house, while they lived in the tight quarters of a trailer.[2] The Singletons continued living in their Neutra house until their growing prosperity, and Singleton's burgeoning wine collection, drove them to search for larger quarters.

BIGGER IS NOT BETTER

Unable to negotiate the purchase of the house Neff had designed for Joan Bennett, where the producer Hal Wallis and his wife, the actress Martha Hyer, were living, Singleton decided to hire Neff to plan a new house. On July 24, 1969, Singleton signed a contract with Neff for the design of the most grandiose house of the architect's career.[3] At $1.2 million, it was certainly the most costly. Singleton had selected a Holmby Hills site sliced by a canyon so large it took two years to fill and grade. Students from the landscape architecture program at nearby UCLA marveled at the transformation, which included the excavation of a small lake. He hoped to enlist the talents of two of the state's leading landscape architects, Edward Huntsman-Trout and Thomas Church, to improve the grounds, but Church took on the project alone after Huntsman-Trout refused to collaborate.

Beyond describing the building's architectural qualities, Neff never publicly discussed the experience of working on the project. He told the *Pasadena Star-News* that Singleton's insistence on materials like walnut parquet, Indiana limestone, and marble brought the cost to fifty dollars a square foot.[4] Even the garage, where guests disembarked, contained a walkway of white marble. Squash, handball, and tennis courts were as state of the art as the table tennis, pool, and billiards facilities. The woodwork on the walls of the large, oval hallway from which all the other rooms radiated was modeled on that of the Petit Trianon at Versailles.

The house was finished in 1970, and it was the antithesis of Neutra's modernist ethos. It affirmed just how far modernism had tumbled. From the halls of the U.S. Senate, where Joseph McCarthy had suggested in 1952 that foreign-born modern architects were carrying subversive ideas into America's classrooms, to the classrooms themselves, where twenty years later, college professors were praising an emerging style called postmodernism, the modern movement had sputtered to a standstill.

Its leading advocate in Southern California, Richard Neutra, died of a heart attack in Germany on April 16, 1970, at seventy-eight. His wife believed he had been slighted by a profession that considered residential architecture second-rate. "In the USA," Dione Neutra said, "bigness counts. How many skyscrapers have you built? How many people do you have in your office?"[5] After decades of animosity, it was finally apparent to Neff that Neutra had been fighting the same battles he had fought.

Now seventy-five years old himself, Neff was having a hard time coming up with an architectural scheme that exhibited originality. Revising the Singleton plan to an even grander scale after having been granted another two hundred thousand dollars to expand his vision, Neff was reprimanded by the contractor, Walter R. Johnson, who had to devote extra time to explaining the new specifications to subcontractors. Johnson kept his pique from Singleton and they remained on good terms until the carpenters coffered the den ceiling, despite Singleton's protests, and Singleton exploded.[6]

Amenities included a wine refrigerator that cost as much as a mid-priced car and hardwood floors worth nearly fifty thousand dollars.[7] The steeply pitched roof and towering chimneys that Neff had relied on throughout his career to evoke country chateaus were combined with battalions of neoclassical columns that would have been more appropriate on a grand public building. The assemblage of vernacular and neoclassical was far afield from Neff's previous efforts at harmonizing scale and proportion. When the mansionization phenomenon began in the mid-1980s,[8] the Singleton House stood as a precedent for the bigger-is-better mentality that wiped out modest houses in favor of ostentatious ones.[9]

HOMAGE TO THE FRENCH AFTER ALL

Neff had already abandoned his allegiance to restraint, however, when he designed the Chandler House in 1960. Ralph Chandler was said to have proclaimed that he wanted to build the last grand mansion in Hancock Park, and he recruited his son, Andrew, to consult on the preliminary design plans. ("This was the best time of my life," Andrew said. "It allowed me to realize all my fantasies.")[10]

Neff had worked for Ralph Chandler during his shipbuilding stint in World War I. After the war, the Chandlers had resided in the Los Feliz neighborhood of Los Angeles, and Chandler had been vice president of the Matson Navigation Company, the cruise and shipping line that had led luxury travel on the Los Angeles-to-Honolulu route. Neff had designed a house for Chandler's cousin Norman a few blocks away.

When the family left Los Feliz for Pasadena, Andrew, whose favorite childhood pastime had been taking the Pacific Electric Red Cars to the beach, had despaired. (Pasadena was "a place where old people brought along their parents when they wanted to have a good time," he said.)[11] In 1960, he finally persuaded his parents to return to Los Angeles. It was at this point that Chandler is said to have decided to build the grandest of the grand Hancock Park residences. Andrew, who was studying drawing, was enlisted by his father to draw plans for an homage to the pavilion at Louveciennes near Versailles, which the French architect Claude Nicholas Ledoux had designed for Madame du Barry in 1771.[12]

The era of Louis XV had become influential in America after the new U.S. government had selected it as the official style for federal buildings in the late eighteenth century. Louis XV style combined the ornateness of the baroque with the precision of the classical. Chandler hired the architect Clyde Burr to draw elevations based on the historic structure. Following Burr's death, Neff was tapped for several reasons: he was a longtime acquaintance of Chandler's, he had studied at MIT (Chandler was known to be skeptical of any architect who had trained at UCLA or USC, where so many local designers had matriculated), and he was willing to put in the time necessary to execute plans for clients who, it transpired, required a great deal of attention.

The neoclassical design the Chandlers aspired to—with its conspicuous use of decoration and profusion of sculpture—was not intended to be entirely true to its model. To accommodate the automobile, Neff devised underground garages. The interior included a grand rotunda entrance and a dining room copied from the Governor's Palace in Colonial Williamsburg.

The best one could do to simulate vast French gar-

The Chandler House

dens in the middle of densely populated Los Angeles was to find a parcel of land on a golf course. Once the Chandlers had purchased a lot on Rossmore Avenue overlooking the Wilshire Country Club, they hired Edward Huntsman-Trout to design the grounds.

Buoyed by his study of drafting, Andrew Chandler worked in Neff's office helping to prepare the drawings. His design for a rotunda was so well proportioned, he said, that Neff's draftsmen worked from it. "Mr. Neff was willing to execute all of my schemes," he claimed. "I was able to manifest my idea of beauty in a hostile world that no longer cares for that kind of thing."[13] But his parents were indecisive and many of the plans had to be redrawn.[14]

Neff's son Arthur often visited the construction site. In 1960, he had met an airline stewardess named Marvine Currey on a flight from Washington, D.C., where he was traveling to promote the Airform, and he was smitten with her. She captured the heart of her prospective father-in-law as well when she recounted an in-flight meeting with the architect Charles Luckman. Luckman, who was renowned for his civic projects, had told her that Neff was the only architect he knew who could devote his architectural practice to residential design without having to chase airport and municipal commissions.[15] (She did not correct him by mentioning the school and college commissions that had kept Neff's office from folding in the 1950s.) On their honeymoon, when she and Arthur visited the pavilion at Louveciennes that had inspired the Chandler House, Marvine joked, "I thought your father designed it."[16]

Stopping at the Chandler site one day to check on the crew, Arthur found them on the roof watching *The George Raft Story* being filmed in the backyard next door. The presence of the curvaceous Jayne Mansfield threatened to push the astounding $450,000 Chandler budget into the half-million-dollar realm. When the

house was finally completed on target in 1961, there was little satisfaction for the architect. "He respected the amount of money being spent, but not the house," his friend Irwin Gellman said.[17] Neff referred to it thereafter as the "Madame du Barry House."[18]

FAMILY CONFLICT

Arthur had become affiliated with his father's practice as an Airform salesman after graduating from Loyola University in 1956 and studying business administration at USC. He had no talent for design, he admitted, and his father's impatience with young architects would have made his life difficult had he decided to enter the field. "Dad told me the architecture students at USC and UCLA couldn't draw a column," he said, describing a sentiment as distinctly antimodern as it was intolerant. Growing up with the limited presence of his father, he said, left all the children in the family emotionally scarred, but he reconciled himself to the situation by concluding that his father was an artist and thus unable to live conventionally. "After my parents separated," he said, "my father did not socialize much. He felt it would have been wrong to bring someone else to a party. He kept company with women who wanted his money. He was an easy mark."[19]

What he lost in familial stability as a child, Arthur tried to make up for as a father. He and Marvine, Arthur Junior, and Andrea resided on Orange Grove Boulevard, the third and fourth generations of Neffs to do so. He had inherited the family house from his aunt Della, and it was filled with furniture from Andrew McNally's Altadena smoking room and Nannie and Ed's era. The library overflowed with photos of Art's acquaintances in Republican politics. The military fascinated him, and a friendship with General Omar Bradley resulted in Art's decision to self-publish a book of Bradley's paintings. The dining table was spread with a breakfast buffet each New Year's Day, when guests began arriving at six o'clock in the morning to watch the Rose Parade as it passed the house.

Art's older brother, Wallace, had graduated from Claremont Men's College in 1953. A single man known as Wally, he lived in Orange County, where he sold real estate. The brothers' relationship had become strained, and as is the case in many wealthy families, money and property were at the core of the friction. They shared a sense of pride in their father's reputation, but each believed he was the ultimate authority on the Neff oeuvre.

By the 1960s, with California in the midst of a phase of big shopping centers and big business, the Neff name conveyed more cachet in social circles than it did in architectural ones. As Dione Neutra had observed, architects' fascination with large-scale projects had focused attention on the Beckets and Luckmans and Pereiras. Among the few in the press who took an interest in Neff's career were columnists covering the social scene.

There was a flurry of coverage of his architectural output when the Frederick Fairbanks Mansion was selected by the Pasadena Junior Philharmonic for its 1967 showcase of interior design, a yearly rite in which interior decorators donated their talents to adorn grand houses in the latest trends, which the *Los Angeles Times* described as "part *haut monde* shindig, part lookyloo's paradise."[20]

The makeover of the 1926 house stunned the architect, who walked silently through its rooms. Its very visible location and high-profile history—from the era of the Fairbanks, to the time of the Hoover family, to the curiosity that followed after the widow of the assassinated Dominican Republic dictator Rafael Trujillo moved in—had made it one of his most talked-about structures. Neff became uneasy as he moved from one boldly painted room to another. Purple or

red, dressed in animal skins or pop art, the rooms were notably disparate. Viewing the painted strawberries as big as human heads that covered the refrigerator in the kitchen, he suggested as delicately as he could the appropriateness of a color scheme that would unite the rooms in harmonious hues. "He did not want to make anyone uncomfortable," the *Los Angeles Times* writer at his side remarked.[21]

When the daughter of the original owner stepped forward to have her picture taken with him, he did his best to be diplomatic. Had she been a younger woman, she speculated, he might have made an effort to be cordial, but as it was, "he stood around with a droll look on his face," avoiding conversation.[22]

Another of his Pasadena mansions, located in the San Rafael district and built around a great auto court for the Milbank Johnsons in 1924, became the showcase house in 1969. This time Neff's inspection left him sanguine after he saw that workmen had removed a false ceiling in the living room to reveal the original. "It will take a face-lift well," he told the group, while a society reporter pulled out her notebook. "Travel makes taste," he was quoted as saying. "Only your eyes can tell you what will clash, what will last, what is good."[23]

Years later, the *Los Angeles Times* columnist Jack Smith, who made a point of covering the showcase house every year, wrote what amounted to an ode to the Neff, McNally, and Libby families. "There has always been a Pasadena myth. We think of Pasadena, in the 1890s and early 1900s, as the private preserve of Midwestern meat packers, soap manufacturers, brewers and Presbyterian bishops who came here in the hope of prolonging their lives in sunshine and orange-scented air. As far as I can tell, the myth is true."[24] Neff, of course, would have gone to any length to avoid admitting that he had been a boy in Pasadena's horse-and-carriage days. His efforts to downplay the aging process included leaving his eyeglasses at home and visiting a hairdresser for color treatments. He ate and drank sensibly, except for a fondness for the dark, strong Lapsang souchong tea, his favored physical stimulant. When he gave it up and the symptoms of withdrawal gripped him, he resumed its consumption.[25]

His reserve about revealing his feelings, dreams, and impressions kept those who sought insight into his motivations from learning much. He mentioned the most thrilling chapter of his life, which took place in 1920s Pasadena and Hollywood, almost as an afterthought when a reporter from the *Pasadena Star-News* visited him in 1974. "I was lucky enough to get in on the rush of the winter people who were moving out here body and soul in the 1920's," the paper quoted him as saying. "The rest just followed."[26]

Neff had found a confidante, however, a year after his daughter's death, in 1963. Melanie Young, fifty years his junior, had been raised in Shanghai by a Chinese father and a German mother, and she met the Neff criteria for physical beauty, for she was the vision of a Raphael painting. She became the sole woman in his life with whom he was able to share a stable, faithful relationship, and he came as close to experiencing emotional fulfillment with her as he had with any woman.

Every weekend she and Neff left town, transporting her pet Pekingese and caged birds in his Cadillac to the Miramar Hotel in Montecito. Neff believed that he was keeping these trips secret, but his draftsmen, among others, couldn't help noticing the weekly ritual. Robert Straus, a client in Santa Barbara, thought the May-December union was undignified. He expected Neff to stay at the Biltmore Hotel, not the down-at-the-heels Miramar, and to select a more demure companion than the outspoken Miss Young.[27]

On Neff's one and only visit to his friend John Elliott's property in Hana on Maui, Hawaii (where Elliott would eventually build a house designed by Neff), Neff told him that Young was "a genuine Manchu princess."[28] At the very least, she inspired him to explore Asian design traditions, for after the visit to Maui, Neff advised Elliott to paint the columns of his house Chinese red (advice that Elliott followed).[29] Hoping to boost Young's credibility in the eyes of his friends, Neff collaborated with her on a humorous guide to China called "Ping & Pong," which they submitted to Rand McNally. It was returned with a polite rejection letter.

In order to keep Young happy, Neff made regular donations to her checking account, which were looked at askance by his sons. They were beginning to keep a wary eye on this woman of no social standing or apparent vocation. Neff's annual eighteen- to twenty-five-thousand-dollar income from the McNally trust provided about half of what he needed to get by, so he turned to friends for four-figure loans.[30] Investments such as his half-interest in the Cloisters health spa in Palm Springs seldom brought financial return, but Neff was too gentle a man to consider making a claim against the partner who had conceived the health-spa idea. His cousin Mary Nevins grew accustomed to his phone calls, but her husband, an attorney, refused Neff's pleas to "break" the McNally trust.[31] Neff took on run-of-the-mill remodeling projects, such as bathroom expansions, to meet the expenses of his reinvigorated life.

Around this time, he was credited with designing a house in a Santa Barbara golf community for Elizabeth Bechtel, who had been married to a son of the founder of the noted construction company, but in fact he was involved in name only.[32] When Thomas Aquinas College acquired the former Doheny ranch in Santa Paula, Neff was paid to review the plans. "I wanted to honor him," the engineer J. Edward Martin said of his decision to consult Neff on the work Albert C. Martin and Associates was doing.

The final design of his fifty-five-year career was built in a development in Newport Beach known as the Big Canyon Country Club, in 1975. Marguerite and Francis Browne, who had hired Neff twice before, could rightfully claim to have used his services longer than any other clients—over a forty-six-year time span. Browne was a retired physician and his wife was a cousin of Neff's wife, Louise. Mrs. Browne and Neff had butted heads when he designed the Brownes' second house in Bel-Air in 1957. This time, however, Neff had to please not only a strong-willed client, but also a design review board. The painted brick structure with a tile roof only vaguely resembled a Wallace Neff house. Mrs. Browne's influence on the construction process, however, produced a house so well built that a 1990s remodeling project had to be scaled back because of the prohibitive cost of tearing out the rocklike walls.[33]

By now, Wallace Neff was almost eighty years old, with hypoglycemia and arteriosclerosis that prevented his once graceful body from moving freely. His male contemporaries were aged or homebound, and it was difficult to find dining companions other than Miss Young. King Vidor could be counted on to ask thought-provoking questions, and the two enjoyed debating the merits of Christian Science, Zen Buddhism, and Judaism. Cary Grant lunched with him from time to time. "He was quiet and reserved," Grant remarked, "courteous and intellectual. I did not know he'd worked on Pickfair until years later, for he never made big claims."[34]

Friends and clients were meeting their demise. Conrad Hilton died in 1979 at his grand Bel-Air estate on Bellagio Road. Groucho Marx died at eighty-six on August 19, 1977, a few months after his brother Gummo died at eighty-three. Mary Pickford was eighty-six when she passed away on May 29, 1979. Paul Williams, who had been called the architect to the stars as often as Neff had, died on January 23, 1980, a month before

The Elizabeth Bechtel House, Santa Barbara

his eighty-sixth birthday, his career distinguished by years of service to municipal and state commissions. Among Neff's acquaintances, the most tragic death was that of the actor Ramon Novarro, who had been murdered in his Hollywood apartment on Halloween in 1968, by young men he probably considered friends.[35] Obituaries had cited his appearance in *Ben-Hur* as his most significant film role.

Four years younger than Novarro had been when he died, Neff was nonetheless vulnerable to being taken advantage of, for he was known for his generosity with money. "It is for someone who is hungry," he told Basha Maxwell, his next door neighbor, when she noticed a fifty-dollar bill sticking out of an envelope taped to his apartment door. He helped pay for the voice lessons she gave to students who could not have otherwise afforded them. "He had a childlike quality," Maxwell said. "Anyone would have loved him."[36]

Neff was *edel*—Yiddish for a gentle, sensitive person—his friend the dry cleaner Irwin Gellman said.[37] He had seen Neff come to work in jackets patched at the elbows, and he noticed that clothing and personal belongings were as unimportant to Neff as where he ate his next meal. Any delicatessen on the block satisfied his friend, even if "he was dining with Cary Grant or Ralph Chandler."[38]

The Hollywood neighborhood where Neff had lived and worked for forty years was sliding into blight. West on Franklin Avenue, closer to the heart of Hollywood, large old houses were available for rent. Joan Didion, who lived in the area in the late 1960s, described it as "a 'senseless-killing neighborhood'. . . peopled mainly by rock-and-roll bands, therapy groups, and very old women wheeled down the street by practical nurses in soiled uniforms."[39]

By the early 1970s, Neff had not had a full-time draftsman in his office for ten years.[40] He purchased groceries and toiletries from the merchants on his block who had known him for decades. Increasingly, he absentmindedly locked his keys in his apartment and had to call a locksmith to get back in. On the morning of June 5, 1972, as he was leaving Melanie Young's apartment on Mariposa Street and heading west on Santa Monica Boulevard to his office, he steered his 1969 Cadillac into the left-turn lane and hit another car. A jury later upheld Marianne Radley's charges that he ran into her 1964 Plymouth. She sought $150,000 but was awarded $10,000.[41]

Soon thereafter, Neff's son Arthur filed a petition to obtain guardianship of his father. Neff was judged incompetent and entrusted to the care of his sons. His expenses were to be reviewed by a bank before he was allowed to sign checks. Sometime in 1973, his sons moved his possessions to his brother Andrew's Bubble House in Pasadena. Rudy Kessman, the locksmith who had assisted Neff when he lost his keys, noticed papers blowing from a dumpster at the curb of the architect's Franklin Avenue office. He later remarked that the departure had been hurried and that the papers looked

as if they had been tossed from Neff's files with little concern for their value.[42]

If there was any consolation for Neff, it was that he was living with his brother Andrew. They kept each other company at the now-fabled Bubble House, where they read *Scientific American* and watched television. Andrew's disenchantment with Roman Catholicism was more pronounced than his brother's, but they had both given up formal penance. Zen Buddhism provided solace, and Neff favored *This Is My God* by Herman Wouk over any other book on the shelf. The brothers enjoyed martinis as they waited for their Stouffer's tuna casseroles to cook in the oven. The kitchen was too small for dining, so they ate at a semicircular coffee table Neff had designed.

The shared interlude of well-being was brief. Flying his airplane at an age when most pilots had long since given up their licenses, Andrew Neff crashed near the San Gabriel Airport. His legs broken, he never regained strength, and a nurse joined the brothers in their cramped quarters. On September 3, 1975, Andrew McNally Neff died, at eighty-three. His achievements in chemical research, music, and aviation were cited in an obituary that inflated the scope of his research at Caltech.[43]

Neff's colleague Cliff May visited him at the Bubble House to console him. The two were natural allies. May's name had become famous because of its association with the postwar mode of suburban living that had elevated outdoor barbecuing to an art. *Sunset* magazine had boosted circulation by publishing May's California ranch houses, although May liked to point out that he had never been licensed as an architect. "I just built one kind of house," he would say (much as Neff used to claim that he just built California houses for California people). "I just had one style."[44] But May was as worried as Neff that his work was being eclipsed by the next trend. The two spent many an afternoon commiserating at May's office on Sunset Boulevard.

Sitting under a map dotted with pushpins designating May's houses and subdivisions, they would plan afternoon excursions to what they considered the best of their houses. "Wallace had no peer in his simplicity of massing," May said. "He wanted to show me the Galli-Curci House at Rancho Santa Fe, but physically he was not up for the trip. We saw the Miller House near the Bel-Air Hotel, and the Wurtzel House on Bellagio Road. Galli-Curci's in Westwood and the Haldemann House on Sunset were his favorites. I admired the confidence he had as a young man to work with the captains of industry. [But] his dream was to find acceptance for his Airform."[45]

Certain that Neff needed all the emotional support his peers could offer, May invited Neff to lunch at his home, where he found Paul Williams, Birge Clark, Gerald Colcord, Vince Palmer, and Walter Johnson awaiting his arrival. The conversation inevitably turned to trade secrets, and Johnson recalled, "Colcord said his secret was in instructing plasterers to apply the material with gloves. Wallace said his secret was insisting that painters use a benzoin aniline stain on woodwork so it would last a lifetime."[46] Johnson, who began and ended his career building Neff designs, remarked later that "the stain was better suited to furniture finishing, it was so time consuming. (It had to be heated.) Painters went along because they liked Neff, and it became one of his trademarks. Wallace used it because he liked the sharp contrast between the white walls and the dark stain."[47]

At the luncheon that day, May noticed that Neff's speech was becoming difficult to understand. He spoke under his breath, "telling himself to calm down."[48] Neff told May that his sons were disputing the terms of his will.

On more than one occasion, May went to visit Neff, only to find that he had been driven to court—and once he witnessed Neff being taken there on a stretcher.[49] Neff was attempting to revoke the 1973 judgment that had declared him incompetent. "My two sons disappointed me," he told a psychiatrist his attorneys called to evaluate him. "They stole together all my Rand McNally funds. There is conflict between my two sons and me." "About what?" the doctor asked. "Stealing my inheritance," he answered.[50] (In fact, they had not "stolen" his inheritance, because it had not yet been distributed.)

Neff was never able to persuade the court to reverse the decision that had him declared incompetent.[51] Today Neff's condition would probably be diagnosed as Alzheimer's disease, but in 1978, doctors called it "Nonpsychotic Organic Brain Syndrome from Senile Brain Disease."[52] Neff often lost track of time, and he missed the significance of September 27, 1981, the day the Andrew McNally trust was finally distributed. When the value of the trust had been determined in court several years earlier, it had been estimated at $11 million, or a stake in excess of $3.5 million for each of the four interests.[53]

Neff was admitted to the Californian Convalescent Hospital on October 4, 1978, at the direction of his doctor.[54] The location two miles north of his beloved Airform on Los Robles Street and one mile east of the Neff house on Orange Grove Boulevard put him in close proximity to family and friends. Louise Neff had lived there for several years, and within hours, Neff was taken to see her. "I wheeled him around to her room," Lynn Maggan, Neff's nurse, recalled. "They talked for about twenty minutes. Their conversation was warm. Mrs. Neff's eyesight was gone, and she was quite infirm. Mr. Neff never saw her again, for her condition grew worse and worse."[55]

When Louise Up de Graff Neff died on October 26 of the following year, at the age of eighty-six, Neff was distraught. For all his infatuations and relationships with other women, he had always respected her. There

Neff's La Mirada birthplace, added to the National Register of Historic Places in 1980

were insufficient funds in her account to cover her funeral mass and burial, and he ordered that they be underwritten by his trust account.[56] Louise was laid to rest where her family and Neff's had been interred, at Mountain View Cemetery in Altadena.

There were still moments of quiet satisfaction for the old architect. His birthplace in La Mirada, now the center of a city park, was added to the National Register of Historic Places in 1980. The American Institute of Architects had granted him emeritus status in 1972, and the Pasadena Arts Council recognized him with a Trustees Special Award, proclaiming, "Wallace Neff has contributed to the beauty of Southern California through his architectural brilliance."[57] Joseph Wambaugh invited him to visit to the Toms House, which Neff had designed in 1924, where the best-selling author now lived. Wambaugh wanted to erect a tennis court in the side yard, but he needed special dispensation to build close to the street. Neff suggested planting Italian cypress trees to create privacy, and the plans proceeded.

Increasingly, his flights of fancy gave him more pleasure than everyday living. The long-ago meeting between a Goodyear Tire salesman and Henry Ford blossomed in his mind into a friendship with Ford. Nurses listened as he reminisced. "He spoke about spending five years in Europe at his grandparents' expense," Lynn Maggan recalled, "and getting schooled at MIT. His favorite house was the Bubble, he said. 'Start building it when the sun comes up,' he warned me." When she learned that a preservation organization was planning a tour of Neff-designed houses, she bought a ticket. "When I told him how impressed people were with his work, he wept."[58]

In 1980, when he was summing up his career in a few sentences for a directory that would include the world's leading architects, he revealed more than he had in his book or in any interview. "I never had any illusion that my work was anything other than 'Californian' in style," he said, distancing himself from the modernists. "Never 'authentic' copies of something alien," he continued, distancing himself also from the Spanish colonial revival, provincial revival, mission revival, and all the rest of the influences that style-conscious clients might have requested. "I was in practice for such a long time that my early work began to be admired in a nostalgic sort of way."

Now his supporters ran the gamut from postmodern architects who lauded revivalism to rank-and-file home buyers exasperated with mass-produced housing at a time when the kind of artisans Neff had once employed—from the classically trained architect to the glass blower and foundry worker—were nearly impossible to find. "My late work was done for people who lived in a different era," he concluded. "I feel it solves the problems of contemporary living."[59]

Ruth Ryon, a writer from the *Los Angeles Times*, interviewed him for the Real Estate section in 1981. A few years before, the attractive young reporter might have charmed him into revealing some of his secrets. Now, she observed, "his arteriosclerosis makes him a man of even fewer words."[60]

"How do you feel when some of the mansions you designed have been torn down?" she asked. "I don't like it," he managed to answer. "What is your favorite home?" she asked. "Galli-Curci's," he replied, not specifying which of the houses he meant. The photograph showed a well-dressed old man with wisps of hair, whose hint of a smile was the same "cookie jar look" a *Times* society reporter had noted twenty years before.[61]

When people came to visit, he sometimes exhibited flashes of clarity. John Elliott brought architecture magazines. A student from Pasadena City College elicited a claim from him that he had designed five hundred houses all told and two hundred in Pasadena.[62] When Clifford Hoskins, Neff's oldest living draftsman, visited in 1981, he found Neff confined to a wheelchair, speechless, after a series of strokes.

It would have been like Neff to suggest that an august institution filled with rare books and art—a place where modernism would not be held in high regard—would become the repository of his architectural papers. Yet the Huntington Library curator who received his documents said it was Neff's sons who had approached the institution in May 1978. The Huntington was not seeking architectural drawings at the time, but its rare-book curator, Alan Jutzi, accepted Neff's papers in the hopes of eventually creating a collection of regional architectural papers.[63]

THE ELUSIVE MEANING OF CALIFORNIA AS A PLACE

On June 8, 1982, after receiving the last rites of the Roman Catholic Church, Wallace Neff died from complications of pneumonia. The private service was arranged for the family only; Melanie Young was not allowed to attend. "There was something vulnerable about those people," Neff's cousin Mary Nevins commented after leaving the Cabot and Sons Funeral Home. "They had a sweet, soft side," she said of Neff, his siblings, and his parents, now all deceased. "They all had talent."[64]

Neff's remains were buried under a coast live oak at Mountain View Cemetery, in view of the Sierra Madre and San Gabriel mountains, where the young Nannie McNally had ridden on horseback a hundred years before. The same burial plot contained her remains, her husband Ed's, Neff's in-laws, Dr. and Mrs. Thaddeus Up de Graff, his brother-in-law, Thaddeus Up de Graff Jr., his daughter, Phyllis, and his wife, Louise.

The strain of California boosterism that had permeated Andrew McNally's guidebooks and maps appeared in several obituaries. The *Pasadena Star-News* listed the names of the famous, like Henry Ford, whom Neff was supposed to have befriended, but with whom he was not really acquainted. Neff was described as having won national awards, when many of them were actually given to him by the local AIA chapter.[65] *Pasadena Heritage*'s obituary noted the hours he had spent in his grandparents' exotic Oriental smoking room and that "in typical California fashion he was exposed to eclectic influences from the start."[66]

A photograph of the Arthur and Emily Bourne House accompanied an obituary in the *Los Angeles Herald Examiner*, along with an image of a handsome, forty-year-old Neff holding a Leica camera. The architecture columnist who wrote the article believed that Neff's Spanish colonial–revival houses outshone the work of modernists like Schindler and Neutra. And there was not even a mention of George Washington Smith, the Santa Barbara architect who was usually given credit for pioneering Mediterranean-style design in California. "Neff was the last living architect in a group—Gordon Kaufmann, Myron Hunt, Reginald Johnson and Roland Coate, among others—that succeeded in building an architecture which captured, even more than the bungalow, tract house or ranch house, the elusive meaning of California as a place," the columnist noted. "California today would somehow be less Californian without this architecture," he wrote, echoing sentiments of the emerging postmodernists, who glorified regionalism.[67]

Neff had been too enfeebled in his final years to know much about postmodernism, but he had seen many other movements in his lifetime, for the practice of architecture had gone through more changes during his eighty-six years than in any other period in history, including the Renaissance. The city he lived in had seen tremendous changes as well: by the end of Neff's life, the population of Los Angeles had reached 2,966,763, within 468 square miles, making it America's second-largest city and the tenth-largest metropolitan area in the world.[68] Through it all, Wallace Neff had remained focused on building houses that expressed the spirit of the region.

The multicultural, multilingual megalopolis he called home has continued to grow and change—just as it was doing in 1895, when he was born—but the grand, romantic houses that are his legacy remain. There is no epitaph on his grave, but his familiar line about building California houses for California people would have suited him nicely in its brevity.

NOTES

CHAPTER ONE

Epigraph. Kate Sanborn, *A Truthful Woman in Southern California* (New York: D. Appleton and Company, 1893).

1. Carey McWilliams, *Southern California: An Island on the Land* (Santa Barbara: Peregrine Smith, 1973), 344.

2. S. N. Behrman, *The Burning Glass* (Boston: Little, Brown, 1968), 314.

3. Nathanael West, *The Day of the Locust* (New York: Random House, 1939), 6–7.

4. Esther McCoy, personal communication, July 16, 1984. "Alas nothing in my files on him," she wrote. "I never met Neff."

5. David Gebhard and Robert Winter, *Architecture in Los Angeles: A Compleat Guide* (Salt Lake City: Gibbs M. Smith, 1985), 486.

6. F. Scott Fitzgerald, "Crazy Sunday," in *Taps at Reveille* (New York: Charles Scribner's Sons, 1935), 202, 211.

7. Wallace Neff, *Architecture of Southern California* (Chicago: Rand McNally, 1964), 3.

8. Kitty Connelly, manager of the Villa Carlotta apartments, personal communication, March 25, 1984; Basha Maxwell, resident of the Villa Carlotta, personal communication, March 13, 1984.

9. Background on Rand from Bruce Grant, "Official History of Rand, McNally & Company" (unpublished paper written for the company centennial, 1955), on deposit at the Newberry Library in Chicago. Among Grant's sources were William B. Rice, *Southern California's First Newspaper: The Founding of the Los Angeles Star* (Los Angeles: Glen Dawson, 1941), and Mary R. Chappell, "A Sketch of the Life of My Father" (unpublished manuscript, n.d.). Rand's participation in the *Los Angeles Star* is documented in Edward C. Kemble, *A History of California Newspapers, 1846–1858* (Los Gatos, CA: Talisman Press, 1962), 233. Rand's obituary in the *New York Times* on June 22, 1915, listed his birth date as May 2, 1828; he was the twelfth child and seventh son of the minister John Rand and his wife.

10. The notice that the *Areatus* had arrived with 139 passengers appeared in the Marine Journal column of the *Alta California* on September 27, 1849.

11. W. H. Brewer, *Up and Down California in 1860–1864* (New Haven, CT: Yale University Press, 1930), 12–15; John Caughey and LaRee Caughey, eds., *Los Angeles: Biography of a City* (Berkeley: University of California Press, 1976), 153.

12. Andrew Rolle, *Los Angeles: From Pueblo to City of the Future* (San Francisco: MTL, 1995), 23.

13. Major Horace Bell, *Reminiscences of a Ranger; or, Early Times in Southern California* (Santa Barbara: Wallace Hebberd, 1927). Page 5 of this most important Los Angeles history describes the Star Building. On page 6, Bell lists Rand as one of the editors, along with John L. Lewis and Manuel Clemente Rojo.

14. Antonio Rios-Bustamante and Pedro Castillo, *An Illustrated History of Mexican Los Angeles, 1781–1985* (Los Angeles: University of California, Chicano Studies Research Center Publications, 1986), 99.

15. Editorial, *Los Angeles Star*, February 26, 1853.

16. According to the February 1956 Rand McNally house magazine, *Ranally World*, Rand became a local hero after he published the name of a gold rush camp killer in the *Star*. When the desperado came to town gunning for Rand, patrons of a local hangout overheard him plotting and convinced Rand to go looking for him. Rand went from saloon to saloon until he found and helped capture the killer. As a result, his stature grew and he was eventually elected to the city council. See Minutes of the Common Council, May 2, 1853, Archives of the City of Los Angeles, California.

17. The relationship between Rand and Reid is covered in Susanna Bryant Dakin, *A Scotch Paisano, Hugo Reid's Life in California, 1832–1852, Derived from his Correspondence* (Berkeley: University of California Press, 1939), 195, 197. See also Rice, *Southern California's First Newspaper*, 14.

18. According to Bruce Grant's Rand McNally history, George Curtis Rand's firm had eight presses that ran day and night to produce three hundred thousand copies of the book. The February 1956 issue of *Ranally* reported that Rand returned to New England in July 1853.

19. Several unpublished profiles of McNally exist in the Rand McNally Archive at the Newberry Library in Chicago. The accounts find McNally working as a journeyman printer in Buffalo, Toronto, and Albany, as well as for a newspaper in Memphis.

20. Bruce Grant, unpublished profile of Andrew McNally, Rand McNally Archive, Newberry Library, Chicago.

21. John Noble Wilford, *The Mapmakers* (New York: Alfred A. Knopf, 1981), 204–5.

22. Mrs. E. D. Neff to Andrew McNally III, February 8, 1952, collection of Marvine Neff Malouf.

23. Sarah Bixby Smith, *Adobe Days* (Los Angeles: Jake Zeitlin, 1931), 1.

24. Martin Ridge, *Atlas of American Frontiers* (Chicago: Rand McNally,

1993), 49.

25. *Pioneer Atlas of the American West* (Chicago: Rand McNally, 1956), 6. Rand McNally's first actual publication is noted in the unpublished company history on deposit at the Newberry Library.

26. Andrew McNally, *The World of Rand McNally* (New York: Newcomen Society in North America, 1956).

27. Andrew M. Modelski, *Railroad Maps of North America: The First Hundred Years* (Washington: Library of Congress, 1984), xix.

28. Editorial, *Los Angeles Evening Express*, July 17, 1877.

29. Ellen Lloyd Trover, ed., *Chronology and Documentary Handbook of the State of California* (Dobbs Ferry, NY: Oceana Publications, 1972), 16.

30. Walton Bean and James J. Rawls, *California: An Interpretive History* (New York: McGraw-Hill, 1988), 488.

31. E. B. McLaughlin, "73 Years of Pasadena Memories Gladden Her," *Pasadena Star-News*, August 29, 1953.

32. "Hotel Arrivals," *San Francisco Chronicle*, March 22, 1880. Other editions show J. B. Lankershim, J. C. Irvine, J. W. Pinkerton, and General U. S. Grant staying at the Palace.

33. E. B. McLaughlin, "Pioneer's 88th Birthday Memoirs of City Told," *Pasadena Star-News*, September 9, 1951.

34. Railroad literature had long touted the success of cooperative settlements like Pasadena (originally called the Indiana Colony), which were owned and irrigated communally.

35. Andrew McNally, "How I Became a Ranchman in California," *Country Life in America*, February 1904, 297–301. According to John E. Baur, *The Health Seekers of Southern California, 1870–1900* (San Marino, CA: Huntington Library, 1959), McNally was the first of the noted Chicagoans to settle in Los Angeles County for health reasons, but at the time his health was not known to have been in jeopardy.

36. Charles S. Gleed, ed., *From River to Sea: A Tourists' and Miners' Guide from the Missouri River to the Pacific Ocean* (Chicago: Rand McNally, 1882).

37. An undated account by his daughter Nannie, from the collection of Marvine Neff Malouf, lists a fifteen-acre acquisition for McNally—five acres each for his friends Armstrong, G. G. Green, and a Mr. Ward. A 1900 map tract book of Pasadena and Altadena, published by Albert G. Thurston, showed only one parcel larger than McNally's—the James A. Scripps grounds.

38. "McNally Will Construct Tunnel in Los Flores Canyon for Water Supply," *Los Angeles Daily Journal*, June 5, 1895. On January 9, 1949, Nannie Neff told the *Pasadena Star-News* the supply came from an Echo Mountain canyon ("Nationally Known Map Maker Chose Altadena as Ideal Home in 1880"). Four years later, on her birthday, she told the paper that she led her father to the underground stream after unearthing quartz speckled with gold.

39. Baur, *Health Seekers of Southern California*, 144–45.

40. "A California Home," *Sunday Chicago Chronicle*, June 5, 1898.

41. McWilliams, *Southern California*, 118.

42. Thomas S. Hines, *Burnham of Chicago* (Chicago: University of Chicago Press, 1974), 62–64.

43. David Woodward, *The All-American Map, Wax Engraving and Its Influence on Cartography* (Chicago: University of Chicago Press, 1977), 37. G. L. Dybwad and Joy V. Bliss, *Annotated Bibliography: World's Columbian Exposition, Chicago 1893* (Albuquerque, NM: The Book Stops Here, 1992), shows eighty-five publications from Rand McNally & Company. The largest map ever printed from a single plate, a 14 1/2 x 9 1/2 foot map of the United States, was exhibited at the fair, along with the electrotype from which it was made.

44. *Los Angeles Evening Express*, June 14, 1893.

45. W. H. Holibard, *Southern California, Its Attractions and Advantages for Small Farmers: A Collection of Facts and Figures* (Los Angeles: Rand McNally, 1888).

46. *Los Angeles Evening Express*, January 18, 1894.

47. "Publisher McNally's Fullerton Place," *Rural Californian*, March

1894, 151.

CHAPTER TWO

Epigraph. Chicago Record, May 16, 1899.

1. *Builder and Contractor*, January 31, 1894, 1. The figure is given as $115,000 by other sources. According to La Mirada historian C. W. Camp, McNally paid a quarter of the purchase price in 1888 and made the last payment in February 1893, when he received deed, title, and recording for his property.

2. Glenn S. Dumke, *The Boom of the Eighties in Southern California* (San Marino, CA: Huntington Library, 1991), 23. In January 1887, the Santa Fe consolidated eight short lines into the California Central Railroad. In 1889, it joined the California Southern and a Redondo Beach line to form the Southern California Railway, "the Pacific division of the great Santa Fe," as *Bancroft's Railway Guide* called it in the July 1890 issue.

3. Rice, *Southern California's First Newspaper*, 36.

4. James M. Guinn, "Los Angeles in the Later Sixties and Early Seventies," *Historical Society of Southern California Annual Publications* 3 (1893): 64.

5. C. W. Camp, "They Walked Before Us" (unpublished manuscript, 1985, City of La Mirada Department of Recreation and Parks), 1, reveals a 1975 discovery of fragmental artifacts.

6. *Pittsburgh Dispatch*, May 31, 1899.

7. C. W. Camp, *La Mirada: From Rancho to City* (Fullerton, CA: Sultana Press, 1970). According to Camp's introduction, he contacted the Mexican consul office for a translation and was told that *la mirada* meant "the look."

8. *The Country Gentleman in California* (Chicago: Rand McNally, 1896).

9. According to Sarah Noble Ives, *Altadena* (Pasadena, CA: Star-News Publishing Company, 1938), 93, McNally's spur gained access to the Altadena Railroad over Mendocino Street.

10. David Starr Jordan, *California and the Californians* (San Francisco: A. M. Robertson, 1907), 34.

11. *Landmarks Club Cookbook* (Los Angeles: Out West Co., 1903). Proceeds were used to preserve, as the book described them, "the remains of the old Franciscan Missions, the noblest and most impressive ruins in the United States" (ibid., 1).

12. Helen Belford, personal communication, January 18, 1986, Laguna Beach, and Mary Nevins, personal communication, October 17, 1984, and August 8, 1993, San Marino.

13. *Inland Printer*, February 1893, 419.

14. Mrs. Fred McNally to Nannie McNally Neff, February 1, 1893, collection of Marvine Neff Malouf.

15. "The Pageant of Roses at the Opera House," *Los Angeles Times*, April 7, 1893.

16. "At Lovely Altadena," *Chicago Herald*, February 17, 1894.

17. "Memo of Agreement, Andrew McNally, Owner, and F. L. Roehrig, Architect, for a 2-Story Frame Dwelling at La Mirada on the Windermere Ranch," *Builder and Contractor*, March 7, 1894, 4.

18. Wallace Neff baby book, courtesy Marvine Neff Malouf.

19. Ibid.

20. Five of her recipes appeared in the *Landmarks Club Cookbook*.

21. Invoices on deposit with the collection of the City of La Mirada.

22. Perhaps no one better epitomizes the dramatic fall from power Hispanic landowners experienced in California during the nineteenth century. Pico rose from poverty to become one of the richest and most powerful men in the region, where he served as governor in 1845. After California became an American state, he served on Los Angeles's city council, building the adobe on his new rancho in 1850 and using it as a country residence while financing the area's first major hotel. His fortunes turned after flood and famine ruined the cattle industry, which had made the land profitable, and by the time he died in 1894, he had lost the adobe.

23. Notice of Green's acquisition of the $64,812 parcel appeared in the *Los Angeles Evening Express* on April 23, 1894.

24. McNally's rail investments included the Altadena Railroad, the Pasadena and Pacific, the Pasadena and Mount Lowe Railway, and the Los Angeles and Pasadena Electric Railway.

25. According to Frank Staff, *The Picture Postcard and Its Origins* (New York: F. A. Praeger, 1966), the first such postcards appeared at the World's Columbian Exposition.

26. "A California Home."

27. Ives, *Altadena*, 93. According to Peterson, *Altadena's Golden Years*, 26, the trees were planted by John Woodbury in 1885. Reynolds Crutchfield, *Pasadena* (Palo Alto, CA: National Press, 1962), credits Thomas Hoad, foreman of the Woodbury Ranch, for planting the Himalayan cedars.

28. "A California Home."

29. Granddaughter Helen Belford believed McNally would have taken what he wanted. An obscure publication on file at the Chicago Historical Society, *Catalogue of Unclaimed Merchandise and Abandoned World's Fair Exhibits*, reveals that three sedan chairs, one porter's saddle, one bundle of palms, and nineteen kegs of anchovies were auctioned when the exhibits came down; conceivably, McNally could have acquired the remnants of a room. David Gebhard believed that of the two Turkish buildings at the fair, the smoking room might have come from what he termed the "minor" one.

30. Roehrig's father was an authority on Islamic culture and the Turkish language. See Robert Winter, ed., *Toward a Simpler Way of Life, The Arts and Crafts Architects of California* (Berkeley: University of California Press, 1997), 111.

31. Oscar O. Winther, "The Rise of Metropolitan Los Angeles, 1870–1900," *Huntington Library Quarterly* 10 (1947): 402.

32. A. Darlow and Harry Brook, *The Rand McNally Guide to California Illustrated via the Overland Route* (Chicago and New York: Rand McNally, 1903), 144–45. By 1934, with Andrew McNally no longer a part of the La Mirada promotion, mapmakers had nothing to hide; that year's California pocket map listed the city's population as three hundred. *Rand McNally California Pocket Map* (Chicago: Rand McNally, 1934).

CHAPTER THREE

Epigraph. Morrow Mayo, "Millionaires' Retreat," in Caughey & Caughey, *Los Angeles: Biography of a City.*

1. Baur, *Health Seekers of Southern California*, 145.

2. Mention of his condition appears in a November 29, 1902, letter from his brother James to Gertrude Potter Daniels, a Rand McNally author, on deposit with the Rand McNally papers at the Newberry Library: "My brother was not feeling well when he left Chicago, and consequently we thought it best not to give him full particulars and to worry him unnecessarily."

3. Joe Hendrickson, *The Tournament of Roses, A Pictorial History* (Los Angeles: Brooke House, 1971), 8.

4. Charles A. Higgins, *New Guide to the Pacific Coast, Santa Fe Route* (Chicago and New York: Rand McNally, 1894).

5. Accounts of McNally's activities appeared in the *Mount Lowe Echo*, edited by George Wharton James, on March 16, 1894, April 21, 1894, and August 25, 1894.

6. "Sorrowing Friends Gather to Pay Last Tribute to Dead," *Chicago Chronicle*, May 15, 1904.

7. "Letter to Fred McNally," in *Memorial Book of Andrew McNally, 1836–1904* (Chicago: Rand McNally, 1904), 122.

8. Resolution of the Board of Directors, Rand McNally & Company, May 16, 1904, in Grant, "Official History."

9. Obituary of William Rand, *New York Times*, June 22, 1915.

10. *Memorial Book of Andrew McNally*, 51.

11. James McNally to Nannie Neff, May 21, 1904, on deposit with the Rand McNally papers at the Newberry Library, Chicago.

12. Will filed in probate court of Cook County, May 26, 1904. Real estate accounted for a hundred thousand dollars, personal property for six hundred thousand. Most of the latter was 5,715 shares of Rand McNally stock, valued at a hundred dollars a share. The investments that failed—such as the Argus Oil Company, which McNally formed with partners in 1901—are not in the will. See *Los Angeles Evening Express*, March 1, 1901.

13. *Los Angeles Evening Express*, December 31, 1898. Bondholders who sold included G. G. Green, E. P. Dewey, M. H. Sherman, J. W. Hugus, and F. C. Bolt.

14. Ives, *Altadena*, 101. The author says the Neffs lived at the A. C. Armstrong House before purchasing Fred Armstrong's residence on Santa Clara Avenue (later renamed El Molino Avenue).

15. An account in the April 7, 1899, *Chicago Tribune* reports that forty passengers narrowly escaped death.

CHAPTER FOUR

Epigraph. Jack Smith column, *Los Angeles Times*, October 10, 1983.

1. *Encyclopedia of American Business History and Biography*, s.v. "Automobile Industry, 1896–1920."

2. Emily Wortis Leider, *California's Daughter: Gertrude Atherton and Her Times* (Stanford, CA: Stanford University Press, 1991), 226.

3. Wallace Neff, interview by Alson Clark and Jae Carmichael, November 7, 1977, Pasadena Oral History Project, Pasadena Historical Society, Pasadena, California.

4. Neff's papers in the Huntington Library include a one-page description of the grade-finder patent.

5. Caspar Ehmcke, personal communication, April 3, 1991.

6. Harold I. Shapiro, ed., *Ruskin in Italy: Letters to His Parents, 1845* (Oxford: Clarendon Press, 1972).

7. Louise M. George, "America for Me," *Maryland-Huntington Life* 11, no. 7 (December 19, 1914): 5.

8. Horace Sutton, *Travelers: The American Tourist from Stagecoach to Space Shuttle* (New York: Morrow, 1980), 128.

9. Neff did not visit the Slavic countries, Scandinavia, or the Iberian Peninsula.

10. George, "America for Me," 5.

11. "Boys Display Rare Form in Rifle Contest, William Neff Grabs Honors of Day," January 6, 1918, clipping from unknown newspaper, collection of Marvine Neff Malouf.

12. Al G. Waddell, "Motor Reserve on Rifle Range," *Los Angeles Times*, August 30, 1915.

13. George W. Robbins and L. Deming Tilton, eds., *Los Angeles, Preface to a Master Plan* (Los Angeles: Pacific Southwest Academy, 1941), 175.

14. Kevin Starr, *Americans and the California Dream, 1850–1915* (New York: Oxford University Press, 1973), 306.

15. Greene & Greene authority Randell Makinson believed the house on Orange Grove Boulevard "suffered from a limited budget which precluded the total design embellishments that were soon to become a hallmark of the Greenes." *Greene and Greene: Architecture as a Fine Art* (Salt Lake City: Peregrine Smith, 1977), 149.

16. Matt Weinstock, *My L.A.* (New York: Current Books, 1947), 72–73.

17. Margaret Stovall, "Famed Architect Neff Serves Wealthy, Poor," *Pasadena Star-News*, February 9, 1974.

18. Ralph Adams Cram, *My Life in Architecture* (Boston: Little, Brown, 1936), 206–12; Robert Muccigrosso, *American Gothic: The Mind and Art of Ralph Adams Cram* (Washington, DC: University Press of America, 1980), 166.

19. Cram, *My Life in Architecture*, 28.

20. Randell L. Makinson, "Greene and Greene," in Esther McCoy, *Five California Architects* (Los Angeles: Hennessey & Ingalls, 1987), 104.

21. Francis Bond, *Gothic Architecture in England* (London: B. T. Batsford, 1905).

22. "Wins Recognition for Artistic Work," *Pasadena Star-News*, June 21, 1917. Nine sketches were used.

23. Neff, interview by Clark and Carmichael. During this interview, Neff discussed being employed by the Chandler Company in the shipping yards.

24. *Friday Morning Club, Los Angeles, California, 1918–19 Directory* (Los Angeles: Fred S. Lang Co., 1918).

25. Maggie Savoy, "Wallace Neff: Father of Showcase Houses," *Los Angeles Times*, April 11, 1969.

26. "E. Wallace Neff Making Progress," *Pasadena Star-News*, April 15, 1922; Stovall, "Famed Architect Neff Serves Wealthy, Poor."

27. Neff, interview by Clark and Carmichael.

CHAPTER FIVE

Epigraph. Harold Kirker, *California Historical Society Quarterly*, 1972.

1. Neff, interview by Clark and Carmichael.

2. *Country Life* 41, no. 1 (November 1921): 70.

3. "A Small California House," *California Southland*, September 1921, 19.

4. Neff, interview by Clark and Carmichael. David Gebhard wrote on November 7, 1983, after searching Smith's papers at the University of California at Santa Barbara Architecture and Design Collection, "I can only conclude that Mr. Neff's admiration for Smith was in his very last years made more concrete than it was in fact," for there was no mention of Neff. City directory listings show Neff, without a Smith or Edwards affiliation, working in Santa Barbara in 1920 and 1921. The evocation of Smith's appearance comes from a 1985 interview with Carl Dumbolton, who was employed in Smith's office and went on to represent building supply manufacturers.

5. David Gebhard, *George Washington Smith, 1876–1930, The Spanish Colonial Revival in California* (Alhambra, CA: Cunningham Press, 1964). See also David Gebhard, *Santa Barbara: The Creation of a New Spain in America* (Santa Barbara, CA: University Art Museum, University of California at Santa Barbara, 1982), 19.

6. E. Wallace Neff, "Impressions of the Santa Barbara Earthquake," *Allied Architects Association of Los Angeles Bulletin* 1, no. 10 (August 1, 1925).

7. *Los Angeles Times*, April 4, 1926. Neff was apparently a member of a panel that prepared restoration plans for the Mission Santa Barbara. The eight-month survey concluded that steel girders and concrete columns sunk into the adobe walls could save most of the structure.

8. McWilliams, *Southern California*, 358.

9. Ibid., 362.

10. Ibid, 359.

11. Elizabeth McMillian, *California Colonial: The Spanish and Rancho Revival Styles* (Atglen, PA: Schiffer, 2002), 32.

CHAPTER SIX

Epigraph. W. W. Robinson, "The Real Estate Boom of the Twenties," in Caughey and Caughey, *Los Angeles: Biography of a City*.

1. Evelyn de Wolfe, "L.A. Developers Recall Early Days," *Los Angeles Times*, March 22, 1987.

2. Kevin Starr, *Material Dreams: Southern California Through the 1920s* (New York: Oxford University Press, 1990), 72.

3. "Who's Doing It," *Southwest Builder and Contractor*, November 21, 1919.

4. Clifford Hoskins and Edna Schoch Hoskins, personal communication, February 27, 1984, and October 29, 1992.

5. Advertisement, *California Life* 19, no. 1 (October 21, 1922): 20.

6. Norman J. Boroughs, "Firm's Meteoric Rise to One of World's Largest Realty Organizations Outlined," *Los Angeles Times*, August 19, 1923. When his health failed in 1941, Meline sold the company to his general manager. Meline died at sixty-nine in 1944. See also Bill Bradley, ed., *Commercial Los Angeles, 1925–1947, Photographs from the "Dick" Whittington Studio* (Glendale, CA: Interurban Press, 1981). Pierce Edson Benedict, ed., *History of Beverly Hills* (Beverly Hills, CA: A. H. Cawston, 1934), positions him as the third-highest selling agent at the Rodeo Land and Water Company.

7. In a 1962 pocket notebook, collection of the author, Neff noted "Meline, 1921–1922."

8. The AIA award Meline received is noted in "Jury Designates Notable Examples of Architecture," *Southwest Builder and Contractor*, April 16, 1920. Nannie Neff saved her son's rendering of the First National Bank design and inserted it into his baby book.

9. Pocket notebook, collection of the author. Today architects are tested on general structures, lateral forces, materials and methods, construction documents, mechanical and electrical systems, codes and access issues, pre-design and building planning, building technology, site design, and oral presentations.

10. *Los Angeles City Directory* (1923), 3359–60.

11. Williams received his license in June 1921. See *Southwest Builder and Contractor*, June 10, 1921.

12. Frank Meline, *Los Angeles, Metropolis of the West* (Los Angeles: Francis H. Webb, 1929).

13. Harry H. Culver, "The Essentials of Selling Real Estate," *Los Angeles Realtor*, June 1925.

14. T. Beverley Keim Jr., "Practical Artistry in Residential Architecture," *Los Angeles Realtor*, June 1925.

15. "Almost all of my clients were sent by William Wilson." Neff, interview by Clark and Carmichael.

16. Hoskins and Schoch Hoskins, personal communication, February 27, 1984.

17. "Thousands of Home Seekers in South," *Pasadena Star-News*, December 15, 1923.

18. "Famous Yachtsman Keith Spalding Has Purchased a Site Opposite the New City Hall to Be Operated by the Maryland Hotel," *Pasadena Star-News*, October 12, 1926.

19. Ralph Hancock, *Fabulous Boulevard* (New York: Funk & Wagnalls, 1949), 127.

20. Dione Neutra, "To Tell the Truth, Dione Neutra," interview by Lawrence Weschler, 1983, Oral History Program, University of California, Los Angeles, California.

21. Gloria Swanson, *Swanson on Swanson* (New York: Random House, 1980), 105.

22. Neff also received AIA awards in 1929, 1938, 1952, and 1954.

23. Hoskins and Schoch Hoskins, personal communication.

24. Neff, *Architecture of Southern California*.

25. Ed Warmington, personal communication, August 18, 1984.

26. Cannon had been a Neff classmate and fraternity brother at MIT.

27. Honnold had a fruitful career. Prior to working in Neff's office, he worked for George Washington Smith. He assisted Cedric Gibbons in the design of Gibbons's art deco–style house in Santa Monica, later writing a guide to Los Angeles for the 1956 national AIA conference.

28. Others Neff employed through the years include Robert Stanton, Charles A. Hill, Frederick C. Marsh, Mark W. Ellsworth, T. L. Pletch, E. Wessel Klausen, William Decker Holdridge, Aubrey St. Clair, E. J. Voight, Jack M. Benson, Robert Eilertsen, Henry Wesley, Michael A. Jordan, Burton F. Lamfrom, and John R. Jarvis.

29. Hoskins, personal communication.

30. Andrea P. A. Belloli, ed., *Wallace Neff, 1895–1982: The Romance of Regional Architecture* (San Marino, CA: Huntington Library, 1989), 112.

31. Hoskins, personal communication.

32. George Brandow, personal communication, June 2, 1987.

33. Hoskins, personal communication.

34. Lucinda W. Pennington, *A Past to Remember, The History of Culver City* (Culver City, CA: City of Culver City, 1976), 28.

35. Starr, *Material Dreams*, 72.

36. Swanson, *Swanson on Swanson*, 82.

37. Anita Loos, *Kiss Hollywood Good-by* (New York: Viking Press, 1974),

30–31.

38. *Southwest Builder and Contractor*, February 11, 1927.

39. Cliff May, personal communication, October 16, 1986.

40. The general contractors who executed Neff's designs during the 1920s and 1930s tended to be single practitioners, many of whom did not survive the stock market crash. "He was very smart about contractors," one of his draftsmen, Peter Liszt, said. "He had two or three he turned to for bids, and he seldom sought others." They included W. J. Jean, William C. Warmington, Carl G. Johnson, Clarence P. Day, Hogan Company, Karl J. Moller, Kemp & Haskett, Lars Swanson, J. V. McNeil, Frederick H. Ruppel, and Walter Johnson.

41. Wallace Neff, interview by Sarah Cooper, 2002, Pasadena Oral History Project, Pasadena Historical Society, Pasadena, California.

CHAPTER SEVEN

1. Kaufmann's clients included Ben Meyer and Milton Getz of Beverly Hills, and Isidor Eisner of Hancock Park. Unlike Neff, Kaufmann saw value in advertising his architectural services and volunteering for community projects like the chamber of commerce's Citizens Committee on Parks, Playgrounds, and Beaches. His La Quinta Resort in Palm Springs was just about the most masterful large-scale example of the California Spanish idiom produced during the 1920s, more striking even than Reginald Johnson's seaside Santa Barbara Biltmore Hotel. "Kaufmann was an excellent businessman," Johnson's son, Joe, observed. (Joe Johnson, personal communication, March 13, 1987.) Neff, discussing Kaufmann's architectural output years later, admitted that he was "probably the best of them all." (Neff, interview by Clark and Carmichael.)

2. H. Roy Kelley, "The California Situation from the Architect's Point of View," *Pacific Coast Architect* 33, no. 11 (November 1928): 37.

3. H. Roy Kelley, "Homes Exhibit Exalts Style," *Los Angeles Times*, July 1, 1928.

4. Neff, interview by Clark and Carmichael.

5. "Down the Street in Search of Beauty," *California Southland*, May 1926, 16.

6. "Mail Invitations to Many Friends," *Pasadena Star-News*, April 9, 1926.

CHAPTER EIGHT

Epigraph. Brendan Gill, *The Dream Come True: Great Houses of Los Angeles* (New York: Lippincott & Crowell, 1980), 87.

1. Loos, *Kiss Hollywood Good-by*, 7.

2. McWilliams, *Southern California*, 331.

3. Swanson, *Swanson on Swanson*, 103.

4. The Assistance League, a charitable organization, earned a fee as an intermediary between property owners and film companies.

5. Ann Lee Morgan and Colin Naylor, eds., *Contemporary Architects* (Chicago: St. James Press, 1987), 644–45.

6. Janet L. Abu-Lughod, *New York, Chicago, Los Angeles: America's Global Cities* (Minneapolis: University of Minnesota Press, 1999), 161.

7. Christopher Gray, "Once the Tallest Building, but Since 1967 a Ghost," *New York Times*, January 2, 2005. Bourne's father, Frederick, died in 1919, leaving an estate of $25 million to his only son. The extent of his stake in the company can only be speculated on.

8. Emily Bourne Boxley, interview by author, March 15, 1985.

9. Accounts of the founding of San Marino and the influence of Henry Huntington include Selena A. Spurgeon, *Henry Edwards Huntington: His Life and His Collections* (San Marino, CA: Huntington Library, 1992), 113; Richard Bigger and James D. Kitchen, *How the Cities Grew: A Century of Municipal Independence and Expansionism in Metropolitan Los Angeles* (Los Angeles: Bureau of Governmental Research, University of California, 1952), 87; James Thorpe, *Henry Edwards Huntington: A Biography* (Berkeley: University of California Press, 1994), 291; John D. Weaver, *El Pueblo Grande: Los Angeles from the Brush Huts of Yangna to the Skyscrapers of the Modern Megalopolis* (Los Angeles, 1973), 48; and Joseph S. O'Flaherty, *Those Powerful Years: The South Coast and Los Angeles, 1887–1917* (Hicksville, NY: Exposition Press, 1978), 150.

10. *Talking about Pasadena, Selections from Oral Histories* (Pasadena, CA: Pasadena Oral History Project, 1986), 12–13. Picturesque and pastoral as San Marino was, its residents had the foibles and prejudices of Caucasians in any other American town. Asians, blacks, and other non-Anglo-Saxon Protestants were forbidden to own land there because of covenants in the city's deeds. Pockets of minority populations emerged around such restricted enclaves: Chinese lived in a Chinatown at Pico Street and Raymond Avenue, and black Pasadenans lived on South Vernon Avenue or in northwest Pasadena. Even a highly respected professional like the African American architect Paul Williams was prohibited by law from living in the neighborhoods where he designed houses; not until the Supreme Court outlawed racially restrictive covenants in 1949 could he or any other member of an ethnic minority have bought land in San Marino.

11. Bourne Boxley, interview. Resort hotels underwrote magazines like *California Life*, which published news of guests' arrivals. The myriad realty companies in the area bought advertising, and the realtors would be asked to refer clients to architects.

12. The Johnson, Kaufmann, and Coate collaborative design appeared in *Architectural Forum* in July 1922.

13. Robert Winter, personal communication during the annual California Historical Society Winter Tour, 1987.

14. "Beautiful Home Under Construction Shown in Miniature Replica Now on Exhibit," *Pasadena Star-News*, November 25, 1924.

15. Rexford Newcomb, *Western Architect*, February 1926, 22–23.

16. Charles Moore, *The City Observed: Los Angeles, A Guide to Its Architecture and Landscapes* (New York: Random House, 1984), 345.

17. Bourne's house in Pocantico Hills, New York, also had an Aeolian pipe organ, more elaborate than even John D. Rockefeller's, for the senior Bourne served as a director of the Aeolian piano and organ company.

18. Cari Beauchamp, "The Women Behind the Camera in Early Hollywood," in Helena Lumme, *Great Women of Film* (New York: Billboard Books, 2002), 113.

19. Frances Marion, *Off with Their Heads: A Serio-Comic Tale of Hollywood* (New York: Macmillan, 1972).

20. Eileen Whitfield, *Pickford: The Woman Who Made Hollywood* (Lexington, KY: University Press of Kentucky, 1997), 423–26.

21. "The One Genius in Pictures—Frances Marion," *Silver Screen* 4, no. 3 (January 1934): 53.

22. David Nasaw, *The Chief: The Life of William Randolph Hearst* (Boston: Houghton Mifflin, 2000), 121.

23. Lumme, *Great Women of Film*, 114.

24. Cari Beauchamp, *Without Lying Down: Frances Marion and the Powerful Women of Early Hollywood* (New York: Scribner, 1997), 128.

25. Andrew Rolle, "From Field to Pulpit to Screen: The Legendary Fred Thomson," *Occidental*, Winter 1985–86, 14–17.

26. Beauchamp, *Without Lying Down*, 161.

27. John O. Pohlmann, "Alphonzo E. Bell: A Biography," *Historical Society of Southern California Quarterly* 46, no. 4 (December 1964): 326.

28. Marion, *Off with Their Heads*.

29. Rexford Newcomb, *The Spanish House for America* (Philadelphia and London: J. B. Lippincott Company, 1927).

30. Greg Mitchell, *The Campaign of the Century: Upton Sinclair's Race for Governor of California and the Birth of Media Politics* (New York: Random House, 1992), 81.

31. Beauchamp, *Without Lying Down*, 244.

32. Charles Lockwood, *The Estates of Beverly Hills, Holmby Hills, Bel-Air, Beverly Park* (Beverly Hills, CA: Hyland & Lockwood, 1989), 75. For years, realtors viewing the unoccupied house rued the difficulty of subdividing the hillside profitably. See Art Seidenbaum, "Life and Cli-

mate at $3.5 Million," *Los Angeles Times*, April 14, 1976.

33. Cari Beauchamp, personal communication, January 25, 2000.

34. Ruth Ryon, "Mogul.com @ $20-Million Site," *Los Angeles Times*, January 4, 1998.

35. Beauchamp, personal communication.

CHAPTER NINE

Epigraph. Reginald Johnson, *California Southland*, February 1926.

1. Neff, *Architecture of Southern California.*

2. His distaste for the style is made clear in his book, *Architecture of Southern California*, in which only one villa-style house—movie producer Sol Wurtzel's—is depicted, while dozens done in the California-Mediterranean style are included.

3. Baur, *Health Seekers of Southern California*, 48.

4. "The bookish erudition of the architects was increasingly matched by the worldly awareness of their clients, who through actual travel or through reading were at least superficially becoming aware of the 'correct' architectural styles." David Gebhard, "The Spanish Colonial Revival in Southern California," *Journal of the Society of Architectural Historians* 26, no. 2 (May 1967): 136.

5. Neff, interview by Clark and Carmichael.

6. McCoy, *Five California Architects*, 18. Bernard Maybeck, another California architect, used other methods of "aging," like throwing pails of muddy water onto new walls.

7. Robert Winter's notes in a printed program for a Da Camera Society concert at the villa in the early 1980s suggest this explanation (collection of the Da Camera Society, Mount St. Mary's College, Los Angeles). Dr. Winter's frequent collaborator, David Gebhard, noted in a lecture on May 10, 1991, at a California Preservation Foundation conference in Santa Barbara, that the coloration was derived from water-based paint sprayed on the structure and sealed with linseed oil or hot wax. Four colors may have been added to create an appearance of patina.

8. Cornelia Fairbanks Vaillancourt, personal communication, September 17, 1985.

9. "The Fairbanks Residence in Pasadena," *California Southland*, November 1926, 17, 27.

10. Lenore Swoiskin, archivist of Sears, letter to author, April 7, 1988.

11. Josephine Leslie, personal communication, June 3, 1988.

12. The same masons fashioned the surround for Neff's Erle M. Leaf House in Hancock Park.

13. John Elliott, personal communication, March 28, 1985, and July 22, 1985. Lilly Anheuser Busch had thirteen children and countless grandchildren, and the funds to keep them all comfortable. It is therefore surprising that one of her grandchildren, Ann Magnus Flannigan, resented her grandmother's gift to her sister Lilly Magnus Berg. Sibling rivalry may have been at the heart of it.

14. John Elliott, letter to author, April 24, 1995.

CHAPTER TEN

Epigraph. Advertisement, *Sunset*, April 1924.

1. Louisa Burrows, *Arthur Albion Libby, Pioneer in the Refrigeration and Canning of Meats* (n.p., n.d.), 8.

2. Obituary of A. A. Libby, *Pasadena Star-News*, July 18, 1899.

3. Libby's son, Dr. Arthur A. Libby Jr., had sold his interest in the company to G. F. Swift in 1888, in order to practice ophthalmology.

4. Louisa Burrows, *Genealogies of William French Burrows and Annie Libby Burrows* (Syracuse: Salina Press, 1970).

5. Marvine Neff Malouf, personal communication, October 1987.

6. James Trager, *The People's Chronology: A Year-by-Year Record of Human Events from Prehistory to the Present* (New York: Holt, Rinehart and Winston, 1979), 750.

7. "Los Angeles Legal Practitioner Making Address at Handsome Residence Situated on Holladay Road," *Pasadena Star-News*, November 12, 1927.

8. F. Scott Fitzgerald, *The Great Gatsby* (New York: Charles Scribner's Sons, 1925), 7–8.

9. "Premiere of a Brilliant Season," *California Life* 19, no. 10 (December 23, 1922): 4. The initial announcement appeared in the *Los Angeles Times* on April 25, 1922.

10. Lucille Miller, personal communication, March 2, 1984.

11. The houses on the grounds of the Huntington Hotel were commissioned by the women's rights leader Clara Burdette and D. M. Linnard, the manager of the Huntington and Maryland hotels. Neither house had a kitchen, since the occupants ate at the hotel.

12. Selena Spurgeon, personal communication, January 5, 1999. Spurgeon, a Huntington biographer, verified that Huntington's sister Caroline, who was married to Ed Burke Holladay, was Helen's mother. Collis Holladay was Helen's brother.

13. "Evening Wedding Is Beautiful Ceremony," *Pasadena Star-News*, June 22, 1923.

14. "Attractive Type of Residences in Homewood Heights Tract," *Pasadena Star-News*, December 1, 1921,

15. Belford, personal communication.

16. "Unexpected End Comes to Wife of Pasadenan," *Los Angeles Times*, August 21, 1926.

17. Arthur Neff, personal communication, October 31, 1983, and January 15, 1985. Arthur said that a generation later his cousin Bill Up de Graff inherited $17 million in Libby stock. Court papers show that Louise inherited $100,000 when her hundred-year-old aunt, Jeanette Libby, died in 1967 (Sup. Ct. C-906892, C-906893).

CHAPTER ELEVEN

Epigraph. McMillian, *California Colonial*, 23.

1. Yoch landscaped Neff's designs for Henry W. Schultz in Pasadena, Amelita Galli-Curci in Westwood, and Henry F. Haldemann in Holmby Hills. Bashford landscaped the Bourne, Schultz, and Miller grounds. Shellhorn designed the Edgar Richards landscape in the 1950s, while Huntsman-Trout planned the Chandler estate in Hancock Park. Church was responsible for Henry Singleton's vast plantings. Hanson worked on the first King Vidor House, the first William-Edith Goetz House, the Fred Niblo House, Pickfair, and Neff's San Marino house. But perhaps the best-trained landscape architect Wallace Neff worked with was Ralph Cornell, the planner of the nascent campus of UCLA.

2. William W. Clary, *History of the Law Firm of O'Melveny & Myers, 1885–1965*, vol. 1 (Los Angeles, 1966), 201.

3. Lee W. Lenz, *Rancho Santa Ana Botanic Garden: The First Fifty Years, 1927–1977* (Claremont, CA: Rancho Santa Fe Botanic Garden, 1977), 7.

4. Ibid.

5. *County Courier*, Orange County Historical Society 29, no. 9 (November 1999): 4.

6. "Albert Yorba: Member of Pioneer Family," *Los Angeles Times*, September 24, 1993.

7. Margaret Redington Reid, "Western Home Building and Modernizing," *Sunset*, April 1935, 44.

8. Alson Clark, "The 'Californian' Architecture of Gordon B. Kaufmann," *Society of Architectural Historians Southern California Chapter Review* 1, no. 3 (Summer 1982): 5.

9. Doyce Nunis Jr., "Los Angeles in the Eye of the Twentieth Century" (lecture, Historical Society of Southern California, Los Angeles, California, November 14, 1999). Nunis cites three national organizations founded to improve reinforced concrete design.

10. *Bienvenidos al Canon de Santa Ana! A History of the Santa Ana Canyon* (Santa Ana, CA: Orange County Board of Supervisors, 1976).

11. Pamela Young, site curator for the Rancho Los Alamitos Foundation, personal communication, August 9, 1994.

12. Ernest Bryant II, personal communication, June 24, 1986.

CHAPTER TWELVE

Epigraph. Leo C. Rosten, *Hollywood, the Movie Colony, the Movie Makers* (New York: Harcourt Brace, 1941); Vachel Lindsay, *The Art of the Moving Picture* (New York: Macmillan, 1915).

1. Obituary of George Elkins, *Los Angeles Times*, February 26, 1993.

2. Eleanor Boardman, personal communication, September 6, 1986.

3. *City of Beverly Hills* (Beverly Hills, CA: Gibraltar Savings and Loan Association, 1970).

4. A. Scott Berg, *Goldwyn: A Biography* (New York: Alfred A. Knopf, 1989), 227.

5. Rhoda Rosen, personal communication, March 23, 1984. A run-in with Joan Crawford seems to have been Neff's one gaffe in the film community.

6. Irving McKee, *"Ben-Hur" Wallace: The Life of General Lew Wallace* (Berkeley: University of California Press, 1947), 188.

7. Harold Grieve scrapbooks, on deposit at the Academy of Motion Picture Arts and Sciences, Beverly Hills, California.

8. "Director Finishes New Home," *Los Angeles Times*, October 16, 1927. The house is described as being "constructed of Calabasas granite, reinforced concrete and stucco."

9. Gebhard and Winter, *Architecture in Los Angeles*, 368.

10. Belloli, *Wallace Neff*, 113.

11. According to Katharine Hepburn's autobiography, *Me: Stories of My Life* (New York: Knopf, 1991), she paid Niblo a thousand dollars a month in rent when she came to Hollywood in 1934. Both the Niblo and Marion-Thomson houses were on the market. "They lived in the house for two years," Hepburn wrote of the Barnes couple, who bought from Frances Marion. "Never paid the taxes. Moved out. And then the house was sold for the taxes—about seventy thousand dollars. That's when I could have bought it. Stupid me" (ibid., 189). For other celebrities who lived in Niblo's house, see Bert Van Tuyle, *Know Your Los Angeles, An Unusual Guide* (Los Angeles: Know Your California, 1938), 44.

12. Cary Grant, interview by author, January 21, 1984; "Sunset Splendor: The Beverly Hills Home of Jules and Doris Stein," *House & Garden*, May 1986, 205.

13. "Sunset Splendor," 205.

14. Gerald Oppenheimer, personal communication, November 10, 1984.

15. Felicia Paik, "Private Properties," *Wall Street Journal*, September 11, 1998.

16. Raymond Durgnat and Scott Simmon, *King Vidor, American* (Berkeley: University of California Press, 1988), 59.

17. Bob Thomas, *Thalberg: Life and Legend* (New York: Doubleday, 1969), 86.

18. King Vidor, *A Tree Is a Tree* (New York: Harcourt Brace, 1953), 101.

19. Fitzgerald, *Taps at Reveille*. Historians have speculated that Irving Thalberg and Norman Shearer were the models, but the description of the house and the marital strife jibe with the Vidors. Fitzgerald scholar Matthew J. Bruccoli corroborates the location in *Some Sort of Epic Grandeur: The Life of F. Scott Fitzgerald* (New York: Harcourt Brace, 1981), 324. Historian Barry Menikoff speculates that the Fitzgeralds picked up the Vidors at their Neff house and went together to a party at the Thalbergs' house (Menikoff, personal communication, June 12, 2003).

20. Durgnat and Simmon, *King Vidor*, 61.

21. Kevin Brownlow, *Hollywood, The Pioneers* (New York: Knopf, 1979), 192.

22. Boardman, personal communication.

23. In fact, the hall widths varied from three feet four inches in the servants' quarters to four feet eight inches in the public passages. The walls were two feet thick.

24. Bernard Brereton, *The Practical Lumberman* (Tacoma, WA: ca. 1921), 31. Although it is widely known as Oregon pine, the correct name is Douglas fir. Knots are objectionable to some because tests demonstrate that beams break at knots, and timber struts will fail.

25. Harry Martin, personal communication, June 3, 1988.

26. Fitzgerald, *Taps at Reveille.*

27. Caspar Ehmcke, personal communication, August 21, 1987.

28. F. Scott Fitzgerald, *The Last Tycoon: An Unfinished Novel* (New York: Charles Scribner's Sons, New York, 1941), 3.

29. Edith Mayer Goetz, personal communication, May 6, 1985.

30. Irene Mayer Selznick, *A Private View* (New York: Knopf, 1983), 194.

31. Betty Lou Young, *Pacific Palisades: Where the Mountains Meet the Sea* (Pacific Palisades, CA: Pacific Palisades Historical Society Press, 1983), 142.

32. Meryle Secrest, *Somewhere for Me: A Biography of Richard Rodgers* (New York: Knopf, 2001), 156.

33. Stephen Farber and Marc Green, *Hollywood Dynasties* (New York: Delilah, 1984), 55.

34. Selznick, *A Private View*, 194. In an advertisement in *Architectural Digest* 10, no. 3: 173, general contractor William C. Warmington credited Neff with having altered the Selznick House. The author is unaware of such a project, but has not reviewed building permits in city records.

CHAPTER THIRTEEN

Epigraph. Gill, *The Dream Come True*, 9.

1. Neff, interview by Clark and Carmichael. Neff got the referral for the Pickfair commission from Clarence P. Day, a Pasadena architect and contractor.

2. Mathis Chazanov, "Pickfair, Relic of Golden Age of Hollywood, Razed," *Los Angeles Times*, April 20, 1990.

3. Savoy, "Wallace Neff: Father of Showcase Houses."

4. Whitfield, *Pickford*, 100.

5. Charles Lockwood, *Dream Palaces: Hollywood at Home* (New York: Viking Press, 1981), 99.

6. Beauchamp, *Without Lying Down*, 124.

7. "Douglas Fairbanks Responds to Story," *Los Angeles Times*, November 15, 1981.

8. Gill, *The Dream Come True*, 9.

9. W. W. Robinson, *Southern California Local History* (Los Angeles: Historical Society of Southern California, 1993), 18.

10. June 25, 1919, building permit, City of Beverly Hills.

11. Dorin Langley Sommer, *Hollywood: The Glamour Years, 1919–1941* (New York: W. H. Smith, 1988), 131.

12. Bob Considine and Bill Slocum, *Dempsey by the Man Himself* (New York: Simon and Schuster, 1960), 112.

13. Kevin Thomas, "Filmmaking Moves West, Creating a New Lifestyle," *Los Angeles Times*, October 7, 1999.

14. Neff worked with a number of other interior designers during his career, including Hazel Rae Davey, William Haines, Betty Barr, and Charles Ray Glass.

15. Arthur Knight, *The Hollywood Style* (New York: Macmillan, 1969), 25.

16. Calculation based on a 1938 list Neff made of his major commissions.

17. Building permit no. 21234, City of Beverly Hills, November 14, 1961. The Nuclear Survival Corporation, which she appears to have financed, did the work.

18. Irving Gellman, personal communication, October 4, 1984.

19. Neff also designed an estate called Rancho Zorro (which included a one-story house for a caretaker) on a twenty-five-hundred-acre tract Pickford and Fairbanks purchased in North San Diego County in 1926. While he was updating Pickfair the same year, he designed a beach house for the couple on a lot in Santa Monica with 150 feet of frontage. Mary's mother, Charlotte, commissioned a Mediterranean-style villa down the hill from Pickfair, near the Beverly Hills Hotel, also in 1926, and in 1931, as the country faced economic hardship, Neff

and Pickford ventured into the field of low-cost housing.

CHAPTER FOURTEEN
Epigraph. Robert Alexander, "Architecture, Planning and Social Responsibility," interview by Marlene L. Laskey, 1989, UCLA Oral History Program, University of California, Los Angeles.
1. David H. Stratton, *Tempest Over Teapot Dome: The Story of Albert B. Fall* (Norman, OK: University of Oklahoma Press, 1998), 20.
2. Meryle Secrest, *Frank Lloyd Wright* (New York: Knopf, 1992), 295. Secrest described the Doheny commissions as "an extraordinary complex of buildings, never built, for the Edward H. Doheny ranch in the Sierra Madre of California." In an interview by the author in May 1998, Albert C. Martin Jr., in jest, called the church his father designed for the Dohenys "the Church of the Holy Oil."
3. Samuel Lunden, personal communication to Barton Phelps, 1983.
4. Dorothy Chandler, who was also a Neff client, originated the Woman of the Year campaign. The Chandlers moved out of the house Neff designed for them in Los Feliz after commissioning Gordon Kaufmann to design a house in Arcadia.
5. Gibson, Dunn & Crutcher to Wallace Neff, June 8, 1960, September 16, 1970, collection of Marvine Neff Malouf. Leases of the McNally property were initiated with Standard Oil Company of California in 1912. As late as 1960, the McNally heirs contracted with a drilling company to seek oil.
6. Charles Lockwood, "Oil Boom Fueled Growth of L.A.," *Los Angeles Times*, August 18, 1985.
7. Paul Schwenzfeier, personal communication, May 3, 1988.
8. Martin, personal communication.
9. Harry Martin, interview by Sarah Cooper, 2002, Pasadena Oral History Project, Pasadena Historical Society, Pasadena, California.
10. Rotten stone was a pumice powder mixed with oil, applied to wood with a soft cloth and then wiped off.
11. Martin, personal communication.
12. Years later, Harriman also remembered overhearing Mrs. Anderson agreeing to pay fifty thousand dollars for a Persian carpet.
13. Martin, personal communication.
14. Carol Hameetman, personal communication, June 3, 1988. Neff told Hameetman this story when she visited him at the Californian Convalescent Hospital.
15. *California Arts & Architecture*, November 1929; *Pacific Coast Architect* 32, no. 3 (August 1927): 2, 28–32; *Architectural Digest* 7, no. 4: 22.
16. Ralph D. Cornell, "Half a Century as a Southern California Landscape Architect," interview by James V. Mink, Enid H. Douglass, and Richard K. Nystrom, 1970, Oral History Collection, University of California, Los Angeles.
17. Hoskins, personal communication.
18. Margaret Leslie Davis, *Dark Side of Fortune, Triumph and Scandal in the Life of Oil Tycoon Edward L. Doheny* (Berkeley: University of California Press, 1998), 246–47.
19. Ibid.
20. Elliott, personal communication, March 28, 1985.
21. King Gillette appears in the memoirs of Upton Sinclair's wife, Mary, *Southern Belle* (New York: Crown, 1957), 224–26. His sole biographer is Russell B. Adams Jr., who wrote *King C. Gillette, The Man and His Wonderful Shaving Device* (Boston: Little, Brown, 1978).
22. *Architectural Digest* 7, no. 4 (1930): 80–82; *California Arts & Architecture*, June 1932.
23. Christopher Silvester, ed., *The Grove Book of Hollywood* (New York: Grove Press, 1998), 143; Salka Viertel, *The Kindness of Strangers* (New York: Holt, Rinehart, and Winston, 1969), 143.
24. John Elliott, personal communication, December 21, 1983.
25. Adams, *King C. Gillette*, 181. A figure of five hundred thousand dollars is cited for the entire project, no doubt at least half of it for the land.

26. Neff, interview by Clark and Carmichael.
27. Adams, *King C. Gillette*, 179–80.
28. Ibid., 181.
29. Aaron Curtiss, "Accord May End Impasse over Parkland," *Los Angeles Times*, March 14, 1996.
30. "A Shopping Center for Home Builders in Pasadena," *California Southland*, October 1928, 21.
31. Martin, personal communication.
32. Abraham Hoffman, "Albert Einstein at Caltech," *California History* 76, no. 4 (Winter 1997): 116.
33. Wallace Neff architectural drawings, on deposit at the Huntington Library, San Marino, California.
34. Building Department records, City of San Marino, California.
35. Just when Neff began referring to his style as Californian is unclear, but architect Rexford Newcomb used the phrase "Californian style" to describe the regional Spanish-colonial revival in *Western Architect*, February 1926, 22.
36. A. E. Hanson, *An Arcadian Landscape: The California Gardens of A. E. Hanson, 1920–1932*, ed. David Gebhard and Sheila Lynds (Los Angeles: Hennessey & Ingalls, 1985).
37. Martin Filler, "Surveying a Century," *House Beautiful*, November 1996, 128.
38. Southland Title Corporation Records (lot 26, tract 9870, book 142, 89–90), Map Records of Los Angeles County, Burbank, California.
39. Hanson, *An Arcadian Landscape*, 12–13.
40. "Stock Debacle Needed Lesson," *Los Angeles Times*, December 15, 1929. Neff designed Baer's Santa Barbara house on La Vareda in 1924.
41. Kate Crane-Gartz, *Seventh Book* (Pasadena, CA: Mary P. Sinclair, 1931), 121.
42. Emily Bourne Boxley, personal communication, March 15, 1985.
43. The Hutchins House is located on Avondale Road in San Marino.
44. Morgan and Naylor, *Contemporary Architects*, 645.
45. Marshall Stimson, *Fun, Fights, and Fiestas in Old Los Angeles, An Autobiography* (Los Angeles: Gordon Stimson, 1966), 282.
46. Elliott, personal communication, March 28, 1985, and July 22, 1985.
47. Bourne Boxley, personal communication.
48. In the *California Register, 1966, Social Blue Book of California* (Beverly Hills, CA: Social Blue Book of California, Inc., 1966), 616, they were listed as "M/M Wallace Neff" on "Alta Vista Ave." in South Pasadena.
49. "Master Detail Series No. 7 California Spanish," *Architectural Forum* 60, no. 3 (March 1934): 218.
50. "The Dream That Came True," *California Arts & Architecture*, April 1932, 25–26.
51. Peggy Hamlin, personal communication, October 1999.

CHAPTER FIFTEEN
Epigraph. David Gebhard and Harriette von Breton, *Los Angeles in the Thirties* (Los Angeles: Hennessey & Ingalls, 1989), 3.
1. Before leaving Pasadena, Neff designed one of the finest houses of his career, in 1931. He punctuated the spare facade of a jewellike Tuscan town house on Orlando Road with an entry alcove, a second-floor loggia, an oval, bottle-glass window, and two ground-floor windows. The composition of the Henry Bertoletti House was so austere that it would surely have won an award, but there was so little construction taking place that juried architectural competitions had ceased to be held. Besides, Neff didn't have the resources to hire a photographer to document his work.
2. Savoy, "Wallace Neff: Father of Showcase Houses."
3. *Los Angeles City Directory* (Los Angeles: Los Angeles Directory Company, 1935), 2454.
4. Marvine Neff Malouf, personal communication, August 19, 1987. John Neff's wife, Lisa, was also involved with the pottery production.
5. Neff's office was listed at this address in the *Los Angeles City Directory* in 1934 and 1935. He lived at the Pasadena Athletic Club and later on

La Loma Road in Pasadena.

6. Hollywood-Western Building (file 87-1741), Los Angeles Historic Cultural Monument no. 336, Recreation, Library, and Cultural Affairs Committee, City of Los Angeles, California.

7. Leonard Mosley, *Zanuck: The Rise and Fall of Hollywood's Last Tycoon* (Boston: Little, Brown, 1984), 105.

8. Mayer earned $1.3 million in 1937, according to Kevin Starr, *The Dream Endures: California Enters the 1940s* (New York: Oxford University Press, 1997), 247. Neff made an entry in his daybook on November 9, 1935, noting that he had paid Mayer twenty-five dollars in rent.

9. Lockwood, *Dream Palaces*, 166.

10. Wurtzel's copious records, collection of Debora S. Rosen, listed a $6.08 garden hose.

11. Sol M. Wurtzel to Lillian Wurtzel, December 24, 1931, collection of Debora S. Rosen.

12. Lillian Wurtzel Semenov, personal communication, November 15, 1985.

13. "Bel-Air Residence of Semicircular Design: Contour of Ground Sets Home Plan," *Los Angeles Times,* November 29, 1931.

14. Debora S. Rosen, personal communication, June 12, 1999. Paul Wurtzel refuted his sister's version. He recalled only two servants—a cook and a houseboy—and an occasional chauffeur (Paul Wurtzel, personal communication, July 1999).

15. Behrman, *The Burning Glass,* 315.

16. Debora S. Rosen, personal communication, November 8, 1999.

17. Sol Wurtzel to Marian Wurtzel (on Twentieth Century Fox Film Corporation letterhead), November 29, 1943, collection of Debora S. Rosen.

18. Records from the collection of Paul Wurtzel show the grand total was $97,447.62, $7,700 of which went to Neff.

19. Raymond Girvigian, *Pan Pacific Auditorium Historical Restoration Report for the Gruen Team Investigation: Feasibility Study, Pan Pacific Recreation Area* (Los Angeles: Gruen Associates, 1980), 1.

20. Charles Abrams, "Housing—The Ever-Recurring Crisis," in *Saving American Capitalism, A Liberal Economic Program,* ed. Seymour Edwin Harris (New York: Knopf, 1948), 183.

21. "Fabricated House Here: First All Factory-Built Cottage Placed on Display," *Los Angeles Times,* July 15, 1934.

22. David Gebhard and Deborah Nevins, *200 Years of American Architectural Drawing* (New York: Whitney Library of Design for the Architectural League of New York and the American Federation of Arts, 1977), 208.

23. *Southwest Builder and Contractor,* February 15, 1935, 16.

24. Diane Kanner, "Architect's Career Spans 64 Years," *Los Angeles Times,* June 9, 1985.

25. "Unification Discussed by Architects Chapter," *Southwest Builder and Contractor,* June 16, 1935, 16. Neff and Lunden were both listed as being present.

26. Warwick Carpenter, "Cottage for Two," *American Home,* November 1934, 365.

27. Between 1929 and 1932, the average American family's income was reduced by 40 percent, from $2,300 to $1,500, according to the Kingwood College Library Web site (http://kclibrary.nhmccd.edu/decade30.html).

28. Sixty years later, the building stands on South Rimpau Boulevard amid towering apartment buildings.

29. "Dwelling Open for Inspection," *Los Angeles Times,* February 24, 1935.

30. Joe Johnson, personal communication, March 13, 1987.

31. It appears Neff conceived of the idea about the time he separated from his wife and moved to Hollywood. A letter from his patent attorney suggests that the formation of the idea took place in June 1934.

32. Gebhard and von Breton, *Los Angeles in the Thirties,* 167.

CHAPTER SIXTEEN

Epigraph. Darrylin Zanuck, personal communication, March 26, 1985.

1. According to Ed Warmington Sr., the son of William Warmington, who built the house, Brigham lived on investments and regularly stayed in Bermuda.

2. Walt Disney selected the country-provincial style for his house in Los Feliz near Disney Studios. While it and some of Neff's houses were almost cartoonish interpretations of medieval forms, they should not be considered "storybook style," as described by Arrol Gellner in his eponymous 2001 book, subtitled *America's Whimsical Homes of the Twenties* and published by Viking Studio.

3. The most outlandishly fanciful house of Neff's career was designed in 1925 for a retired Midwestern physician in Pasadena who held chamber music concerts in his home. The roof of the Doane House dipped so close to the ground on one side that the eaves were purported to be a mere six feet from the soil.

4. Ehmcke, personal communication, August 21, 1987, and April 3, 1991.

5. Rosten, *Hollywood,* 206.

6. Starr, *Americans and the California Dream,* 411.

7. William J. Mann, "Wisecracker William Haines," *Architectural Digest* 55, no. 4 (April 1998): 96.

8. James J. Yoch, *Landscaping the American Dream: The Gardens and Film Sets of Florence Yoch, 1890–1972* (New York: Harry N. Abrams, 1989), 183.

9. Neff notebook, November 1936–April 1937, Wallace Neff Papers, Huntington Library, San Marino, California.

10. Liesel Reisch, personal communication, February 8, 1988. According to Reisch, she was packing to disembark in New York when Louis B. Mayer "dragged" her to the deck to see the Statue of Liberty.

11. Ibid.

12. Ibid.

13. Ibid.

14. Cary Grant, personal communication, October 30, 1983.

15. *Federal Writers' Project of the Works Progress Administration of Northern California: California, A Guide to the Golden State,* 5th ed. (New York: Hastings House, 1947), 199.

16. Advertisement, *Architectural Digest* 10, no. 3: 173.

17. Joan Bennett, *The Bennett Playbill* (New York: Holt, Rinehart and Winston, 1970), 256. Later owners Hal Wallis and wives Louise Fazenda and Martha Hyer altered it, according to Hyer, personal communication, June 20, 1985.

18. *Los Angeles Times,* May 1, 1943.

19. Claudette Colbert, personal communication, November 20, 1985. On August 21, 1987, Caspar Ehmcke said that once Colbert saw Bennett's house, she decided to commission Neff to remodel her own.

20. Colbert, personal communication.

21. Warmington, personal communication. See Evelyn de Wolfe, "Warmington Clan Celebrates," *Los Angeles Times,* September 11, 1983. Colbert continued expanding the house for the next twenty years. Permits show she even moved the garage and guesthouse from one end of the property to the other.

22. Florence Eldridge, personal communication, May 17, 1985.

23. Robert Westbrook, *Intimate Lies, F. Scott Fitzgerald and Sheilah Graham: Her Son's Story* (New York: HarperCollins, 1995), 94.

24. Sam Jaffe, personal communication, March 14, 1994. Jaffe sold the house for sixty-five thousand dollars. Sammy Davis Jr. later purchased it, and after his death it was sold for $2.5 million.

25. Neff notebook, July–December 1938, Wallace Neff Papers, Huntington Library.

26. Joe Morella and Edward Z. Epstein, *Paulette: The Adventurous Life of Paulette Goddard* (New York: St. Martin's Press, 1985), 85.

27. Paul J. Karlstrom, review of *Painting on the Left: Diego Rivera, Radical Politics, and San Francisco Public Murals,* by Anthony W. Lee, *Southern California Quarterly* 83, no. 3 (Fall 2001): 345.

28. Maxwell, personal communication.

29. Neff notebook, November 1936–April 1937, Wallace Neff Papers,

Huntington Library.

30. Ibid.

31. Gellman, personal communication.

32. Frank Jamison, personal communication, September 13, 1984. Neff did not win the Taylor-Stanwyck commission.

33. Ibid.

34. "Contract Let for Cinema Executive's Coastal Dwelling," *Los Angeles Times*, February 28, 1937.

35. Angela Fox Dunn, "Bill Goetz: The Greatest of Them All," *Los Angeles Times*, April 20, 1980.

36. Carl Johnson, personal communication, December 5, 1985.

37. Lili Zanuck, personal communication, October 14, 1985.

38. Goetz, personal communication.

39. Walter Scott, personal communication, March 2, 1985.

40. Goetz, personal communication.

41. Neff notebook, July–September 1937, Wallace Neff Papers, Huntington Library.

42. Bob Adler, personal communication, October 23, 1985.

43. Ibid.

44. Darrylin Zanuck, personal communication.

45. Ibid.

46. Ibid.

CHAPTER SEVENTEEN

Epigraph. Mark Daniels, *Architect and Engineer*, January 1941, 19.

1. James F. O'Gorman, "Neff and Neutra: Regionalism Versus Internationalism," in Belloli, *Wallace Neff*, 51.

2. Ehmcke, personal communication.

3. Alson Clark, "The Californian Architecture of Gordon B. Kaufmann," *Society of Architectural Historians Review* 1, no. 3 (Summer 1982):

4. Neutra's name appears on plans for Kaufmann's Eisner House.

4. Ehmcke, personal communication.

5. Ibid.

6. McWilliams, *Southern California*, 344.

7. Ehmcke, personal communication.

8. At MIT, the retired architecture dean's reaction to modernism imbued his memoirs with vitriol. Ralph Adams Cram blasted Salvador Dali, the Museum of Modern Art, and modern churches alike: "They adapt themselves with scant sympathy to the purposes of any religion other than that of Voodooism, fetishism, and similar psychopathic manifestations," he wrote, calling "cubist, dimaxion functional houses a vicious assault on the basic principles of a sane and wholesome society."

9. Neutra, interview by Weschler.

10. This century's most important architectural exhibition is described in Holger Cahill and Alfred H. Barr Jr., eds., *Art in America in Modern Times* (New York: Reynal & Hitchcock, 1935), 132.

11. Lucille Terry Hobart, "Life in Los Feliz," unpublished manuscript, 1985.

12. Diane Kanner, "Living in a Work of Art and Feeling at Home," *Los Angeles Times*, December 5, 1983.

13. He and Neff also differed on the subject of which came first, the plan or the elevation: "The plan is everything," Ehmcke said. "The elevation will fall into place. Wallace worked the elevation first. Some people build for advertisement, others for living practically." Ehmcke, personal communication.

14. Ibid.

15. Ibid.

16. Gilbert Morgan, personal communication, July 17, 1984; David Gebhard, *Schindler* (San Francisco: William Stout, 1997), 155.

17. Bylaws of Southern Skis (revised May 28, 1992), 2, collection of Mrs. Jo Anne Jordan.

18. Hedda Hopper column, *Los Angeles Times*, November 11, 1938.

19. Cecilia Rasmussen, *L.A. Unconventional: The Men and Women Who Did L.A. Their Way* (Los Angeles: Los Angeles Times, 1998), 138.

20. "Increased Building Activity Noted by Local Architect," *Los Angeles Times*, July 9, 1939.

21. W. Averell Harriman, personal communication, October 11, 1984.

22. *Golden Anniversary*, press literature (Sun Valley, ID: Sun Valley Company, Winter 1985–86), 1.

23. Ibid., 2.

24. P. J. Ognibene, "At the First Ski Spa, Stars Outshone the Sun and Snow," *Smithsonian* 15, no. 9 (December 1984): 108–14.

25. *Golden Anniversary*, 2.

26. Dorice Taylor, *Sun Valley* (Bethany, CT: Ex Libris Sun Valley, 1980), 31. Lawrence McNeil was the contractor.

27. Ehmcke, personal communication.

28. Mrs. Donald W. Fraser, personal communication, June 6, 1985. Underwood's work was documented in the January 1938 issue of *Architectural Record*.

29. Ehmcke, personal communication.

CHAPTER EIGHTEEN

Epigraph. Gill, *The Dream Come True*.

1. Arthur Neff, personal communication, October 5, 1983; Cliff May, personal communication, October 20, 1983.

2. A fifth, undocumented, house may have been built in Lake Arrowhead in 1940.

3. Michael Raeburn, *The Chronicle of Opera* (New York: Thames and Hudson, 1998), 174–75.

4. Undated clipping from unknown newspaper in the Neff-McNally Collection, City of La Mirada, Community Services Department, Historic Files, La Mirada, California.

5. "Delightful Home's Intimate Corner," undated clipping from unknown newspaper, Neff-McNally Collection, City of La Mirada.

6. Paul Robinson Hunter and Walter L. Reichardt, eds., *Residential Architecture in Southern California* (Los Angeles: Southern California Chapter, American Institute of Architects, 1939), 15, 18, 20.

7. Galli-Curci to Wallace Neff, undated letter, collection of Marvine Neff Malouf.

8. Katherine Haldemann, personal communication, February 26, 1986.

9. "Tell Me, What Is Modern Architecture?" *House & Garden*, April 1940, 46–60.

10. "Home Investment Estimated Around $100,000," *Los Angeles Times*, January 8, 1939.

11. Yoch, *Landscaping the American Dream*, 65.

12. Steve Chawkins, "Developer to Buy Part of Camarillo Seminary Land," *Los Angeles Times*, May 6, 2004.

13. Starr, *Material Dreams*, 337.

14. Father William Ward, personal communication, March 1, 1984.

15. Miller, personal communication.

16. Starr, *Material Dreams*, 337–42.

17. Edward Doheny Sr. had died on September 8, 1935, at seventy-nine, a relatively old age considering the emotional toll of the Teapot Dome trials and the death of his son. His wife, who had served as his personal secretary after he suffered a series of strokes, knew where he stood on the disposition of his business and personal papers. Hours after his funeral service, she, her sister, Daysie, and her trusted secretary, Lucille Miller, went to the basement of the Chester Place house and threw the documents into the furnace, according to Martin R. Ansell, *Oil Baron of the Southwest: Edward L. Doheny and the Development of the Petroleum Industry in California and Mexico* (Columbus, OH: Ohio State University Press, 1998), 243. Had the Los Angeles archdiocese historian of future years, Msgr. Francis J. Weber, been there, he said, he would have tried to stop the inferno. "Burning the papers," he said, "has proven to be the single most disastrous decision she ever made." (Weber, personal communication, June 5, 1984.)

18. Wallace Neff's House of Studies for Vincentian seminarians at Catholic University in Washington, D.C., was also dedicated in the name of Edward L. Doheny. Institutional living was a new problem for Neff. He used the courtyard plan that worked so well with houses, giving the students privacy in the busy area, and applied a Lombard-Italian style to the brick structure.

19. Miller, personal communication.

20. Schwenzfeier, personal communication.

21. Sister Mary Irene Flanagan, "The Historical Development, Design, and Furnishings of Doheny Hall, the Residence of Mr. and Mrs. Edward L. Doheny, Now the Doheny Campus of Mount Saint Mary's College, Los Angeles, California" (master's thesis, San Jose State College, 1967), 54.

22. Ibid.

23. Neff, *Architecture of Southern California*, 122.

24. Miller, personal communication.

25. Neff notebook, March–June 1940, Wallace Neff Papers, Huntington Library.

26. Starr, *Material Dreams*, 342.

27. Russell Chandler and Sam Enriquez, "L.A. Archdiocese to Auction Off Its Gutenberg Bible," *Los Angeles Times*, February 28, 1987. In the story, a spokesman for the archdiocese said that while some of the funds generated by the sale would be used for capital improvements, most of them would go toward the training of initiates into the priesthood.

28. Paul Dean, "A Pumpkin Bread That Tastes Divine," *Los Angeles Times*, November 22, 1986.

29. Lucille Miller note on a 1951 statement documenting Neff's work for Mrs. Doheny that year, Wallace Neff Papers, Huntington Library.

30. Hancock, *Fabulous Boulevard*, 137.

CHAPTER NINETEEN

Epigraph. Airform construction fact sheet, 1970, Wallace Neff Papers, Huntington Library.

1. Peter Liszt, personal communication, April 6, 1985.

2. Friends like Rhoda Rosen say the Airform was his most frequent topic of conversation. (Rhoda Rosen, personal communication.) Neff told Melanie Young that the Pasadena Airform his family owned was worthy of being turned into a museum. (Melanie Young, personal communication, June 12, 1985.)

3. Neff's defense of the Airform appears in an Airform construction fact sheet, September 1960, collection of Marvine Neff Malouf.

4. Andrew F. Rolle and John S. Gaines, *The Golden State: A History of California* (Arlington Heights, IL: AHM Publishing, 1979), 12.

5. The Los Angeles ice cream igloo was photographed for a special issue of *California History*; see also Robert Winter, "The Architecture of the City Eclectic," in *Los Angeles, 1781–1981* (San Francisco: California Historical Society, 1981), 72–73.

6. In a September 1958 paper Neff wrote titled "The Pneumatic Form," he credited K. P. Billner of Philadelphia as having invented the spherical balloon shape built with steel forms. Billner's mistake, Neff said, was applying the concrete from the bottom up. As the load reached the top, deformation occurred around the bottom. Neff's approach was to apply the concrete from the top down, using five pounds per square inch in air pressure. Collection of Marvine Neff Malouf.

7. Neff notebooks, 1940–41, Wallace Neff Papers, Huntington Library.

8. According to Westbrook, *Intimate Lies*, 52, Vidor offered the house—and marriage—to columnist Sheilah Graham before settling on Elizabeth Hill. Durgnat and Simmon, *King Vidor*, 96, blames Vidor's affair with Hill on the set of *Bird of Paradise* in Hawaii for being what finally broke up his second marriage, to Eleanor Boardman.

9. Vidor's letters to Goldstein in Washington are on deposit with the King Vidor Papers at the USC Archives of Performing Arts.

10. Bascom N. Timmons, *Jesse H. Jones, The Man and the Statesman* (New York: Holt, 1956).

11. Jesse Jones to King Vidor, February 2, 1941, King Vidor Papers, Archives of Performing Arts, University of Southern California.

12. Attorney William Campbell represented the Neff Airform interests in Los Angeles.

13. Jack Linforth to Wallace Neff, November 12, 1941, Wallace Neff Papers, Huntington Library.

14. "Important dates," mimeographed document, Wallace Neff Papers, Huntington Library.

15. Wallace Neff notebook, November–December 1941, Wallace Neff Papers, Huntington Library.

16. "Ballyhooed Balloon," *Architectural Forum* 75, no. 6 (December 1941): 421.

17. "Balloon Houses," *Catholic Digest*, January 1942, 80–81.

18. The most wide-reaching publicity Neff ever received came when *Life* published "Balloon Houses Designed for Defense Workers Bloom under Virginia Trees" on December 1, 1941.

19. Advertisement, *Newsweek*, January 26, 1942, 34–35.

20. "Jones Approves Balloon Houses on Inspection," *Washington Post*, n.d.

21. "A Fresh Approach to Housing," *Architectural Forum* 74, no. 2 (February 1941): 88–89.

22. "General Outline of Developments, Concrete Balloon Type Structures," mimeographed document, Wallace Neff Papers, Huntington Library.

23. Ibid.

24. *The Children's Encyclopedia: The Book of Knowledge* (New York: Grolier Society Inc., 1943).

25. King Vidor to Robert Goldstein, March 3, 1942, King Vidor Papers, Archives of Performing Arts, University of Southern California.

26. Thomas E. Sheridan, *Arizona: A History* (Tucson: University of Arizona Press, 1995), 272.

27. Arthur C. Verge, *Paradise Transformed: Los Angeles during the Second World War* (Dubuque, IA: Kendall/Hunt Publishing, 1993), 7.

28. Ibid.

29. David M. Kennedy, *Freedom from Fear: The American People in Depression and War, 1929–1945* (New York: Oxford University Press, 1999), 465.

30. Despite his flourishing Hollywood clientele, Neff's debts were mounting: past due office rent, patent attorney fees, car and furniture loans, and real estate loans are all documented in Wallace Neff notebook, October 1942–March 1943, Wallace Neff Papers, Huntington Library.

31. "Circumventing Rubber Shortage: Bomb Shelter Built Around Bubble of Air Tested Here," *Los Angeles Times*, June 29, 1942.

32. "Inflated Bag Forms Let It Down," *Engineering News Record* 131, no. 23 (December 2, 1943): 55.

33. Wallace Neff, "Concrete Dome" (letter to the editor), *Engineering News Record* 133, no. 6 (August 10, 1944): 77.

34. Ibid.

35. Airform box 2, Wallace Neff Papers, Huntington Library.

36. Skidmore, Owings & Merrill, *Study and Evaluation of Various Types of Prefabricated Housing*, prepared for the Chief of Engineers, Department of the Army, November 30, 1949.

37. In 1958, an inflatable form with a twenty-four-foot diameter cost $4,300, and one with a diameter of almost thirty feet cost $5,000.

38. "30 Percent of Textiles Serve Industry," *New York Times*, October 14, 1956.

39. "French West Africa," *Time*, August 18, 1958, 24–28.

40. Neff promotional literature, collection of Marvine Neff Malouf.

41. Wallace Neff to Manuel Reachi, July 9, 1953, Wallace Neff Papers, Huntington Library. During one six-month period, Neff's patent expenses amounted to four thousand dollars.

42. Wolf Von Eckardt, ed., *Mid-Century Architecture in America: Honor Awards of the American Institute of Architects* (Baltimore: Johns Hopkins

Press, 1961), 241.

43. Daniel I. Vieyra, *Fill'er Up: An Architectural History of America's Gas Stations* (New York: Macmillan, 1979), figs. 95–96.

44. "Beautiful Bubbles," *Time*, June 22, 1953, 62; "Air-Formed Concrete Domes: House Hobe Sound, Florida," *Progressive Architecture*, June 1954, 116–19.

45. C. A. Blum to Wallace Neff, n.d., Wallace Neff Papers, Huntington Library.

46. Airform box 2, Wallace Neff Papers, Huntington Library.

47. John Elliott, personal communication, March 2, 1994.

48. Elliott, personal communication, December 21, 1983.

49. Stovall, "Famed Architect Neff Serves Wealthy, Poor."

50. "The noise of the air compressor was so loud, my husband took me for a ride for relief, and when we came back, it was quiet. By the light of the house next to it, I could see that the dome house had collapsed." Mrs. Somerville Higgins, personal communication from the house on Wallis Street where she had lived since 1941, June 12, 1986.

51. Elliott, personal communication, March 2, 1994.

52. Lee Howard, "Outwitting Mars," *Los Angeles Times Home Magazine*, April 13, 1947, 3, 26.

53. Brandow, personal communication.

54. Coldwell Banker and Tennies & Associates, "The Wallace Neff Bubble House," n.d. A March 15, 1998, advertisement by realtors Mossler Deasy & Doe in the *Los Angeles Times* listed the Airform at $289,000.

55. Randy Nerenberg, personal communication, July 23, 1985.

56. Marilyn Nerenberg, personal communication, January 3, 1991.

57. Jorge de Mattos, personal communication, January 18, 1986.

58. Neff, interview by Clark and Carmichael.

59. Thomas Herzog, *Pneumatic Structures: A Handbook of Inflatable Architecture* (New York: Oxford University Press, 1976), 183.

60. Matthys Levy and Mario Salvadori, *Why Buildings Fall Down: How Structures Fail* (New York: W. W. Norton, 1992), 38.

61. Neff, interview by Clark and Carmichael.

CHAPTER TWENTY

Epigraph. Sunset Boulevard, directed by Billy Wilder (Hollywood, CA: Paramont Pictures, 1950); Alan Jay Lerner, *The Street Where I Live* (New York: W. W. Norton & Co., 1978), 34.

1. Knight, *Hollywood Style*, 8.

2. McCoy continued her homage to the Greenes, Wright, and others in "Seven Pioneers Who Showed the Way," *Los Angeles Times Home Magazine*, September 9, 1956, 24.

3. David Gebhard and Robert Winter, *A Guide to Architecture in Southern California* (Los Angeles: Los Angeles County Museum of Art, 1965), 12. Neff was credited with designing his own house in San Marino, Galli-Curci's in Westwood, and the 1963 Eaton House at Hope Ranch in Santa Barbara. By the time Gebhard and Winter published the third and fourth editions of their guide in 1985 and 1994, they took pains to point out that they had been shortsighted in slighting period-revival architecture. "We left a back door open when we noted that the book might become 'a period piece,'" they wrote in the 1985 edition, "but we did not realize how right we were" (ibid., 6).

4. Elliott, personal communication, March 28, 1985.

5. Three-page overview of Neff's work, collection of Marvine Neff Malouf.

6. "Loyola University," *Tidings*, August 31, 1945.

7. "Work Speeded on Pomona Gym," *Los Angeles Times*, April 16, 1950; "College Building Honors War Dead," *Los Angeles Times*, November 10, 1950.

8. Father Richard H. Trame, personal communication, October 14, 1985.

9. Liszt, personal communication. Neff's notes in the archive at the Huntington Library show a $36,329 commission.

10. David Gebhard, "William Wurster and His California Contempo-
raries: The Idea of Regionalism and Soft Modernism," in *An Everyday Modernism: The Houses of William Wurster*, ed. Marc Treib (Berkeley: University of California Press, 1995), 164.

11. Wallace Neff, handwritten, two-page description, Wallace Neff Papers, Huntington Library.

12. De Mattos, personal communication.

13. Elliott, personal communication, December 21, 1983.

14. Gloria Ricci Lothrop, personal communication, October 26, 1994.

15. Gellman, personal communication.

16. Structural engineer George E. Brandow's records, job 52201, December 3, 1952. (Because Hilton developed low-cost housing projects, it is safe to assume that Neff approached the hotelier for Airform support.) In 1953, Leonard Firestone selected Neff to remodel his office, but hired William Pereira to design his vacation house.

17. Permit, July 3, 1953, San Marino City Hall, San Marino, California.

18. Anna Bing Arnold, personal communication, March 1, 1985.

19. Liszt, personal communication.

20. Shirle Duggan, "Swiss Modern," *Los Angeles Examiner*, January 13, 1952; "34 Architects of Southland Given Awards," *Los Angeles Times*, November 10, 1954.

21. "Six L.A. Architect Firms Selected for AIA Awards," *Los Angeles Times*, May 1, 1955.

22. Wallace Neff to American Institute of Architects, April 19, 1956, American Institute of Architects Archive, Washington, D.C.

23. In 1927, Neff designed a house on Arden Drive in Beverly Hills for L. G. McNeil. If there is a connection to the church contractor, it is unknown to the author.

24. *Los Angeles Times*, April 11, 1969. Neff said, "Zeppo wanted his house sexy. Never did know what he meant by that, so I built his house around a pool. He liked it."

25. Maxine Marx, *Growing Up with Chico* (Englewood Cliffs, NJ: Prentice-Hall, 1980), 100.

26. Susan Marx, personal communication, March 20, 1985, and March 28, 1985.

27. Ibid.

28. Savoy, "Wallace Neff: Father of Showcase Houses."

29. "Mrs. Neff Dies at 95; Resident Since 1884," *Los Angeles Times*, January 30, 1959. The cash realized by the trustees of her estate was $358,324. An appraisal of Wallace Neff's portfolio, in which he invested his McNally trust proceeds, was $137,678 on January 9, 1961. W. Francis Burke, accountant, to Wallace Neff, February 4, 1961, collection of Marvine Neff Malouf.

30. "The Passing of Edwin D. Neff," *Pasadena Star-News*, November 24, 1943.

31. Nannie Neff's will specified that the house was to be shared by all her children, although Della, who died in 1969, was the only one who lived there.

32. "Debs of Generation Ago Relive Holiday, Debut Parties," *Pasadena Star-News*, December 18, 1955. Louise Neff is identified by her married name. For the most public of announcements, Wallace Neff used his wife's address.

33. Wallace Neff, interview by Dr. Barlow Smith, October 25, 1979, Case No. P625152, Superior Court of California, County of Los Angeles.

34. Naneen Boot Levinworth confirmed her father John's alcoholism in a personal communication on March 19, 1994. Bill Neff's condition was mentioned to the author by a number of people interviewed for this book, including John Elliott.

35. Henry Wesley, personal communication, July 26, 1985.

36. Neff, interview by Smith.

37. Rosalinde Gilbert, personal communication, May 20, 1985.

38. Harry Clow, personal communication, March 19, 1985.

39. Neff, *Architecture of Southern California*.

40. Harold Kirker, "California Architecture and Its Relation to Contemporary Trends in Europe," *California Historical Quarterly* 51, no. 4

(Winter 1972): 292.

41. Elsa Kunin, personal communication, March 28, 1985.

42. Neff, *Architecture of Southern California.*

43. Clow, personal communication.

44. Review of *Architecture of Southern California,* by Wallace Neff, *Los Angeles Times Home Magazine,* May 16, 1965.

45. Wallace Neff, "Biological Age in Art and Nature" (unpublished manuscript), collection of Marvine Neff Malouf.

46. Grant, personal communication.

47. Belford, personal communication; "McNally Test Scheduled by Atlantic," *Los Angeles Times,* March 8, 1952.

48. Camp, "They Walked Before Us" (unpublished manuscript), City of La Mirada Recreation and Parks Department, Historic Files, La Mirada, California.

49. D. J. Waldie, *Holyland: A Suburban Memoir* (New York: St. Martin's Press, 1997), 1.

50. Walter and Cordelia Knott were the first among the established landowners to find fortune. Their boysenberry-pie stand had pioneered jam-and-jelly venture capitalism in the 1920s, and in the following decades they began to serve chicken dinners out of the family kitchen. By the time Knott's Berry Farm, the family's amusement park, was born in 1968, Buena Park had incorporated to stave off nearby Anaheim's ambitions to host the park. But once Disneyland opened on July 17, 1955, Anaheim was poised for riches of its own.

51. Camp, *La Mirada,* 60.

52. Belford, personal communication.

53. John Anson Ford, *Thirty Explosive Years in Los Angeles County* (San Marino, CA: Huntington Library, 1961), 51.

54. "Big Crowds Reported at La Mirada Project," *Los Angeles Times,* August 18, 1957.

55. The La Mirada map was underwritten by various local individuals and businesses and was distributed by the *Lamplighter.* Collection of the City of La Mirada Recreation and Parks Department, Historic Files, La Mirada, California.

56. Advertisement for La Mirada Woods, *Long Beach Press Telegram,* January 9, 1955.

57. Charles Moore, "You Have to Pay for the Public Life," *Perspecta* 9–10 (1965): 65.

CHAPTER TWENTY-ONE

Epigraph. David Brodsly, *L.A. Freeway, An Appreciative Essay* (Berkeley: University of California Press, 1981), 132.

1. Richard Neutra, *World and Dwelling* (New York: Universe Books, 1962), 147.

2. The Fletcher House was built in 1962 on Chalon Road. The Fletchers requested a contemporary version of Neff's country-French vernacular after he told them he preferred the style to all others.

3. Records show Neff's standard commission was 10 percent for new work, 12 percent for remodeling, and 8 percent for projects he designed but did not oversee, Wallace Neff Papers, Huntington Library.

4. Stovall, "Famed Architect Neff Serves Wealthy, Poor."

5. Neutra, interview by Weschler.

6. Walter R. Johnson, personal communication, December 5, 1985.

7. "A Major Local Wine Collection Goes on Sale," *Los Angeles Times,* May 12, 2000. At an auction of Singleton's wine collection in May 2000, Christies' wine expert called it "the most significant private cellar we have had the privilege of handling in Los Angeles since we started wine auctions on the West Coast."

8. Diane Kanner, "'Demolition Derby' Grips the Westside," *Los Angeles Times,* June 21, 1987.

9. Neff's work itself fell victim to the mansionization trend in 1985, after producer Aaron Spelling tore down the house he purchased from the Shick shaving magnate Patrick Frawley, a house Neff had

remodeled in 1972.

10. Andrew Chandler, personal communication, January 15, 1985.

11. Ibid.

12. The Chandler House on Rossmore was not modeled after the Petit Trianon, Europe's most elegant small building, as some surmised.

13. Chandler, personal communication.

14. Lizst, personal communication.

15. Marvine Neff Malouf, personal communication, February 20, 1991.

16. Ibid.

17. Gellman, personal communication.

18. Ibid.

19. Arthur Neff, personal communication, October 31, 1983.

20. Shawn Hubler, "The Junior Phils' Many Mansions," *Los Angeles Times,* April 16, 1996.

21. Anne Sonne, personal communication, September 24, 1998.

22. Vaillancourt, personal communication.

23. Savoy, "Wallace Neff: Father of Showcase Houses."

24. Jack Smith column, *Los Angeles Times,* October 10, 1983.

25. John Elliott, personal communication, March 15, 1994.

26. Stovall, "Famed Architect Neff Serves Wealthy, Poor."

27. Robert Straus, personal communication, March 3, 1986.

28. Elliott, personal communication, December 21, 1983.

29. Elliott, personal communication, December 21, 1983, and March 28, 1985.

30. Case no. P-625, 152 (Cal. Superior Ct. 1972) authorized Security Pacific National Bank to pay debts due: five thousand dollars to John Factor and two thousand dollars to John C. Elliott.

31. Nevins, personal communication, October 17, 1984.

32. Plans show that Santa Barbara architect Richard Bliss Nelson was the architect.

33. Debbie Foster, personal communication, July 29, 1999.

34. Cary Grant, personal communication, January 21, 1984.

35. "Ramon Novarro, 69, Dies of Blows, Slayer Unknown," *Variety,* November 6, 1968.

36. Maxwell, personal communication.

37. Leo Rosten, *The Joys of Yiddish: A Relaxed Lexicon of Yiddish, Hebrew and Yinglish Words Often Encountered in English . . . From the Days of the Bible to Those of the Beatnik* (New York: Pocket Books, 1970), 106.

38. Gellman, personal communication.

39. Joan Didion, *The White Album* (New York: Simon and Schuster, 1979), 15–17.

40. Liszt, personal communication.

41. *Marianne Radley v. Wallace Neff,* CS7979, P596592. Arthur Neff filed a petition for conservatorship of his father on September 7, 1973, because Wallace Neff was "in ill health and . . . unable to properly care for himself or his property," Case No. P596592, Superior Court of California, County of Los Angeles.

42. Rudy Kessman, personal communication, January 22, 1999.

43. "Dr. Neff, Noted Scientist of Pasadena, Dies," *Pasadena Star-News,* September 5, 1975. A letter from Caltech to the author on October 5, 1999, states that Andrew Neff was not a professor. "Music and Arts Helped by Caltech Researcher," *Pasadena Star-News,* November 21, 1936, confirms that Andrew visited Caltech, but did not teach.

44. May, personal communication.

45. Cliff May, personal communication, December 22, 1985.

46. Walter Johnson, personal communication.

47. Ibid.

48. May, personal communication, December 22, 1985.

49. May, personal communication, October 20, 1983.

50. Dr. Barlow Smith to Lee Dicker, Simon & Sheridan Attorneys, November 1, 1979, recounting October 26, 1979, examination of Neff, Case No. P625152, Petition for Restoration to Capacity, Probate Code Section 1470, Superior Court of California, County of Los Angeles.

51. Ibid.

52. Scott L. Carder, M.D., to Stanley Hahn and Clark Byam, November 23, 1979.

53. Cameron S. Avery, of Bell, Boyd, Lloyd, Haddad & Burns, to Stanley L. Hahn, Wallace Neff's attorney, April 11, 1978, Case No. P625152, Superior Court of California, County of Los Angeles.

54. With Neff in the convalescent hospital and his brother Andrew deceased, his son Wally sold the Bubble House.

55. Lynn Maggan, personal communication, July 30, 1985.

56. Case no. P-625152 (Cal. Superior Ct., County of Los Angeles, February 26, 1980).

57. "Gold Crown Awards Honor Pasadena Arts and Culture," *Pasadena Star-News*, May 5, 1978.

58. Maggan, personal communication.

59. Morgan and Naylor, *Contemporary Architects*, 644–45.

60. Ruth Ryon, "Architect Wallace Neff Looks Back," *Los Angeles Times*, December 6, 1981.

61. Savoy, "Wallace Neff: Father of Showcase Houses."

62. Cheryl Graunke, personal communication, January 1980.

63. Neff's papers include plans for eighty-five projects and miscellaneous records.

64. Nevins, personal communication, August 8, 1993.

65. Vera Danielson, "Veteran Architect to Be Remembered for his Showplaces," *Pasadena Star-News*, June 10, 1982. Neff could not have been Henry Ford's friend, for they never met.

66. Obituary of Wallace Neff, *Pasadena Heritage Newsletter* 6, no. 1 (Spring 1982): 7.

67. Joseph Giovannini, "Architects Shaped a California Tradition," *Los Angeles Herald Examiner*, June 14, 1982.

68. Rolle, *Los Angeles*, 2.